The Crime Scene

ELSEVIER *science & technology books*

Companion website:

http://booksite.elsevier.com/9780128129609/

The Crime Scene: A Visual Guide
Marilyn T. Miller and Peter Massey

Resources for Professors:

- Instructor support materials for *The Crime Scene: A Visual Guide*, including videos, test banks, lecture slides and lab exercises.

TOOLS FOR ALL YOUR TEACHING NEEDS
textbooks.elsevier.com

ACADEMIC PRESS

The Crime Scene
A Visual Guide

Second Edition

Marilyn T. Miller
Peter Massey

ACADEMIC PRESS

An imprint of Elsevier

Academic Press is an imprint of Elsevier
125 London Wall, London EC2Y 5AS, United Kingdom
525 B Street, Suite 1650, San Diego, CA 92101, United States
50 Hampshire Street, 5th Floor, Cambridge, MA 02139, United States
The Boulevard, Langford Lane, Kidlington, Oxford OX5 1GB, United Kingdom

Library of Congress Cataloging-in-Publication Data
A catalog record for this book is available from the Library of Congress

British Library Cataloguing-in-Publication Data
A catalogue record for this book is available from the British Library

ISBN: 978-0-12-812960-9

For information on all Academic Press publications visit our website at
https://www.elsevier.com/books-and-journals

www.elsevier.com • www.bookaid.org

Publisher: Stacy Masucci
Acquisition Editor: Elizabeth Brown
Editorial Project Manager: Kathy Padilla
Production Project Manager: Mohana Natarajan
Designer: Matthew Limbert

Typeset by TNQ Technologies

Last digit is the print number: 9 8 7 6 5 4 3 2 1

Dedication

Marilyn T. Miller

As I look through the many textbook offerings about crime scene investigation, I never cease to be amazed. I will never believe that one television series or one celebrity trial is responsible for the explosion of interest in crime scene investigation. I believe it is a public awakening of law enforcement centered on using physical evidence and not just solving a case by confession or eyewitnesses. The explosion has helped keep me working with amazing crime scene professionals and equally amazing students who cannot wait to get the job done! I dedicate this textbook to those professionals and students. Thank you for wanting to learn and to always wanting do the best job. This textbook is the result of a "war storytelling" session with Pete. On my goodness, how I treasure our friendship! Patience and pride from family is important too! So, to my family, thanks for the encouragement and space. It is my hope to always make you proud.

Peter Massey

We have spent countless hours teaching and training students and professionals the proper and correct way in which to recognize, evaluate, document, and collect evidence from forensic scenes. It is for those past students and those who will follow that drive the passion to offer this book. To my children, Emily, Abigail, Rebecca, and Zachary—you are never too old to grow and learn and to give back. To Brooke and Sharon, thank you for your contributions. Marilyn—mere words cannot express my love and respect for you and for your support and guidance throughout our friendship. To my best friend, soul mate, and absolute love of my life, my wife Sandy, thank you for all of your support and sacrifices for me.

Contents

Foreword

I appreciate the opportunity to introduce this new textbook on crime scene investigation and procedures by a pair of authors who have long and varied theoretical and practical experience in this area. This book emphasizes the visual—principles are highlighted and discussed using crime scene visuals as centerpieces. This approach follows the idea that the use of visuals with text is a more effective instructional tool than text alone—an idea with considerable support in the learning techniques literature.

The book is divided into three parts, each containing several chapters. Part I introduces basic concepts upon which crime scene investigation is based and discusses all important Fourth Amendment search-and-seizure rules. Preliminary scene procedures are included in this part. Part II is primarily about scene and evidence documentation, as well as searching. Its title, "Making a Scene Relevant," summarizes the importance of these activities. In Part III, Concluding Processes, we learn about reconstruction activities, current technologies, and some concluding remarks by the authors.

Chapter 1 covers important basic concepts. It is important for investigators to consider the types of physical evidence that might be found at scenes and also their uses, i.e., how might a physical evidence item help inform the case. The scientific basis for crime scene investigation is the Locard's exchange principle, the idea that when things come into contact, they exchange some matter. The issue in crime scene investigation is whether or not these mutual exchanges are recognizable or detectable. In some instances, such as where a fingerprint is deposited or a DNA-containing body fluid trace left, the matter is comparatively easy. In others, such as where small quantities of trace may be left behind, it is not so easy. An important point is that recognition of physical evidence at a scene is the sine qua non for everything that follows. In the search for evidence, a scientific approach involves hypothesis formation. There can be more than one hypothesis and more than one set of events and circumstances that could have led to the scene at hand. The hypothesis—the "educated guess" as to what might have happened—can inform the search for evidence. It is this approach that separates crime scene investigation from crime scene processing. Chapter 1 also discusses the Fourth Amendment to the US Constitution which governs legal aspects of search and seizure. Physical evidence is not useful by definition unless it is admissible. Crime scene investigators do not have to be lawyers, but they have to understand the constraints governing admissibility, when a search warrant is required. Chapter 2 looks at initial procedures. Highlights here include the actions of first responders, initial scene survey, and security implementation. Multilevel scene security procedures insure that the core scene is properly protected while still providing work and staging areas for authorized personnel.

In Part II, Chapters 3–5 cover scene and evidence documentation. There must be a good and recoverable record of a scene's initial condition and the location in context of every relevant item of physical evidence. In a case of perfect documentation, a scene could literally be "reconstructed" from the documentation. Documentation includes notes, photography, videography, and sketching. Each has a specific role, and none of them is replaceable by another one. Crime scene investigators must be familiar with the detailed technical aspects of video, photography, and sketching. With the exception of items actually collected from a scene, only the documentation record will be available later after the scene has been released. Complete documentation is thus a requirement. Sometimes, video records, photographs, and finished sketches are presented as evidence at trials. These are the only ways the trier of fact can understand how the scene appeared. Chapter 6 discusses searching for evidence at the scene. There are different "methods" of searching, applicable to different scenes and circumstances. But as noted, the key to thorough searches is a consideration of the overall scene and circumstances. Specialized lighting and other equipment or specialized chemicals may also be helpful or necessary. In recent years, laboratory analytical methods have gotten more and more sensitive. This development makes it necessary for crime scene investigators to don protective clothing and footwear to keep any of their own traces from contaminating the scene (as well as to protect them from any potentially hazardous materials within the scene).

Part III, the final part, discusses Concluding Processes. Chapter 7 is about reconstruction. Good crime scene investigators, in collaboration with lab scientists and other forensic specialists like pathologists, anthropologists, etc., can do reconstructions. Good reconstructions are based on good scene investigation and documentation. Reconstructions arise from hypothesis formulation and testing. The physical evidence record informs the hypothesis, and the "best fit" hypothesis to all the physical and investigative information represents a reconstruction. Many (probably most) reconstructions are incomplete—not everything that happened will be known. It is important to distinguish between things that are actually known and things that are part of a "best fit hypothesis." An investigator may know for certain what caused a certain blood pattern, for example, but might not know when in a sequence of events that pattern was formed. Reconstructions are not scientific records of what actually happened overall. They are models which comport with all the available physical and investigative information. Chapter 8 is about newer technologies, including those for software-based scene documentation, for measurement, and lab techniques that may be used at a scene. There is a general trend toward the development of sophisticated technologies (such as DNA profiling) that are portable and can be taken to and used at crime scenes. Realization and implementation of these will have a huge impact on crime scene investigation efficiency and case resolution. Settling questions such as whose blood made a pattern, what drugs are around, whose fingerprints are on an item, etc. at a scene, instead of weeks or months later after lab analysis, would revolutionize case processing. Chapter 9 is a recap of the crime scene process emphasizing important principles. This thinking hearkens back to the uses of physical evidence discussed earlier. To be useful to the case, the physical evidence must have probative value, i.e., it must be able to tell investigators something relevant about the case.

Each chapter is complete with learning objectives and discussion questions. Overall, the book is an outstanding introduction to crime scene investigation. The visual approach, which is novel, should be helpful to practicing and aspiring crime scene investigators on many levels and will be an important pedagogic addition to the crime scene investigation literature.

R.E. Gaensslen, Ph.D.
Professor Emeritus, Forensic Science University of Illinois, Chicago

Writers' Note:
Many thanks as always to Bob Gaensslen for his Foreword to the first edition of this text. Based on his comments and others, a chapter on the collection and packaging was added. His insights shall always guide both of us in all we do.

Introduction

PURPOSE FOR TEXTBOOK

There are a plethora of excellent books already in print on how to instruct individuals on what may be called generally accepted practices in processing a crime scene. The basic fundamentals for most of these texts are legal search, evidence recognition, enhancement as part of a search, documentation, and collection/packaging. While these books have filled bookshelves and have been used in many academic courses, as well as in service training classes, practical experience has indicated that while individuals are trained the "correct way," many continually operate in an "incorrect" mode. This textbook has a unique method for correcting the "incorrect" processes that continue. It will indicate, using actual photographs, errors, mistakes, and improper techniques and then will also visually indicate the "correct" way in which to process a crime scene. The result will be less crime scenes and physical evidence compromised. There are currently no books available in print using this style of instruction.

This textbook has a basis as presented because it represents the combined experience of almost 70 years in crime scene investigation as primary responders and consultants giving testimony in all levels of courts in the United States. Additionally, the textbook is presented in such a manner so as to present academically sound pedagogy by use of learning objectives and critical thinking exercises.

TEXTBOOK ORGANIZATION

For each of the topics presented in the chapters, actual crime scene photographs are presented to illustrate the improper or incorrect procedures that have been used in actual investigations. For comparison and corrective purposes, examples of the correct procedures are present.

The chapters are organized into three majors parts based on Part I—Preliminary Preparations, Part II—Making a Scene Relevant by Documentation, and finally, Part III—Concluding Processes.

Part I—Chapter 1, Crime Scene Investigations, discusses the use and significance of physical evidence found at crime scenes. The importance of the Locard's exchange principle and legal implications for crime scene investigators is presented. Chapter 2, Initial On-Scene Procedures, presents procedures and use of first responders and discusses the proper use and setup for scene security, and the correct utilization of the preliminary scene survey.

Part II—Chapter 3, Notes and Videography, presents two of the components for documenting a crime scene. This chapter compares correct and incorrect methods with challenges for taking notes and using the video for a visual record of a crime scene. Chapter 4, Photography, again compares the correct and incorrect methods with challenges or barriers. Additionally, because photography is the major technique for documenting a crime scene and its evidence, Chapter 4 discusses the issue of redundancies with photographs. Documentation process of sketching is presented in Chapter 5. The various methods of sketching with their challenges are discussed. Chapter 6 shows methods for intensive searching of crime scenes for evidence based on its composition along with on-scene testing. Chapter 7 has been added to provide the user with proper packaging and collection based on the type of evidence found at the crime scene.

Part III includes discussions of final or off-scene processes done as part of a crime scene investigation and future considerations of crime scene investigation methodologies based on the physical evidence found at the scene. Chapter 8 looks at reconstruction activities; Chapter 9 identifies some current technologies; and Chapter 10 includes final thoughts on the probative value of physical evidence at the scene.

USERS

The target users for this text are any current crime scene investigators, potential crime scene investigators in training, law enforcement officers, criminal justice majors in college, law enforcement academies, medico-legal investigators, forensic science laboratories, colleges or universities that have forensic science programs, fire fighters and investigators, accident investigators, private and corporate investigators, and even criminal attorneys and their investigators.

Part I

Preliminary Preparations

Chapter 1

Crime Scene Investigations

Chapter Outline

Learning Objectives

On completion of this chapter, the reader should be able to

- Identify various types of physical evidence found at a crime scene and the usefulness of the evidence in a criminal investigation.
- Discuss and apply the Locard's exchange principle to the investigation of crime scenes.
- Identify and utilize a variety of general processes and procedures to begin a crime scene investigation.
- Understand and apply legal requirements as part of a crime scene investigation.

TYPES OF PHYSICAL EVIDENCE AND CRIME SCENES

Any attempt at identifying all the types of physical evidence that could be found at a crime scene would be folly. See Photo 1.1.

Physical evidence can be anything. It is oftentimes not always visible to the investigator. Visualization and enhancement to assist searching for physical evidence at scenes must be done and become part of every scene investigation. Just using your sight is not enough. This is especially true with bloodstained impressions. (See unenhanced bloody footwear impression and enhanced bloody enhancement in Fig. 1.1 below.)

The physical evidence can range in size from huge to microscopic. It can be animal, vegetable, or mineral. The crime scene investigator must expect the unexpected and more. By identifying the categories of physical evidence at the crime scene, it assists the investigator determine the collection method. Regardless of the type of physical evidence found at the crime scene, the scene investigator must always consider that it is the physical evidence that will make or break an investigation.

Because any item found at a crime scene can be physical evidence, it is can be labeled "the debris of criminal activity." Although there is considerable overlap of identifications of evidence, it can be categorized into the following broad groups based on its origin, composition, or method of creation:

1. *Biological evidence*—any evidence derived from a living item. It includes physiological fluids, plants, and some biological pathogens.
2. *Chemical evidence*—any evidence with identifiable chemicals present.
3. *Patterned evidence*—any evidence with a pattern or predictable pattern of appearance or origin.
4. *Trace evidence*—any evidence of such a small size so as to be overlooked, not easily seen or not easily recognized.

The Crime Scene. https://doi.org/10.1016/B978-0-12-812960-9.00001-9

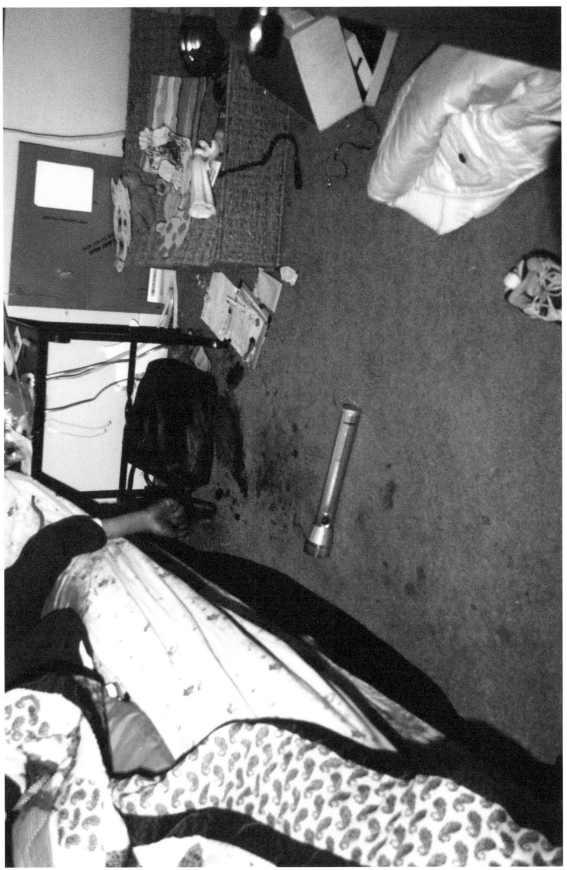

PHOTO 1.1 Crime scene with a variety of different types of physical evidence.

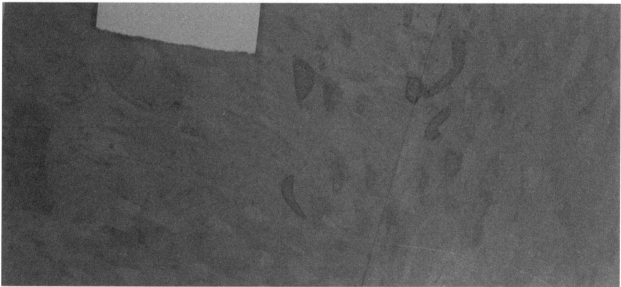

FIGURE 1.1   Unenhanced and enhanced bloody footwear impressions.

USE OF PHYSICAL EVIDENCE FOUND AT THE CRIME SCENE

In addition to identifying the type of physical evidence found at a crime scene, it is possible to obtain valuable source and investigative information from the analysis of the physical evidence. The types of information that can be obtained from the physical evidence are as follows:

- Determination of *corpus delicti*—the evidence is used to determine if a crime has taken place. For example, a red-brown stain on a wall in a kitchen may not be human blood. It may just be dried tomato sauce. A broken window may not always mean a breaking and entering has occurred (see Fig. 1.2).
- *Modus operandi* identification—criminals repeat behavior. Repeated methods of entry, for example, by kicking in a back door with the same shoe leaving the same footwear impressions throughout the crime scene (see Fig. 1.3).
- Association or linkage—the Locard's exchange principle—transfer of evidence by contact. See the next section to follow.

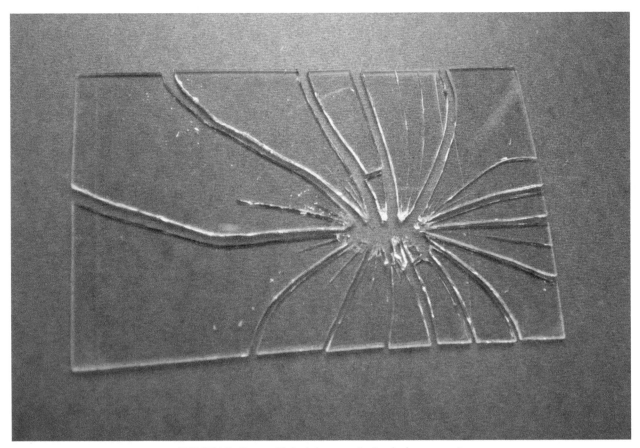

FIGURE 1.2 Reassembled window pane (broken by lawn mower).

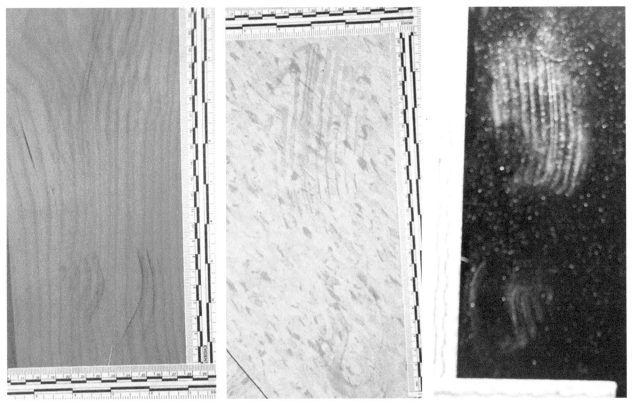

FIGURE 1.3 Consistent footwear impressions.

- Disproving/supporting victim/suspect/witness statements—the evidence may or may not support what these groups say. For example, an eyewitness may say that the suspect fled the crime scene wearing tennis shoes but the only footwear impressions and shoes found at the scene are bloody slippers (see Fig. 1.4).
- Identification of suspects/victims/crime scene location—fingerprints and DNA can be used to identify who was present at a crime scene (see Fig. 1.5).
- Provide for investigative leads for detectives—the use of the physical evidence to give information to detectives that will assist them in locating victims and suspects. An example would be to determine the make, model, and year of the vehicle involved in a hit and run that left paint chips at the crime scene (see Fig. 1.6).

LOCARD'S EXCHANGE PRINCIPLE

The Locard's exchange principle forms the foundation for why crime scenes are searched for physical evidence to be used in a criminal investigation. The Principle states that whenever two objects are in contact there will always be a mutual exchange of matter between them. Generally, the physical evidence found at a crime scene will link the suspect to the scene, the victim to the scene, and the suspect to the victim (and vice versa). In the example shown below, the Locard's exchange principle links or associates the bleeding victim to the suspect, the vehicle, and the foyer of the house by use of the physical evidence found at the various crime scenes (see Photo 1.2 below).

1. Victim's blood is found on the suspect's shoes and shorts;
2. A bloody trunk liner was found 10–15 feet from a vehicle. The trunk liner has victim's blood, and the trunk liner matches the vehicle;
3. Impact blood spatter from the victim is found in the foyer of the house.

GENERAL PROCESSES AND PROCEDURES AT THE CRIME SCENE

Scientific crime scene investigation is not just going to a crime scene, taking a couple of pictures, taking some notes, and collecting some physical evidence. It is the first step and the *most crucial step* of any criminal investigation. The foundation of all crime scene investigations is the ability of the crime scene investigator to recognize the potential and importance of physical evidence, large and small, at the crime scene. The subsequent identification of the physical evidence along with determination of its source or origin is the next step in the investigation. Proper crime scene investigation is the starting point for the process of establishing what happened and who did it. Because of the legal requirements in any criminal investigation and for the correct analysis of the evidence by the crime laboratory, careful processing, documentation, and collection of physical evidence are integral parts of the "investigation process" and the crime scene investigation.

Contrary to the way it is portrayed in popular media, crime scene investigation is not glamorous or accomplished in an easy or lackadaisical manner. It is an organized, methodical, systematic, and logical process—it is scientific in nature. It is based on an understanding of the scientific nature of the physical evidence and the use of the physical evidence in a criminal investigation. It is a discovery process, subject to review and refinement. If done properly, it requires not only adequate training, current and ongoing, and experience on the part of the investigator but also necessitates a managed and coordinated team effort. Crime scene investigation must never restrict the flow of information from the scene, it must provide for an opening of communication between scene investigators and all other law enforcement personnel.

Scientific Crime Scene Investigation

Most of the textbooks currently in the field limit crime scene investigation to the recording of the crime scene and the subsequent collection of the physical evidence. These steps are historically called "crime scene processing" and have given the crime scene investigator the role of being a technician, someone who just follows a checklist and only does their job without thinking. Recording or documentation of the crime scene and the collection of physical evidence are important aspects of the crime scene investigation and must be properly done. However, these activities are purely mechanical tasks. Any investigator with minimum training might be able to perform them correctly. However, the issue remains that mistakes are frequently made. The result-crucial evidence is lost, contaminated, or even suppressed. The completion of these crime scene tasks is essential for the integrity of the physical evidence and the ultimate conclusion of criminal investigation (see Fig. 1.7).

Skillful crime scene investigation is a systematic and methodical approach. It is not haphazard or "lucky." It begins with the initial response to a crime scene and continues through the scene security, the preliminary crime scene survey, the

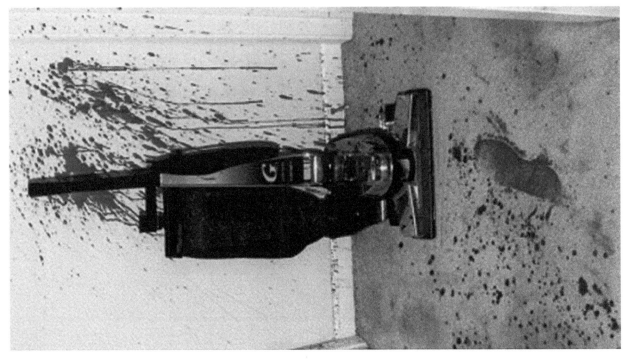

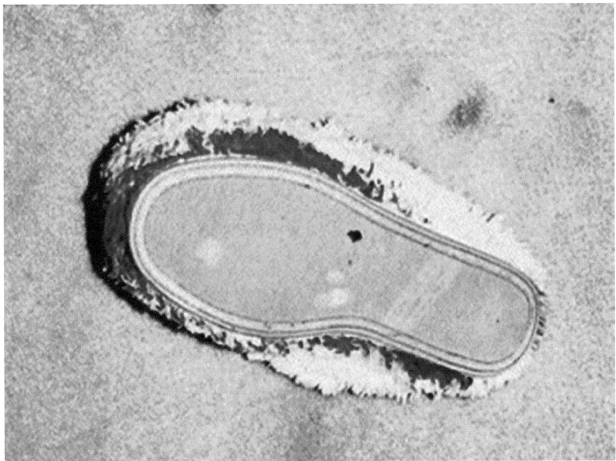

FIGURE 1.4 Bloody slipper and impression.

LATENT PRINT

ROLLED PRINT

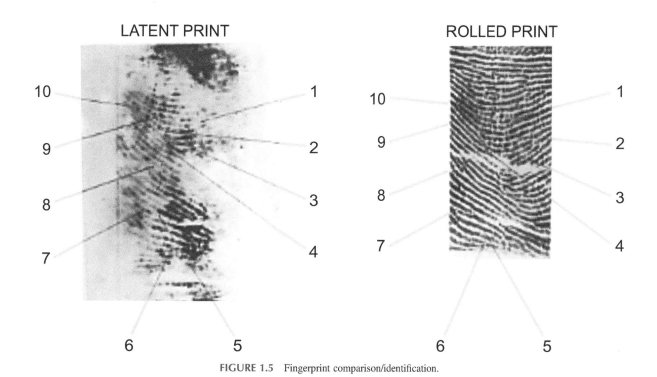

FIGURE 1.5   Fingerprint comparison/identification.

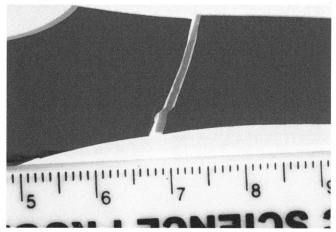

FIGURE 1.6   Automotive paint evidence.

PHOTO 1.2 Victim's blood on suspect's shoes and shorts; blood on trunk liner from victim; trunk liner from car; and impact spatter from victim in house.

recording or documentation of the crime scene, intensively searching for physical evidence by enhancement or visualization, the collection, packaging, and preservation of physical evidence, the search of the crime scene one last time, to, finally, the reconstruction of the crime scene (see Table 1.1). Systematic crime scene investigation is based on the principles of the Locard's exchange principle, basic logical analysis, and the utilization of scientific knowledge with forensic techniques of physical evidence examination to generate investigative leads that will ultimately solve the crime.

FIGURE 1.7   Crime scene investigators and their vehicle.

TABLE 1.1 Steps of Crime Scene Investigation

1. Use of first responder
2. Establishment of scene security
3. Preliminary scene survey
4. Scene recording or documentation
5. Intensively searching for evidence
6. Collection and packaging
7. Final scene search
8. Reconstruction

LEGAL CONCERNS FOR THE CRIME SCENE INVESTIGATOR

Even with the advent of advanced evidence recording and searching, there will be major problems with the crime scene investigation, if those results are not admissible in any subsequent judicial proceeding. The most commonly used means to diminish the value of a particular piece of physical evidence is to demonstrate that the evidence was obtained illegally. If a court determines that the evidence was obtained illegally or did not follow legal or scientific requirements for collecting or preserving the evidence, then, in most circumstances, the item of evidence will be deemed as inadmissible. This suppression of evidence is based on the Constitutional protections against unreasonable searches and seizures, as declared in the Fourth Amendment to the United States Constitution, as well as similar provisions in state constitutions. This Fourth Amendment protection has been enforced through application of the Exclusionary Rule in a series of well-established cases by the United States Supreme Court, including the landmark case of *Mapp v. Ohio* 367 US 643 (1961). Furthermore, any secondary or additional evidence derived from the inadmissible evidence may also be deemed as inadmissible through the "Fruit of the Poisonous Tree Doctrine," *Nardone v. United States*, 308 US 338 (1939) (See Fig. 1.8).

FIGURE 1.8 Serving search warrant.

Legal implications regarding a crime scene search and seizure of physical evidence from that scene fall into two general areas. First is the actual search of the premises lawful, and second is the seizure of a specific piece of evidence within the confines of a legal seizure. When evaluating the legality of conducting crime scene searches and seizing evidence, there is a central legal decision that dictates lawful conduct, *Mincey v. Arizona*, 437 US 385 (1978). (See Mincey Warrant template at the end of the chapter.)

In the *Mincey* investigation, a narcotics raid of the defendant's apartment occurred. An undercover police officer was shot and killed and the defendant was wounded. Homicide detectives proceeded to the scene and conducted a warrantless search of the apartment, lasting 4 days. During that search, detectives seized hundreds of pieces of evidence used in the defendant's trial. On review of this case by the United States Supreme Court, the Court held that law enforcement personnel responding to a crime scene could essentially conduct three functions legally, without consent from the owners, prior court authorization, search and seizure warrant, or other exigent circumstances.

First, officers could enter the scene to search for victims and to render aid to those in need. The scope of this search is restricted to those areas where a victim could reasonably be located. In addition, just because one victim is readily located, officers are not precluded from conducting a reasonable search to ascertain if additional victims may be present.

Second, first responding officers may also enter the scene to search for the perpetrator/s. As with a search for victims, the scope of this search must be reasonable and restricted to areas where a perpetrator could be hiding. Again, locating one perpetrator within the scene does not prohibit officers from continuing their search to ensure that no additional perpetrators are present.

Third, while the officers are legally within the premises for the purpose of either rendering assistance to victims or searching for suspects, they may seize any evidence in plain view. There are limitations to this plain view exception. The item to be seized must be easily determined to be of evidentiary nature and no additional manipulation is allowed.

An example, it is not permissible to pick up an item and examine it for any identifiable information (serial number) that is not the readily visible, in an effort to determine if that article is stolen property, *Arizona v. Hicks*, 480 US 321 (1987). It is not recommended to seize an object under the plain view exception while searching for victims and/or perpetrators, as it somewhat shortcuts the complete documentation and potentially proper collection and preservation of that piece of evidence. Therefore, plain view seizures conducted by first responding officers should be avoided unless there is a significant risk that the evidence may be lost, destroyed, or altered. Examples of that situation might be a bloody footwear impression in the only point of entry to the structure (see Fig. 1.9). In this scenario, the greater need is to protect the evidence from destruction or disappearance.

Once these three functions are completed, any additional search and seizure activities will probably be deemed illegal. Officers are allowed to secure that scene and prevent access to that area while they seek search warrants or written permission from the lawful owner to proceed with a detailed crime scene search. If "permission to search" is given, it must be determined that the consenting individual has the legal capacity to grant permission to search the desired areas. There is no time limit as to how long first responding officers may be on the premises before securing a search warrant or consent, but it must be reasonable based on the prevailing circumstances.

A final legal consideration for the crime scene investigator is the determination of the scope of the search even if the actual search has been court authorized by permission or by exigent circumstance. To obtain a valid search warrant, the participants need to describe specific physical evidence or types of evidence that they will seek during the search. The physical evidence sought must be based on a written application of probable cause to believe that the evidence may be present at the location and, hence, that the scene will be searched. Once the search is commenced, only items within the scope of the search warrant or by the written permission of the owner may be subject to collection. Items falling outside the scope of the warrant/permission may still be legally seized so long as they are inherently items of contraband or fall within a class of other, very limited exceptions. The scope of the areas to be searched must be articulated within the search warrant or written consent document. Common examples include searches of vehicles located on the crime scene, but not listed as areas to be searched, or the search of unattached buildings or structures, also not mentioned in the warrant.

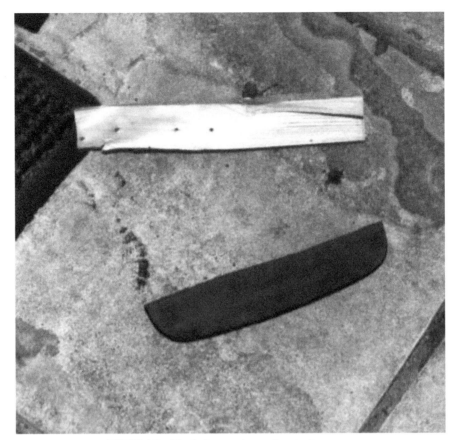

FIGURE 1.9 Bloody footwear impression at crime scene.

Crime scene investigators should possess the necessary legal training to properly evaluate the legality of a particular search and seizure for their scenes. If questions arise, investigators should consult the prosecuting authorities within a particular jurisdiction. In addition, the investigator may be aware that provisions in state constitutions and case precedence may differ substantially from federal rulings. Investigators need to be always aware of the dire consequences of seizing evidence unlawfully.

DISCUSSION QUESTIONS

1. Searching, finding, and collecting physical evidence found at the crime scene is the basis for investigating crime scenes. What are various significant uses of physical evidence for the case investigation?
2. Give a practical example of each of the uses of physical evidence used in Question #1.
3. Define "scientific crime scene investigation."
4. Discuss the basic principle of crime scene investigations and the basic steps of scientific crime scene investigation.
5. Using a practical example of a crime scene, how does a scene investigator get access to begin the on-scene investigation?

Homicide/Mincey/Joyce Search Warrant

Blood, semen, saliva, physiological fluids and secretions, hair, fibers, fingerprints, palm prints, footprints, shoe prints, gunshot residue (GSR), weaponry and firearms including pistols, rifles, revolvers, shotguns, hatchets, axes, knives, cutting instrument and cutting tools, blunt force instruments, projectiles, ammunition, bullet casings and fragments, dirt, dust and soil, paint samples, glass and plastic fragments, marks of tools used to gain access to locked premises or containers, and items containing traces of any of the abovementioned articles or items.

(Example: FOR ARSON/HOMICIDE related Cases—Any items containing traces of accelerants including lighters, flame torches, flares, and matches or any above-mentioned articles, many of which are minute.)

(The evidence will be collected and submitted to the State Forensic Science Laboratory for physical examination, scientific testing, and forensic analysis.)

(Use this language on the bottom of page 1, top of page 5, and top of page 6) Note: Give an accurate description of the person, place, or thing being searched.

*You *must* also describe the person, place, or thing to be searched within the body of the Affidavit that is identical to pages 1, 5, and 6.

(NUMBER your paragraphs and begin your narrative section with the Affiants qualifications and establishing your probable cause. Describe the underlying crime and pertinent facts.)

Narrative Section of Search Warrant:

1. Your Affiant, **(Title & NAME)**, is a duly sworn Police Officer for the **(Town of)**, Connecticut, and have been for the past **(List Years)**. I am currently assigned to the **(Your Position)** and have been for the past **(List Years).** I have investigated numerous violent crimes, **(if applies including attempted murder, or murder)**, and have processed and collected physical evidence from scenes of violent crimes, including murder. I have received specialized training in the investigation of violent crimes, **(if applies including attempted murder, or murder)** and how to process the scenes of such crimes. I have personal knowledge of the facts and circumstances herein related as a result of my own investigative efforts and those of other police officers who reported their findings to me.

2. Your affiant, **(co-affiant's name and the same info as above paragraph, etc.)**

Please Read the Following Information Before Continuing

You must adapt the information below to your investigation including on pages 1 and 5 of your search warrant. *For example*, if you know firearms are involved, you should leave out the any references to knives, hatchets, accelerants, paints, etc. If there is other evidence you wish to seize from a scene include them in the list of items you're searching for, also support that information in the Affidavit section below.

The Next Five Paragraphs Should Be in Conclusion Part of Every Mincey Warrant

(Does State's Attorney require a Lab location? If not, delete it below in all areas) Your Affiants have personal knowledge, based upon their experience and training, that crimes of violence involve a struggle, a break, the use of weapons and other instrumentalities, and/or the element of unpredictability; the person or persons participating in the commission of a violent crime is/are in contact with physical surroundings in a forceful or otherwise detectable manner; there is often an attempt to alter, destroy, remove, clean up, or cover up evidence of a crime. That traces may be left in the form of blood, semen, saliva, physiological fluids and secretions, hair, fibers, fingerprints, palm prints, footprints, shoe prints, weapons and firearms including pistols, rifles, revolvers, shotguns, knives, hatchets, axes, cutting instruments and cutting tools, blunt force instruments, projectiles, ammunition, bullet casings and fragments, gunshot residue (GSR), dirt, dust and soil, paint samples, glass and plastic fragments, marks of tools used to gain access to locked premises or containers and items containing traces of any of the above mentioned articles. Many of the above items are minute and/or microscopic, thus requiring additional specialized examination by forensic science laboratory techniques *(by the State Forensic Science Laboratory).*

Your Affiants also have personal knowledge, based upon their experience and training, that a crime scene, such as described above, will contain physical evidence, hereinbefore itemized, which will aid in establishing the identity of the perpetrator(s), the circumstances under which the crime was committed, and/or which in general will assist in the discovery of the pertinent facts and that such evidence requires a systematic search to locate, seize, record and process. That trace evidence left in the forms mentioned above is easily transferred between participants and inanimate objects such as surroundings, including their home or motor vehicle. That it is reasonable to believe and expect that a person responsible for committing a crime, such as the one described in this affidavit, would come in contact with these forms of trace evidence and transfer them to their surroundings.

Your Affiants also have personal knowledge that the *(State Forensic Science Laboratory location)* has the equipment, personnel and expertise necessary to conduct physical examination, scientific testing and forensic analysis, including but not limited to biological and chemical testing, instrumental analysis, firearms, photography, biochemistry, DNA, criminalistics, fingerprints, in order to locate, identify, compare and reconstruct items of evidence and trace evidence to aid in establishing the circumstances of the crime and identity of the participants involved in the crime. The *(State Forensic Science Laboratory)* will use standardized and documented procedures to extract, amplify and detect DNA from evidentiary items and samples taken from known individuals. The resulting DNA profiles from the evidentiary items will be compared to the known individuals' profiles and the results documented in a laboratory report.

Based upon the facts and circumstances described above, your Affiants have probable cause to believe that evidence of the crime of murder, in violation of State Gen. Stat. ##, will be found within **(LIST THE ADDRESS),** State of offense, and its curtilage, or upon the person of **(NAME OF VICTIM, dob 00/00/00)**, or **(NAME OF SUSPECT, dob 00/00/00).** *(In some cases you may have to list both.)*

Therefore, your affiants are requesting a Search and Seizure warrant be issued for **LIST ADDRESS HERE AND ANY PERSONS.**

(Use this laboratory language in proper box on pages 3 and 5 of a search warrant) (The evidence collected will be submitted to the State Forensic Science Laboratory located at address for physical examination, scientific testing and forensic analysis.)

Chapter 2

Initial On-Scene Procedures

Chapter Outline

Learning Objectives

On completion of this chapter, the reader should be able to

- Identify the duties and common problems of first responders at a given crime scene.
- Identify and utilize multilevel scene security.
- Define, discuss the steps of, and utilize the preliminary scene survey to a crime scene.

FIRST RESPONDERS AT THE CRIME SCENE

The crime scene investigator is rarely the first person at a crime scene. Private citizens, emergency medical personnel, fire fighters, and law enforcement usually arrive on crime scenes first. Most first responders work on reflex or instinct at the scene. Their tasks are to save lives or apprehend suspects. Unfortunately, that may mean that physical evidence at the scene may be inadvertently altered, changed, or lost because of the actions of a first responder. The crime scene investigator needs to communicate with the first responders to determine if any changes or alterations have occurred at the scene before the scene investigator arrived.

Notice in the photograph (see Fig. 2.1) that a chair has been placed over drops of blood and a bloody footwear impression found at the scene. Without information from the first responder, it would never be known as to whether the emergency medical services (EMS) moved the chair or if it was moved by the victim or suspect as part of the scene activities.

On further inspection, it is possible to see that medical assistance was provided. Often these medical procedures will cause used supplies and appliances that may be left behind at the scene and also on the bodies. See Fig. 2.2.

In another investigation, a large number of EMS and fire fighters were on a crime scene to provide medical assistance to the victims and to make the scene safe and preserve the condition of the scene, a fiberglass boat. As Fig. 2.3 shows, the crime scene was changed and altered with good intentions and purpose but the scene was changed nonetheless.

In addition to the shore events in the above investigation, there were numerous passengers on the boat. All of the passengers required medical treatment by a variety of EMS people. It may become significant to identify passenger locations at the time of the accident. This investigative task can be accomplished by the communication with the first responders. See Chart 2.1.

With the advent of touch DNA identifications, this case can also illustrate the need for information gathering from medical responders. Subsequent DNA analysis of bloodstains on the boat may show the presence of DNA mixtures at the scene because even with gloves being worn by EMS, there may be trace amounts of EMS personnel DNA on the scene. Prior acquisition of DNA standards from first responders may assist with interpretations of the DNA mixtures found in sample swabbings (see Fig. 2.4).

As the above cases illustrate, it is very important for the crime scene investigator to communicate well and find out everything from the first responders as the scene investigation begins.

The Crime Scene. https://doi.org/10.1016/B978-0-12-812960-9.00002-0

FIGURE 2.1   Moved chair.

FIGURE 2.2   Plastic bag used to hold emergency medical supplies left at the crime scene.

FIGURE 2.3 Numerous first responders at a crime scene.

Check List for Information from First Responders

Case Number: _____ Agency: _____

Case Detective: _____ Date of Incident: _____

Victim(s): _____

CS Investigator: _____

First Responder(s): _____ Agency: _____

_____ Phone: _____

_____

The following information is to be obtained from the first responder(s):

Time of dispatch: _____Time of arrival: _____Time cleared:_____

Others present on scene at arrival with their agency name:

_____

_____

_____

_____

_____

Did you move any objects at the scene, what, and how?

_____

_____

_____

Did you move the victim(s), and how?

_____

_____

_____

Was anything changed or left at the scene while you were there?

_____

_____

Other information:

CHART 2.1   Information from first responders.

FIGURE 2.4 DNA results show a mixture of DNA profiles in the swabbings taken from this area due to EMS activities.

CRIME SCENE SECURITY

Because we know that the Locard's exchange principle is the basis for the use of physical evidence in a criminal investigation, it is extremely important for the crime scene to be made secure and restrict the access to the crime scene by nonessential people. This is a difficult task. Many agencies allow easy access to crime scenes by anyone in the agency. Most media persons are kept out, but agency personnel can cause changes to the scene and evidence can potentially change in attempts to protect victims. This commonly occurs when blankets or barricades are erected on the crime scene. The basic idea is sound, but the potential for evidence alteration or contamination must always be considered, too.

A multilevel approach to scene security places may have layers of protection between the target area scene and the other people who may appear at the crime scene (see Figs. 2.5–2.10).

PRELIMINARY SCENE SURVEY

The preliminary scene survey or walk-through is the crime scene investigator's first opportunity to view the target area crime scene. A simple visual search for obvious physical evidence can be accomplished at this time. Should any changes to the crime scene have occurred or even be suspected, then it is a good idea to include first responders in this preliminary search activity. The use of evidence markers occurs during the survey. It is during this first viewing of the crime scene that the scene investigator should note any transient or temporary items of evidence and protect them immediately. Melting snow footwear impressions are examples of this transient evidence. See Fig. 2.11.

Likewise, footwear impressions near any points of entry or exit may inadvertently be changed, altered, or destroyed because of their location in the crime scene. See Fig. 2.12. With consultation with the first responder and other crime scene investigators on scene, the transient evidence can be protected immediately.

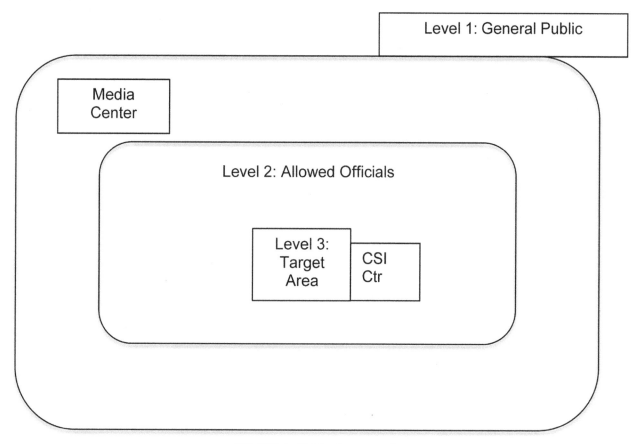

FIGURE 2.5   Multilevel scene security.

FIGURE 2.6 Investigators and noncrime scene investigators do not belong in the innermost target area.

FIGURE 2.7 Well-intended officers in the target area should not happen.

FIGURE 2.8   Quantity does not equal quality for crime scene security.

FIGURE 2.9   Witness interviews must occur away from the crime scene.

FIGURE 2.10   Barriers may prevent viewing by media but their placement may interfere with evidence at the crime scene.

FIGURE 2.11   Snow footwear impressions.

FIGURE 2.12   Bloodstain patterns at point of entry/exit.

FIGURE 2.13   Forensic anthropologists at crime scene.

The preliminary scene survey is also the time for the crime scene investigators to determine if specialists are necessary. Examples of these experts would include the use of hazardous material experts, scuba divers, forensic anthropologists, forensic odontologists, or forensic entomologists. All assistance by experts can be determined at the conclusion of this preliminary survey and, therefore, can be initiated early in the on-scene investigation. See Figs. 2.13—2.16. The same rules apply to them in that their presence must be documented and the prevention of evidence loss must occur.

In summary, the use of first responders, the establishment of scene security, and the preliminary scene survey are the first steps of the crime scene investigator. The preservation and prevention of alterations to the physical evidence at the scene is paramount. These three activities are the beginning to the scene investigation and must receive the scene investigators undivided attention.

DISCUSSION QUESTIONS

1. What is the most important use of the first responder in crime scene investigation?
2. How can a first responder insure that not additional changes or alterations occur at the crime scene?
3. Give an example of the three levels of the multilevel approach to crime scene security.
4. What type of information should be minimally included in the security log?

FIGURE 2.14   Scuba divers will be needed at this crime scene.

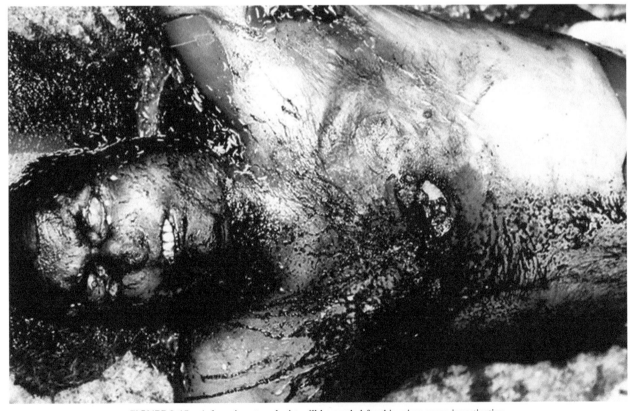

FIGURE 2.15   A forensic entomologist will be needed for this crime scene investigation.

FIGURE 2.16   Hazardous materials at a crime scene.

5. A dish of melting ice cream in the apartment of a homicide victim is an example of what type of evidence that might be found during a preliminary scene survey? What should be done with this type of evidence?
6. At the conclusion of a preliminary scene survey, a crime scene investigator has observed several 55-gal drums of leaking chemicals, what and who needs to be called to the crime scene? What would be another example of a specialist that should respond to this scene?

Part II

Making a Scene Relevant-Documentation

Chapter 3

Notes and Videography

Chapter Outline

Learning Objectives

Upon completion of this chapter the reader should be able to:

- Explain the significance and importance of "documentation in the documentation" in notes, videography, still photography, and sketching.
- Identify the ingredients of note taking at the crime scene.
- Use the proper structure to prepare a crime scene report.
- Use and/or demonstrate the process of videography at the crime scene.

DOCUMENTATION AT THE CRIME SCENE

To show the relevancy of the crime scene investigation, the crime scene itself and the physical evidence present at the crime scene must be permanently and accurately recorded. The current preferred methods for recording the crime scene are note-taking, videography, still photography, and sketching. These methods are written, visual, and quantitative in nature. The methods are detailed and continuous. Each method, if done correctly, has sufficient content to stand alone, but each method is intended to supplement the other methods. All of these methods or techniques of documentation must also contain relevancy and reliability. The relevancy and reliability is accomplished by the use of "documentation within the documentation." Simple recording of case number, date(s), time(s), and name(s) minimally can fulfill the documentation of the documentation method. Each of the documentation methods to be discussed in this chapter and the next will include the method by which the documentation can be documented along with the scene evidence.

NOTE-TAKING AT THE CRIME SCENE

The written record of the crime scene investigation includes overall observations of the scene. The observations include a *detailed* description of the scene, the body (if a death investigation), and any items of physical evidence found by the preliminary scene survey. An easy process to follow to assist the scene investigator is to answer the following questions when describing the scene, etc.: How many (quantity)? What is it (name or other identifier)? Where is it (location)? What does it look like (appearance, color, construction, size, condition)? Is it unique (serial numbers, signatures, brand or model name, etc.)? Who is at the scene? Who is a potential witness?

    The notes are the written record of on-scene activities, location of physical evidence, descriptions of people at the scene, and the condition of the crime scene. The notes are not only crucial for initial crime scene investigation but are also important for subsequent investigations. Accurate crime scene reporting in the notes is essential in the successful completion of an investigation and case resolution from a relevancy and reliability viewpoint.

There is no set process or procedure for crime scene note-taking, but some minimum requirements that should be found in the notes are:

1. Notification and arrival information.
2. Description of the scene:
    a. weather (temperature, winds, rain, etc.);
    b. location (interior/exterior, first floor/second floor, car/house, etc.);
    c. vehicles, buildings, or other major structures;
    d. evidence easily identified (prior to preliminary scene survey) and especially the transient (smells, sounds, sights) and conditional (light switches, HVAC controls) evidence.
3. Description of victim(s)—The victim's body is the single most important piece of evidence in a death investigation. Its condition as it exists at the scene is the last time it will be in that condition. It requires significant documentation prior to removal from the scene. Any movement or disruption of the body at the crime scene must be with the authorization or approval of the appropriate authority. Once given, the following may be included in the notes:
    a. position or location;
    b. lividity or rigidity;
    c. wounds;
    d. clothing, footwear, jewelry, forms of identification;
    e. weapons at scene;
    f. any physical evidence deposited on the body—patterned evidence, trace evidence, etc.
4. Descriptions of the crime scene investigation team:
    a. duty assignments—notes, video, photography, sketching, evidence collection, processing or searching responsibilities, etc.;
    b. preliminary scene survey information—from the "walk-through";
    c. start and ending times for the scene duties;
    d. evidence searching, processing or enhancement, collection, packaging, and transportation/storage.

At the conclusion of on-scene note-taking the crime scene investigator will need to prepare a report of the "crime scene investigation." While there is no set format for these final summary reports, information from the on-scene investigators notes are the only reliable source to fulfill legal and scientific needs. If the notes are incomplete, then there may be significant information easily forgotten or changed (see Fig. 3.1).

A complete note-taking report includes all details and can include basic sketches or drawing to supplement the verbiage of the report. Remember, "a picture equals a 1000 words." See Fig. 3.2. Recording of the crime scene activities must occur as they happen should be done and should not be based on fallible memories. Until expertise in recording the details of the on-scene investigation is attained, the use of some checklists may assist the crime scene note-taker (see Appendix 2).

In addition to the detail properly done in the above crime scene report, the report also shows the appropriate use of the documentation within the documentation that represents the relevancy of the report. See this short crime scene report (Fig. 3.3) to show that the process of note-taking does not end when the original scene work is finished. It is always necessary for all activities related to the on- and off-scene work. The scene work is not just the work while at the scene but subsequent workup until the investigation concludes.

VIDEOGRAPHY AT THE CRIME SCENE

Videography is the "virtual reality" format of crime scene documentation. It is an orientation format intended to allow the viewer to be virtually "at the scene." Videography at crime scenes should be one of the first steps after the walk-through (or preliminary scene survey). The notes by the videographer should start with the recording of the information on the equipment used in addition to the basic notification and location information.

The process for the videography of crime scenes starts with recording a placard for documentation within the documentation. The placard information should include, minimally, the case number, the date, time, location, type of investigation, and any other information deemed necessary by the videographer. See Fig. 3.4.

The videography of the entire crime scene should be without any subjective audio recording. It is important to prevent added subjectivity to the crime scene documentation, making sure that all law enforcement personnel are not videotaped on the scene.

Crime Scene Notes
CSInvestigator Michelle Ward, 0600
Case #: 2015-02376
January 13, 2015

Address: Palm Terrace
Scene: Second story apartment, CBS construction, dry wall/plaster, front door locked but pried open, carpet, ceramic tile and hardwood floors, heater at 77 deg, windows closed and draperies drawn closed. Female body in back south bedroom. Rooms appear ransacked. Purse on kitchen table with contents spilled. Red-brown stains in area of front door (only POE).

Body Description: face up, hands by sides, legs crossed at ankles. Blue jeans, turtle neck shirt, shoes and shocks present. No obvious wounds but bruising around the neck. Laying next to the fully made bed. Throw rug under the body. Possible hairs in the right hand.

Team members are: Miller, Smith, Ward and Jones.
First responder at scene: EMS Daren Watson

Walk Thru Done: Smith
Lead Detective: S. Holmes, CID

Documentation started: Miller 0630

FIGURE 3.1   Incomplete details in notes.

Begin the orientation videography with a general view of the areas surrounding and leading into or away from the crime scene, especially roads and intersections. The use of the four compass points will insure that all general viewpoints are recorded. The videography throughout the crime scene should be done in the wide-angle view format. Close-up views of the evidence are not usually done with the videography because still photography is better suited for that purpose. The videography of the crime scene should also include a view of the crime scene looking from the victim's point of view. Putting the video camera on a tripod near the victim's location and recording 360 degrees can achieve this viewpoint and oftentimes is useful for further investigation. Do not destroy evidence or alter the victim's position when attempting this step. It is not good practice to walk while recording instead use a tripod for the 360-degree views. This practice will also allow for ease in panning throughout the crime scene. See Fig. 3.5.

A good plan of action before doing the actual recording is essential. This plan can be easily accomplished by the use of a map. The Internet map applications and good old-fashioned road maps work well for visualizing all surrounding roads, intersections, and points of entry or exit. See Fig. 3.6 for an example of using a map for setting up a plan of action for video recording at the crime scene.

Videography of the crime scene, once completed, should never be edited or altered. There is nothing wrong with repeating recordings of the crime scene, especially as new evidence is located or found. Digital video cameras can be examined by viewing through the viewfinder, evaluated immediately, and the entire scene rerecorded if necessary. Videography as a documentation method can provide a perspective of the crime scene that is more easily perceived than by notes, sketches, or still photographs. Remember, however, that it is a supplemental technique and not a replacement for the other techniques. Use the video record as a means for allowing nonessential personnel to view the scene without them actually being on the scene.

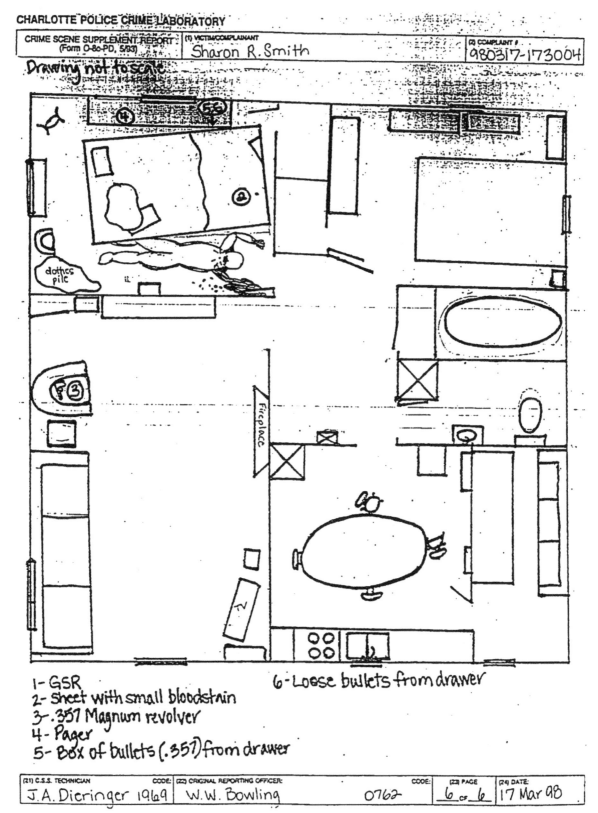

CHARLOTTE POLICE CRIME LABORATORY

CRIME SCENE SUPPLEMENT REPORT (Form O-8c-PD, 5/93)	(1) VICTIM/COMPLAINANT Sharon R. Smith	(2) COMPLAINT # 980317-173004

Drawing not to scale

1- GSR
2- Sheet with small bloodstain
3- .357 Magnum revolver
4- Pager
5- Box of bullets (.357) from drawer
6- Loose bullets from drawer

(21) C.S.S. TECHNICIAN J.A. Dieringer	CODE: 1969	(22) ORIGINAL REPORTING OFFICER: W.W. Bowling	CODE: 0762	(23) PAGE 6 of 6	(24) DATE: 17 Mar 98

FIGURE 3.2   Sketch in crime scene report.

NEW HAMPSHIRE STATE POLICE
CONTINUATION OF INVESTIGATION REPORT

1. CASE NO. MC-13-9423	2. INVESTIGATING TROOPER Sgt. Jeffrey Ladieu	3. I D. NO. 873	4. TOWN OF CRIME Charlestown	5. TN. CD. XXX	6. DATE OF INCIDENT 06-27-2013

EXECUTION OF *'BODY WARRANT'* ON
MR. James R. ROBARGE
(DOB: 12-28-1969)

On Friday, June 28th 2013, at approximately 1630 hours, I, Jeffrey Ladieu, was on duty as a Detective Sergeant assigned to the New Hampshire Department of Safety, Division of State Police, Investigative Services Bureau, Major Crime Unit. At that time I was in the town of Claremont, New Hampshire, within the Claremont Police Department, assisting with a missing persons investigation related to, one;

Kelly ROBARGE
Race: WHITE Gender: FEMALE
DOB: 10-02-1970
124 Happy Acres Road
Charlestown, NH. 03603

During the course of the mentioned investigation I was assigned to execute a search warrant, or 'Body Warrant,' on the following subject, identified as, one;

James R. ROBARGE *(HUSBAND)*
Race: WHITE Gender: MALE
DOB: 12-28-1969
124 Happy Acres Road
Charlestown, NH. 03603

Also assigned to the task of executing this search warrant was the following;

Trooper/Detective Matthew KOEHLER
NH. State Police – Major Crime Unit
33 Hazen Drive
Concord, NH. -03305
(603) 223-3856

		SIGNED		DATE
	Page 1 of 2		Sergeant Jeffrey Ladieu	09-3-2013

DSSP 102 (Rev. 08/94)

FIGURE 3.3 Even short reports require note-taking.

NEW HAMPSHIRE STATE POLICE
CONTINUATION OF INVESTIGATION REPORT

1. CASE NO. MC-13-9423	2. INVESTIGATING TROOPER Sgt. Jeffrey Ladieu	3. I.D. NO. 873	4. TOWN OF CRIME Charlestown	5. TN. CD. XXX	6. DATE OF INCIDENT 06-27-2013

Throughout the course of the execution of this search warrant Trooper/Detective Matthew KOEHLER and I gathered and/or collected the below listed items as evidence;

ID	Item	Purpose
JDL-1	(1) Knife – Black in Color	Hold
JDL-2	(1) Knife	Hold
JDL-3	New Balance Sneaker (L) (w/stain)	Hold
JDL-4	New Balance Sneaker (R) (w/stain)	Hold
JDL-5	Jean Shorts (w/ small stain)	Hold
JDL-6	Underwear	Hold
JDL-7	(1) White sock (L)	Hold
JDL-8	(1) White sock (R)	Hold
JDL-9	Buccal Swab	Hold
JDL-9a	Buccal Swab	Hold
JDL-10	Pulled body hair from head 'several'	Hold
JDL-11	Major Case Prints	Hold
JDL-12	Fingernail clippings	Hold
JDL-13	Earring (Cross)	Hold

I also took various photographs during the process of executing this search warrant, along with an audio recording of the entirety of such. Attached to, and incorporated within this report are the CD-R discs' of such photos and recording.

At the conclusion of executing this search warrant Mr. ROBARGE was provided with a zip-up Tyvec style suit, complete with attached booties. He was then released from State Police custody.

The above listed items of evidence were packaged, sealed, and transferred to the custody of the New Hampshire State Police Major Crime Unit (SP91) 'same date.' Attached to, and made part of this report are the Evidence Examination Request forms (DSSP20).

- **END OF REPORT.**

	Page 2 of 2	SIGNED *7.Hoffli* Sergeant Jeffrey Ladieu	DATE 09-3-2013

DSSP 102 (Rev. 08/94)

FIGURE 3.3 cont'd

Case No. 15-061

February 14, 2015   0615

CS Overalls

mtmiller
Videographer

FIGURE 3.4   An incomplete placard. What is missing?

FIGURE 3.5   Always use a tripod for videography.

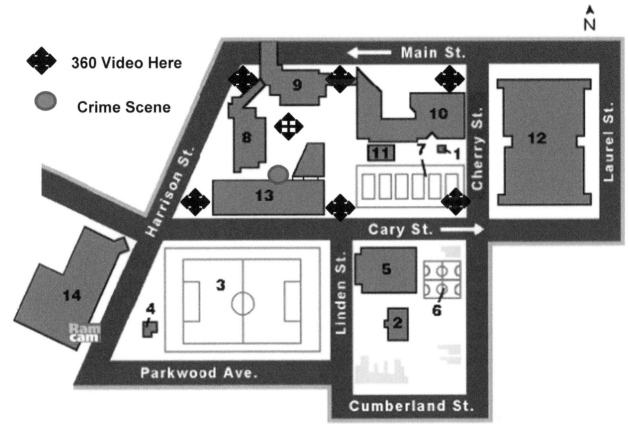

FIGURE 3.6   Using a map for a video plan of action.

DISCUSSION QUESTIONS

1. Why is it important to document the crime scene and the physical evidence found in the scene?
2. What is the purpose for note-taking and videography as methods of crime scene documentation?
3. What should be included for good note-taking at the crime scene?
4. The videography of a crime scene has what essential role in the documentation of crime scenes?

Chapter 4

Crime Scene Photography

Chapter Outline

Learning Objectives

On completion of this chapter, the reader should be able to

- State the purpose and processes of photography as a component of crime scene documentation.
- Identify the type of equipment best suited for crime scene photography.
- Explain and apply the two-step documentation process of overall, general photographs to close-up photographs at the crime scene.
- Define and apply the use of examination or evidence quality photographs as a means for documenting certain types of evidence at the scene.
- Discuss the advantages and disadvantages of the various aspects of digital photography at the crime scene.
- Discuss and apply various types of lighting as part of crime scene photography.
- Explain the use of and contents for photo logs as part of crime scene photography.

PURPOSE

The documentation of crime scenes and evidence found at the scene is arguably the most important aspect of the overall process of crime scene documentation and processing. Crime scene photography has been developed to provide a visual record of the scene and related areas, to record the initial appearance of the crime scene and physical evidence, to provide investigators and others with a permanent record for subsequent analysis of the scene, and to provide the permanent record for the courts. This description places an enormous burden on the forensic photographer to ensure that the documentation is done properly because of the today, tomorrow, and future applications. This burden exists for legal purposes, too. The first rule to follow as the crime scene photographer is to not to destroy the scene, including not to contaminate the scene. All forensic scenes are different and dynamic; the investigator should not have an idea of how many images to capture. There is no set number of images, the right number changes each and every time. Rule of thumb is to take more than not enough, and if in doubt, shoot it!

Proper dress is critical (see Fig. 4.1).

The Crime Scene. https://doi.org/10.1016/B978-0-12-812960-9.00004-4

FIGURE 4.1   Proper dress for the crime scene photographer.

PROCESS: EQUIPMENT

The process of crime scene photography as a visual form of documentation naturally follows after documenting the scene via videography. The ability to record images cannot be accomplished without a discussion on the types of equipment required or desired. This equipment can range from a few hundred to several thousand dollars. At the very least, a basic crime scene photography kit includes a camera, recording medium, external flash, and a tripod. The preferred camera would be what is known as a single lens reflex (SLR) or a digital single lens reflex (DSLR). These cameras can be basic to high end and include a variety of compatible, interchangeable lenses. The crime scene investigator should have four basic lenses: the lens that came with the camera body, usually a 50-mm lens, a zoom lens to take photos from longer distances, a macro lens to allow for close-up photos, and a 28-mm wide-angle lens to allow for a broad view image capture. Photo 4.1 illustrates the evolution of the camera to the current state of DSLR cameras.

Using a good quality, stable tripod is essential for better photographic images at the crime scene. Additionally a photographer should have a hard shell camera kit, a shutter release cord, a separate electronic flash unit, and a sync cord for the flash unit.

PHOTO 4.1 Evolution of cameras.

Additional materials are required to properly document the crime scene. These include a title page placard, photo log, and several different types of measuring devices such as an L-scale, tape measure, ruler, and adhesive backed scales.

PROCESS: GENERAL TO SPECIFIC PHOTOGRAPHS

The media formats for crime scene photography have changed over the years—film to digital—but the need for a true and accurate record of the crime scene and the physical evidence remains the same. This is one of those areas where a case can be made or lost.

The crime scene photographer needs to remember that photographic images of the crime scene help refresh memory of witnesses and victims, present the crimes to people sitting on juries, and even show a reconstructionist the different perspectives that existed at that scene. Each image captures but a moment in time, but aids in telling the story.

The first photograph taken by the crime scene photographer is that of the case placard. As was done with videography, this photograph insures the documentation within the documentation process (sets relevancy). See Placard 4.1 for an example of good documentation of the photographic documentation.

To properly document the crime scene, the photographer should use the "general to specific" or "overall to close-up" method or process. This allows the viewer to gain a full perspective of the crime scene and the evidence. See Figs. 4.2A—D and 4.3A—D.

Just as with video documentation, a plan of action utilizing a map or overhead image of the crime scene location will insure that the investigator gets complete coverage of the surroundings, intersections, and points of entry or exit. See Map 4.1 for an example of a photographic plan of action. This example is only for the surroundings but a similar plan could be used for the scene target area too. Remember to take all four compass point directions for objectivity.

PROCESS: EMS PERSONNEL IN CRIME SCENE

As discussed in earlier chapters, the scene needs to be secured and absent of all personnel and crime scene equipment to ensure the integrity of the crime scene and to avoid destroying or moving evidence. Recall that because of the necessary presence of medical personnel at the scene there may be medical waste left behind (see Figs. 4.4 and 4.5). This contamination of the scene will be discussed later regarding probative evidence.

NEW HAMPSHIRE STATE POLICE

Photographer: M. Bonilla

Date: 7.5.13   Time: 10:25

Location: 124 Happy Acres, Charlstown

Incident: Missing Person   MC13.9423
                                (CASE NUMBER)
ROLL# Digital

DSSP 135 (04/92)

PLACARD 4.1   Actual case photography placard.

PROCESS: SURROUNDINGS, ROADS, AND STRUCTURES

If the crime scene is in a structure, then the crime scene photographer should document the areas surrounding and any areas leading into and out of the crime scene. These photos should include the exterior of the building to include doors, windows, points of entry and exit, and landmarks (see Fig. 4.6A—D). Many different perspectives should be taken so that the photographic documentation is complete. These photographs can include view of witnesses to affirm or refute their depiction of the events that occurred.

Photograph the address and street information of the crime scene (see Figs. 4.7 and 4.8).

The adjoining neighborhood area should also be photographed using the overall, compass point method. This process can indicate the possible entry—exit track, escape path, and locations where evidence can be left behind and allows for the continued objectivity of recording all of the crime scene and surroundings through photographic documentation. See Fig. 4.9A—D for examples of photographic documentation of the roads in and out of a crime scene.

PROCESS: PHOTOGRAPHING VEHICLES AND CONDITIONS

The photographic documentation of a vehicle or boat follows the same process as a structure. Photograph the entire vehicle with use of the four corners (like compass points). See Fig. 4.10A—D. In addition, to properly document a vehicle, the crime scene photographer should always include the license plate, vehicle identification number, any decals, and other identifying marks.

Always remember that the condition of the structure or vehicle may be important and should be documented thoroughly as well. See Fig. 4.11.

The photography of suspicious fire scenes must also include the documentation of the structural condition. See Fig. 4.12.

PROCESS: POINTS OF ACCESS

Crime scene documentation of a structure should include all the points of access to the scene (see Figs. 4.13—4.15).

(A)

(B)

FIGURE 4.2 (A) Overall photograph of scene and path; (B) closer overall of path to scene; (C) midrange view of scene; (D) close-up or specific photograph of evidence.

(C)

(D)

FIGURE 4.2 cont'd

(A)

(B)

FIGURE 4.3 (A) Overall view of store entrance; (B) closer overall view of entrance; (C) midrange view into store; (D) midrange view of ransacked office in store.

(C)

FIGURE 4.3 cont'd

(D)

FIGURE 4.3 cont'd

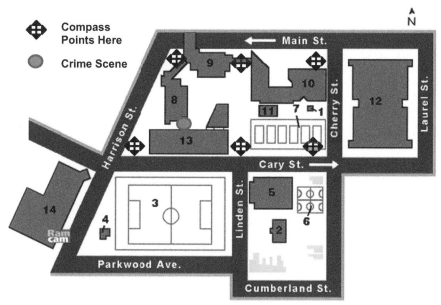

MAP 4.1 Using a map for a photographic plan of action.

FIGURE 4.4 Medical waste at a crime scene.

FIGURE 4.5 EMS equipment left at the crime scene.

(A)

(B)

FIGURE 4.6   (A and B) Four sides of a building.

(C)

(D)

FIGURE 4.6 (C and D) cont'd

FIGURE 4.7 Photograph showing scene address.

FIGURE 4.8 Photograph any street signs or intersections.

FIGURE 4.9   (A) View of surrounding road at crime scene; (B) one direction view of surrounding road; (C) another view of surrounding road at crime scene; (D) final view of surrounding road at crime scene.

(C)

(D)

FIGURE 4.9 cont'd

(A)

(B)

FIGURE 4.10 (A—D) Four views of boat.

(C)

(D)

FIGURE 4.10 cont'd

FIGURE 4.11   Interior condition of a vehicle.

FIGURE 4.12   Photographic documentation of the structural condition at a fire scene.

FIGURE 4.13   Possible access point to crime scene—overall view.

FIGURE 4.14 Possible access point to crime scene—close-up view.

FIGURE 4.15 Possible access point to crime scene.

PROCESS: AERIAL PHOTOGRAPHY OF CRIME SCENES

As discussed above, all crime scenes should be photographed to show all surrounding roads or over access possibilities. These overall photos can be supplemented with aerial images to show pathways, movements, vegetation, and other nearby structures. Dependent on the investigation, the aerial views will even show how desolate a crime scene may be. Aerial photographs are especially useful for juries who may not be familiar with the areas in question. See Figs. 4.16 and 4.17. The future use of drone photography at crime scene can accomplish easily affordable and accessible aerial photographs.

PROCESS: PHOTOGRAPHY OF INTERIOR CRIME SCENES

The crime scene photographer should use an "overlapping" technique by using the four compass points or four corners of the interior of the scene to assist in complete scene documentation (see Fig. 4.18).

Midrange photographs are used to show the relevance and orientation of evidence to the scene and their location in that scene. These midrange photographs show the evidence and its location relative to its surroundings. The specific information regarding those items is not yet documented. These are the intermediate photographs that show the transition from the overall view to closer views in the crime scene. When taking midrange shots, the scene photographer should position the object (evidence) and a fixed feature in the crime scene so that they are of the same distance from the photographer. The shape of the isosceles triangle is an example of this technique. See Fig. 4.19A–E.

FIGURE 4.16   Aerial view of crime scene.

FIGURE 4.17   Aerial view of crime scene.

PROCESS: CLOSE-UP AND EXAMINATION QUALITY PHOTOGRAPHS OF EVIDENCE

Close-up photographs document the individual items of evidence along the item's characteristics and details. The photographs provide specific information on the particular item of evidence. Close-up photographs should always be taken at a 90 degrees angle with respect to the item of evidence, regardless of how that item lays at the scene. This location oftentimes requires the crime scene photographer to contort in any number of poses and may require the use of a tripod, monopod, or perhaps a selfie stick (see Fig. 4.20).

The use of a scale in your image is of a critical importance. The scale allows for accurate size reproduction with the photograph. These types of photographs are necessary in scenes where there is damage due to a projectile occurs, wound dynamics or injury documentation is needed, and patterned evidence-like fingerprints or bloodstain patterns result. The examination quality photograph is vital if there is any chance of item distortion or alteration on collection. The crime scene investigator should take the photograph without a scale (see Fig. 4.21) and with a scale (see Fig. 4.22).

The scale must be placed so that the scale markings are adjacent to your image and are readable (see Fig. 4.23).

If the photograph is not shot at that 90 degrees angle, it allows for distortion in the size of the object and makes reconstruction virtually impossible (see Fig. 4.24).

The goal of these photographs is to produce examination or evidence quality photographs. That is a photograph that is sharp, focused, properly exposed, evidence properly framed, have proper lighting, and have documentation within the documentation. See Fig. 4.25.

Examination or evidence quality photographs are essential for future laboratory examinations and comparison. Without these photographs it is very difficult, if not impossible, to get identifications or be used for possible reconstruction purposes. Figs. 4.26—4.30 illustrate ineffective or improper examination or evidence quality photographs.

FIGURE 4.18   Overlapping or compass point views of crime scene.

FIGURE 4.18 cont'd

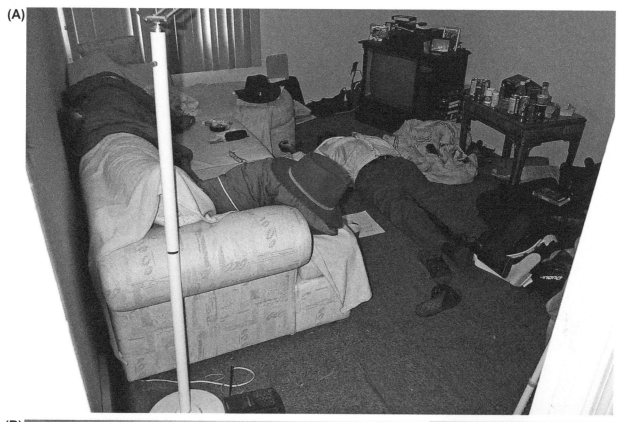

FIGURE 4.19   (A) Overall view of crime scene; (B) overall view of crime scene; (C) midrange view of crime scene; (D) midrange view of crime scene; (E) midrange view of crime scene.

(C)

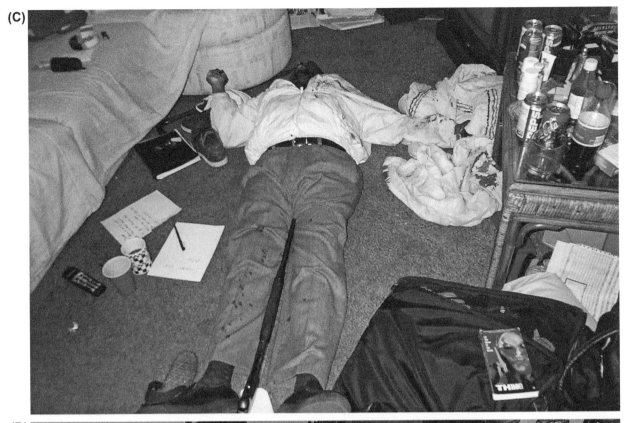

(D)

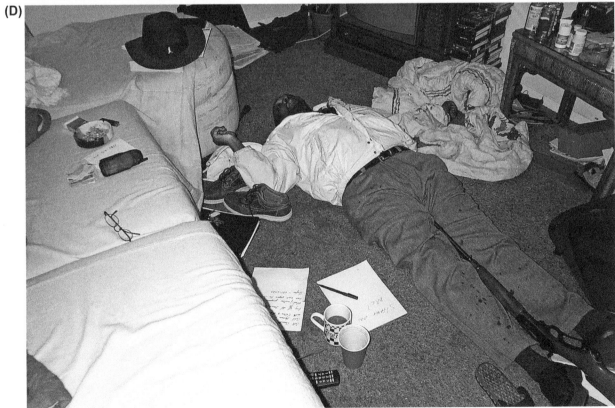

FIGURE 4.19 cont'd

(E)

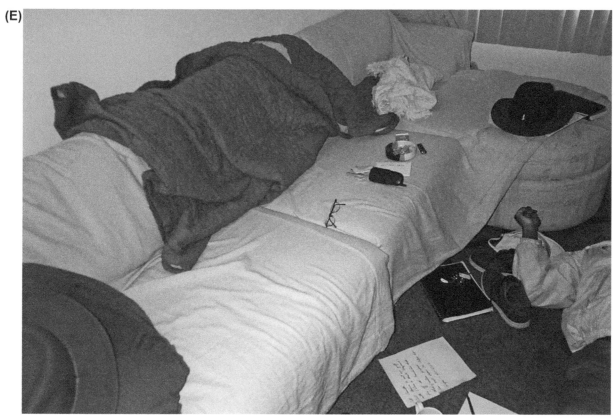

FIGURE 4.19 cont'd

PROCESS: ADDITIONAL PHOTOGRAPHS OF MARKED EVIDENCE

The preliminary scene survey identified items of potential evidence. The photographs of the surrounding points of access and eventually the overall to specific evidence photographs document the crime scene as it was found, hopefully still in its most pristine state and undisturbed. It is at this time that those items deemed of evidentiary value were marked and identified. There are a wide variety of products that can be used as the evidence markers. Figs. 4.31 and 4.32 show a couple of the commonly used types.

These placards are utilized to denote evidence items and act as identifiers to avoid future mistakes. The most critical component is that whatever has been identified during the preliminary walk-through, will be marked with the evidence placard, must be photographed, and will be eventually collected.

PROCESS: EVIDENCE MARKERS AND DIFFERENT SITUATIONS

There may be times when the sequence of how the crime scene is photographed will be altered. Examples of this would be weather, difficulties in scene security, or the potential destruction of the evidence. Generally, the practice is such that the overall photographs are not taken once the evidence placards have been deployed. Clearly, if it assists in showing a pattern, or can aid in documenting a possible reconstruction of the crime scene, then it should be photographed immediately regardless of the preferred sequence. See Fig. 4.33.

The crime scene photographer must always be cognizant of the meaning of an image. The mere placement of an evidence marker without any other relevant photographs may call into question that which is being depicted in the photograph. See Fig. 4.34.

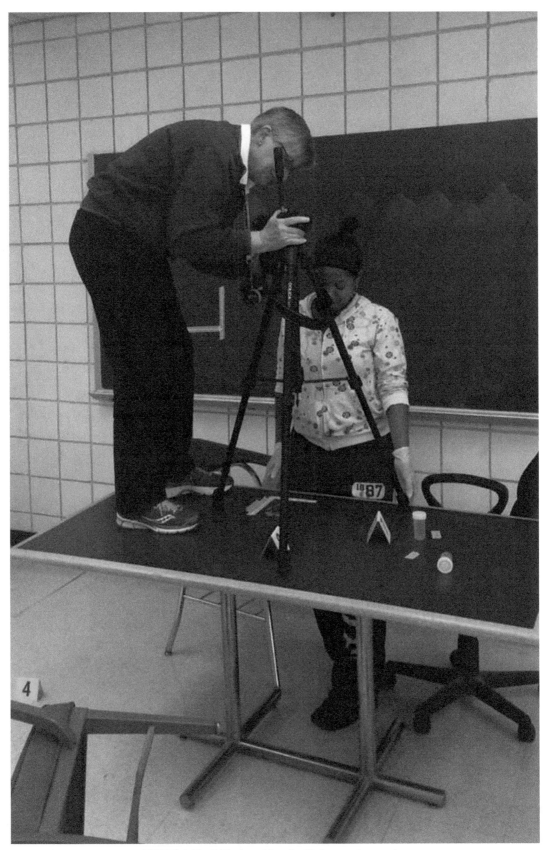

FIGURE 4.20 Difficult positions for 90 degrees photographs.

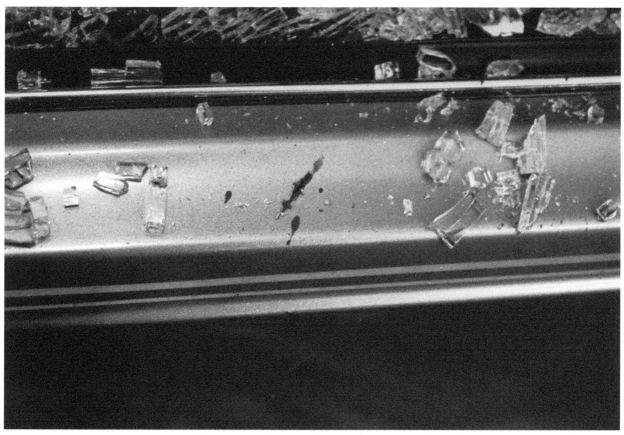

FIGURE 4.21   Photograph of bloodstain without scale.

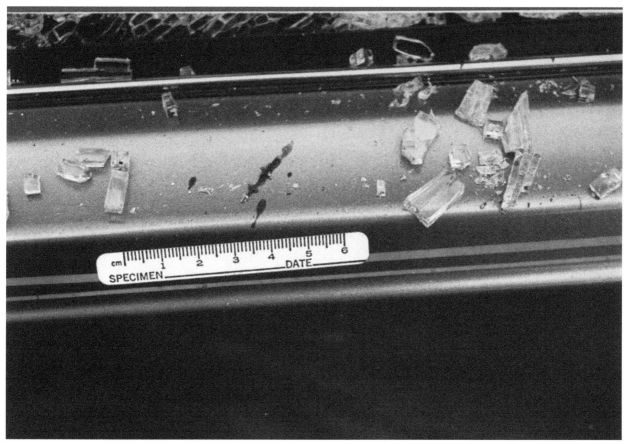

FIGURE 4.22   Photograph of bloodstain with scale.

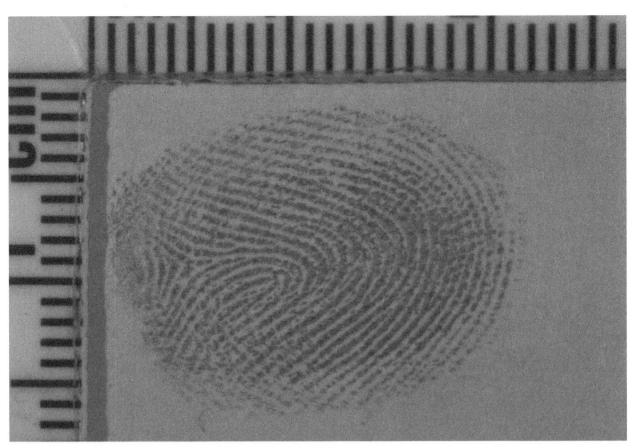

FIGURE 4.23 Readable scales beside evidence.

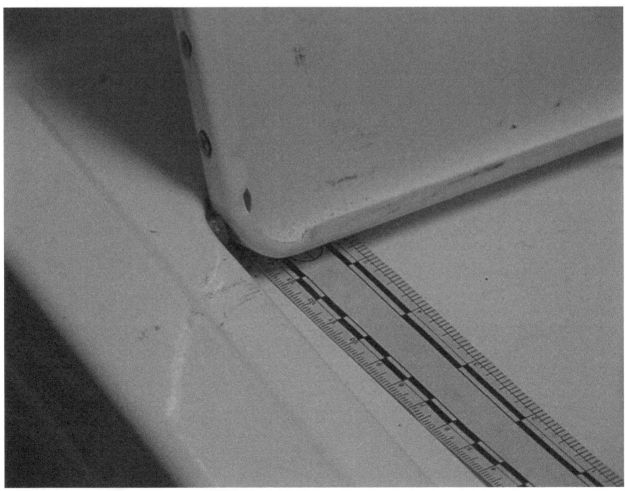

FIGURE 4.24 Photograph of bloodstain not at 90 degrees.

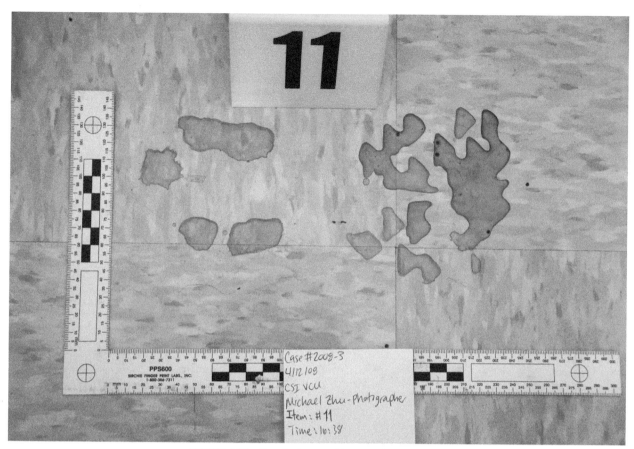

FIGURE 4.25   Examination or evidence quality photograph.

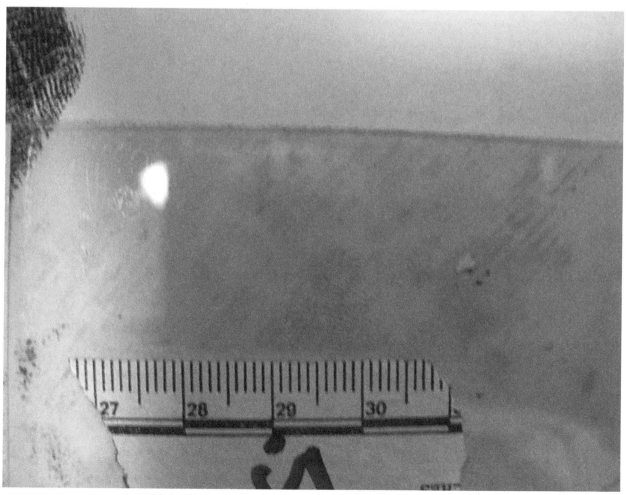

FIGURE 4.26   Improper lighting for an evidence quality photograph of fingerprint.

FIGURE 4.27   Improper lighting for evidence quality photograph.

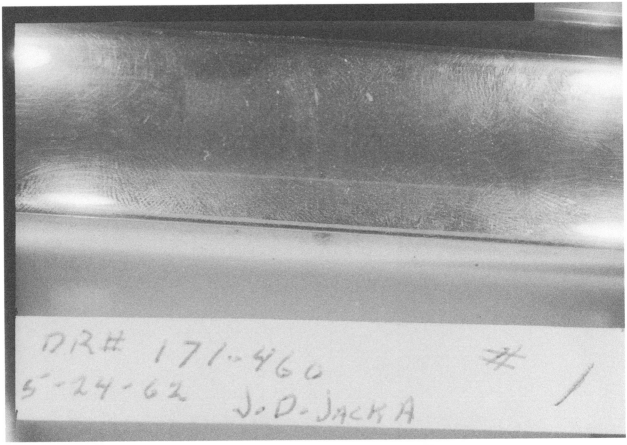

FIGURE 4.28   No scales in evidence quality photograph of latent.

FIGURE 4.29   Improper lighting, no doc in doc in evidence quality photograph of cigarette butt.

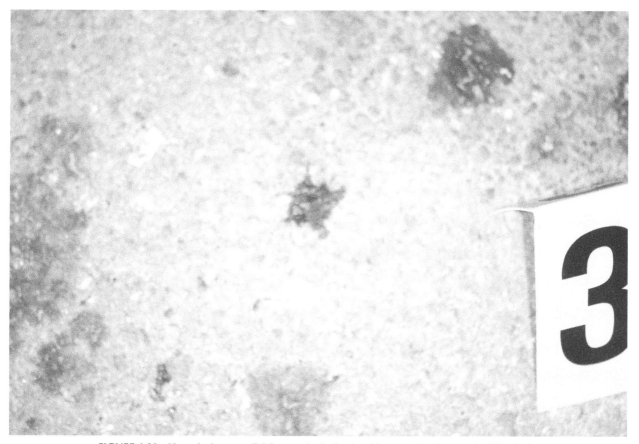

FIGURE 4.30   No scale, improper lighting, no doc in doc in evidence quality photograph of bloodstain.

FIGURE 4.31   Yellow, tent-like evidence markers.

FIGURE 4.32   Red, cone-like evidence markers.

FIGURE 4.33   Evidence markers used in overall photographs of scene.

FIGURE 4.34   Evidence marker placed without any information as to what is being identified or depicted. Which stain?

PROCESS: DOCUMENTATION WITHIN THE DOCUMENTATION OF CLOSE-UP AND EXAMINATION (EVIDENCE) QUALITY PHOTOGRAPHS

Close-up photographs should, as practical as possible, show the evidence marker. Examination (evidence) quality photographs must have the information about case number, item number, initials, date, and time within the photograph and not show the evidence marker. There may be concerns about admissibility or reconstruction when there is no reference or an inadequately marked reference in the photography. See Figs. 4.35–4.37, where there are no identifiers of evidence number and other necessary documentation to establish relevancy for the evidence. Evidence identifiers are necessary for assisting to effect an identification with fingerprints.

The photographic documentation of bloodstain patterns can be difficult. The use of the same two-step technique of general to specific with midrange photographs works well. The overall photographs should contain scales around the edges of the bloodstain pattern. This use of scales on the edges of a stain pattern is known as "road mapping." See Fig. 4.38. Once the pattern road map has been done, then midrange and close-up photographs of stains to be collected should follow. See Fig. 4.39.

These close-up images would denote those stains taken for further biological examination. The crime scene photographer cannot take for analysis and document every specific bloodstain. These close-up images might be able to show important information to the investigator or reconstructionist such as pattern type, force involved, and angle of impact.

For close-up and examination quality photography, the item of evidence must fill the frame. Failure to fill the frame detracts from the purpose of the photograph and will make an actual size photo impossible for the laboratory to create for their comparisons. See Fig. 4.40A and B for examples.

PROCESS: THE PHOTO LOG AND DIGITAL IMAGE FORMATS

To ensure reliability and relevancy and to allow for quick access to an image, every photograph taken at the crime scene must be recorded or documented in a photo log. The photo log contains all the information about the photographer's equipment and for every photograph taken (see Fig. 4.41).

FIGURE 4.35   No evidence identifiers in this photograph.

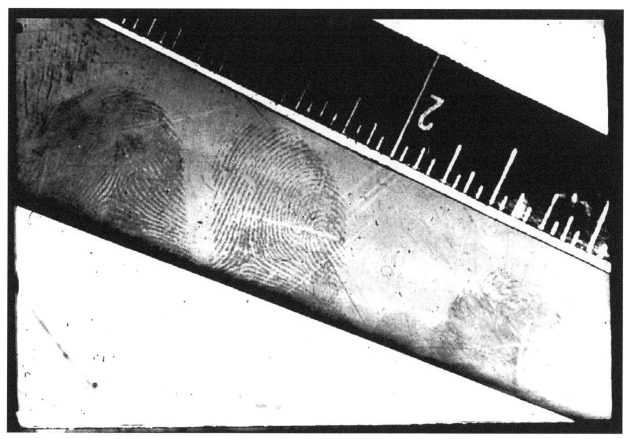

FIGURE 4.36 Without any evidence identifiers in this photograph there can be no reliability as to affecting an identification with the fingerprint.

It is critical that under no circumstances should an image be deleted. Not every image is going to be in focus, utilize light properly, or be that perfect image. They are numbered in the camera, which can be verified using the exchangeable image file format (EXIF) data. A gap may indicate an integrity issue. It is better to not be subjected to questions about what someone may think is important, but rather justify that it is a bad image. There is no justification as to a deleted image.

Fortunately for most digital images taken at a scene and in common file formats such as .jpeg, .tiff, and .wav, the photo log information is embedded in the digital file itself. It contains a variety of information. This is called EXIF. This information, which may require special software to extract, can include: the original file format, date and time the image was taken, the GPS or geolocation, and the unique ID number of the device capturing the image, including the brand and model of the DSLR. See Fig. 4.42.

The crime scene photographer has to make a decision as to which digital file format will be used to capture the images at the crime scene. There are three file formats that are commonly utilized: .jpg; .raw; and .tiff. For images requiring extreme detail or high definition photography such as those images of footwear impressions, friction ridge impressions, tool mark impressions, and close-up images of blood spatter patterns, the best option for the image is .raw or .tiff. These are uncompressed file formats. A .jpg file format will automatically eliminate pixels that are believed to be not necessary. This elimination may change important characteristics, such as a nick in the footwear or bifurcation of a fingerprint. Digital image storage space is very inexpensive. Utilize multiple data cards and never mix cases on the same card.

Digital photography as a form of documentation of crime scenes has achieved far-reaching acceptance across the criminal justice system in the United States. Originally this acceptance was difficult because of the ease in the manipulation of digital images (see Fig. 4.43A and B).

FIGURE 4.37 No evidence identifiers to show relevancy for this impression.

Digital images should be archived as soon as practical after the incident in a redundant type system. Preferably there will be software in place to allow for detailed record keeping as to who is opening the image and when it occurs. It should also lock out the ability to change the original image in any way. The original image should never be used to perform any type of enhancement. Always use a copy of that original.

PROCESS: LIGHTING

Lighting can be very critical when documenting crime scenes and its evidence. Oftentimes it is important to show depth and detail in a three-dimensional impression, an indentation, by the use of a light held above the same plane as the impression. A light at approximately the same plane as the imprint illuminates imprint impressions that are two-dimensional in nature. See Figs. 4.44 and 4.45.

There are several concerns with using flash photography. If the flash is perpendicular to the evidence in question, it can often obscure any detail. See Fig. 4.46.

In places where there has been a fire, the blackness of the char soaks up the light producing the same results as too much light—inability to ascertain details—in this case, not enough light. Additional lighting is essential. See Fig. 4.47.

FIGURE 4.38   Road mapping of bloodstain pattern on a wall.

PROCESS: PHOTOGRAPHING THE USE OF ALTERNATE LIGHT SOURCES

Physical evidence at a crime scene may not be seen clearly enough in visible light. The use of variable wavelength alternate light sources (ALS) may be required. Chapter 6 addresses the use of ALS for visualizing and enhancing evidence to facilitate searches at crime scenes. The use of a colored filter is part of this technique to enhance the evidence. If the evidence is visualized using the ALS and a colored barrier filter, then that same colored filter needs to be used with a camera when photographing the item of evidence. There are commercially available filters that screw on to the camera lens, and placing the colored barrier flush against the lens opening will work too. See Figs. 4.48–4.50 for examples of various filters that work with ALS visualization.

PHOTOGRAPHIC DOCUMENTATION OF A CRIME SCENE—RULES TO FOLLOW

Rule # 1 Do Not Disturb the Scene

- **This is the cardinal rule of forensic scene photography**
- Investigators and jurors need to see the scene as it was when the police arrived
- After the scene has been photographed in its original state, you may shoot a second series of pictures with minor changes occurred during the photography

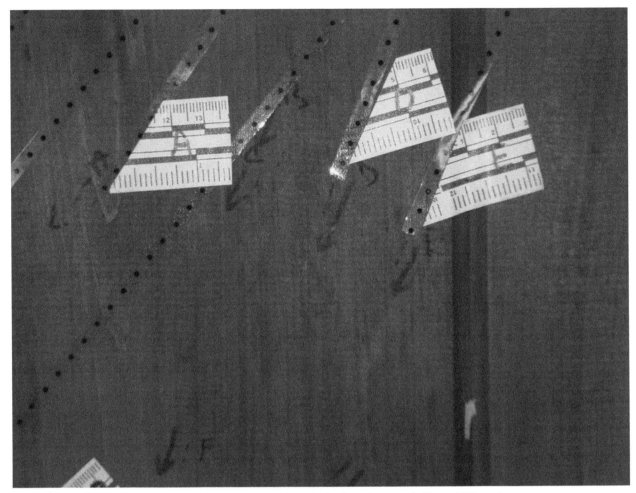

FIGURE 4.39   Close-up photographs of bloodstains from the pattern in Figure 4.38's road map.

Rule # 2 Complete Set of Photographs

- You have to move around the scene to see everything—so should the camera
- Generally speaking, each important object in the scene should appear in at least three pictures
- The **overall** photographs should cover the entire scene to show the entire scene and to record the relationships between the objects. The **midrange** shot shows an important object and its immediate surroundings. Finally, each **close-up** shows a key detail clearly

Rule # 3 Pay Attention to Angles

- Relationships of size and distance may be distorted by the wrong viewpoint of the photograph
- Most photographs are taken with the camera at eye level. This is the height from which people normally see things and that makes it easier to judge perspective but do not forget to change your perspective
- Ask yourself questions such as:
  - Does this picture reveal the true position of the evidence to the crime?
  - Does this photograph distort the object?
  - Does the photograph give the perspective of an observer?

(A)

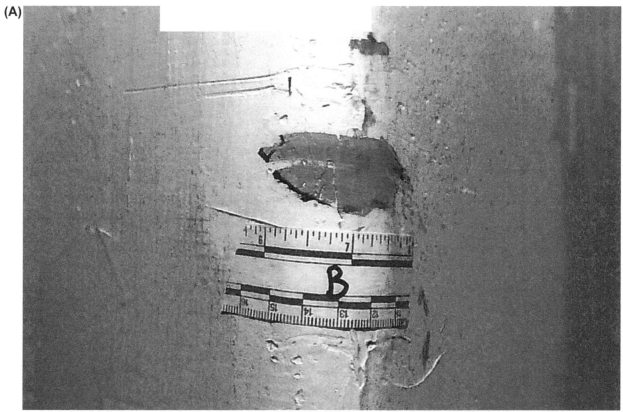

(B)

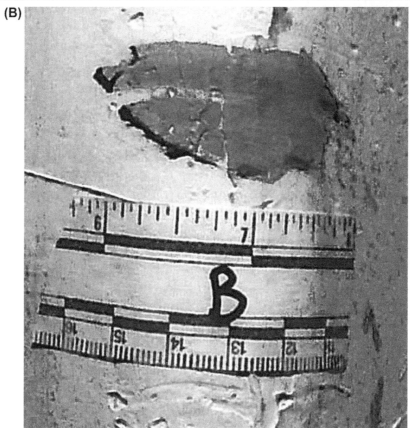

FIGURE 4.40 (A) Examination quality photograph that does not fill the frame; (B) filling the frame with the evidence.

Agency Name: _____ Investigator: _____ Date: _____

Case No.:_____ Location: _____

Image Number	Description	Location

FIGURE 4.41 Photo log example.

File name:IMG_0132.JPG

File size: 246582 bytes (1440x960, 1.4bpp, 17x)

EXIF Summary: 1/2s f/22.0 ISO400 50mm (35mm eq:80mm)

Camera-Specific Properties:

Equipment Make:	Canon
Camera Model:	Canon EOS D30
Maximum Lens Aperture:	f/2.8
Sensing Method:	One-Chip Color Area
Firmware Version:	Firmware Version 1.02
Serial Number:	0203687616
Owner Name:	Andrew P. Scott

Image-Specific Properties:

Image Orientation:	Top, Left-Hand
Horizontal Resolution:	180 dpi
Vertical Resolution:	180 dpi
Image Created:	2010:07:28 13:54:37
Exposure Time:	1/2 sec
F-Number:	f/22.0
ISO Speed Rating:	400
Lens Aperture:	f/22.0
Exposure Bias:	0 EV
Subject Distance:	0.00 m
Flash:	No Flash
Focal Length:	50.00 mm
Color Space Information:	sRGB
Image Width:	1440
Image Height:	960
Exposure Mode:	Manual
Focus Type:	Auto
Metering Mode:	Evaluative
Sharpness:	Normal
Saturation:	Normal
Contrast:	Normal
Shooting Mode:	Manual
Image Size:	Small
Focus Mode:	Manual
Drive Mode:	Single
Flash Mode:	Off
Compression Setting:	Normal
Macro Mode:	Normal
White Balance:	Auto
Exposure Compensation:	3
Sensor ISO Speed:	224
Image Number:	101-0132

FIGURE 4.42 Embedded information for digital images.

Resolution Unit: i
Chrominance Comp Positioning: Centered
Exif IFD Pointer: 178
Compression Scheme: JPEG Compression (Thumbnail)
Horizontal Resolution: 180 dpi
Vertical Resolution: 180 dpi
Resolution Unit: i
Offset to JPEG SOI: 2036
Bytes of JPEG Data: 5120
Exif Version: 2.10
Image Generated: 2010:07:28 13:54:37
Image Digitized: 2010:07:28 13:54:37
Meaning of Each Comp: Unknown
Image Compression Mode: 2
Shutter Speed: 1/2 sec
Metering Mode: Pattern
Focal Plane Horiz Resolution: 1614 dpi
Focal Plane Vert Resolution: 1613 dpi
Focal Plane Res Unit: i
File Source: Digital Still Camera
Lens Size: 50.00 mm
ISO Speed Rating: Unknown
Digital Zoom: None
Self-Timer Length: 0 sec
Canon Tag1 Length: 64
Subject Distance: Unknown
Flash Bias: 0.00 EV
Sequence Number: 0
Canon Tag4 Length: 50
Image Type: IMG:EOS D30 JPEG
Custom Function: Sensor cleaning - Disabled
Custom Function: Shooting Set button function - Not Assigned
Custom Function: Menu button return position - Previous (Volatile)
Custom Function: Fill flash auto reduction - Enabled
Custom Function: Lens AF stop button - Operate AF
Custom Function: Shutter curtain sync - 1st-Curtain Sync
Custom Function: AEB sequence/auto cancellation - 0,-,+/Enabled
Custom Function: Av mode shutter speed - Auto
Custom Function: AF-assist light - Auto
Custom Function: Tv/Av and exposure level - 1/2 Stop
Custom Function: Mirror lockup - Disabled
Custom Function: Shutter/AE lock buttons - AF/AE Lock
Custom Function: Long exposure noise reduction - On

FIGURE 4.42 cont'd

(A)

(B)

FIGURE 4.43   (A) Original crime scene photograph; (B) altered crime scene photograph.

FIGURE 4.44 Indentation impression lighting.

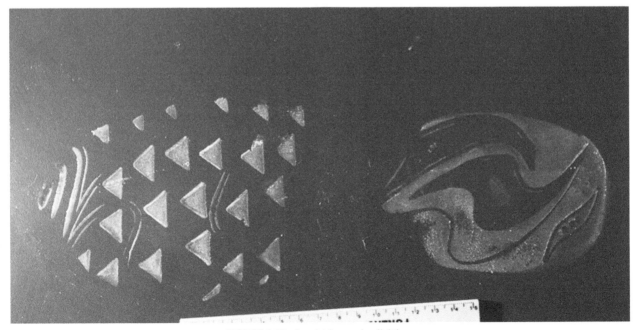

FIGURE 4.45 Imprint impression lighting.

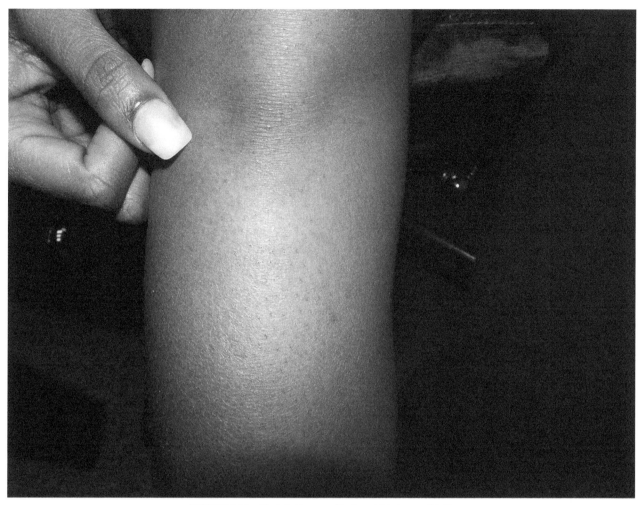

FIGURE 4.46 Flash held perpendicular might obscure detail.

TYPES OF PHOTOGRAPHS BY THE TYPE OF CRIME

Homicide or Death Investigation

1. Four compass points of scene
2. Original position and condition of body before removed
3. Trace evidence
4. Hands and face of victim
5. Any wounds, bruises, or injuries
6. Entire area surrounding scene—signs of struggle
7. GSR or bloodstain patterns
8. Relative location of evidence (gun, bullet)
9. Detailed coverage of victim

FIGURE 4.47   Fire scenes absorb lighting to obscure details.

Suicide

1. Four compass points of scene
2. Original position of body and condition before removal from scene
3. Entire area surrounding scene
4. GSR or bloodstain patterns
5. Any wounds, bruises, or injuries
6. Relative location of evidence (gun)
7. Suicide note
8. Knots in ropes
9. Hesitation wounds
10. Detailed coverage of victim

Motor Vehicle Accident

1. All vehicles in original positions
2. Aerial or high angle views
3. Debris patterns
4. Any special hazards or contributing factors
5. Path of each vehicle
6. Dash board and pedals
7. Detailed exterior and interior of each vehicle
8. Detailed coverage of victim

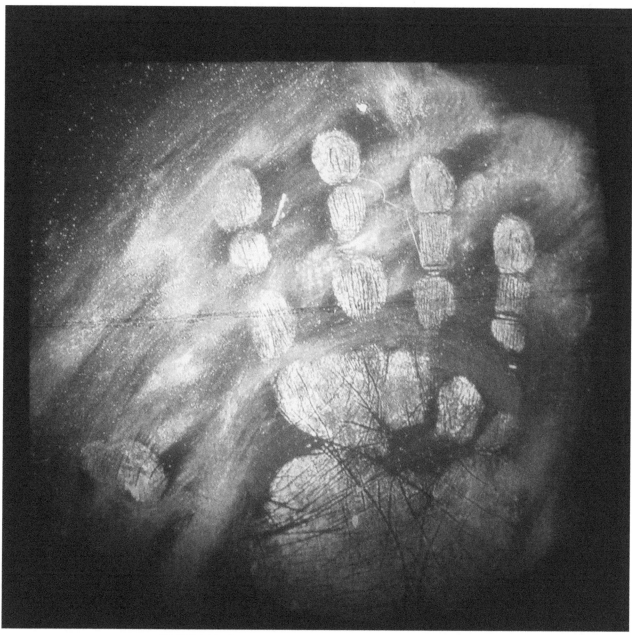

FIGURE 4.48 Photograph of alternate light sources-enhanced palm print.

Fires

1. Overall scene
2. All directions of scene
3. Signs of forced entry
4. Suspicious items (gas can)
5. Wounded persons
6. Crowd photos
7. Burn patterns
8. Any fire burning and smoke
9. Debris patterns
10. Suspected point of origin
11. Trailers or pour patterns

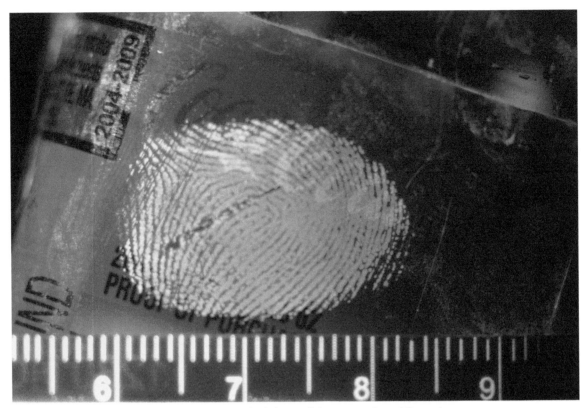

FIGURE 4.49 Photograph of alternate light sources-enhanced fingerprint.

FIGURE 4.50 Photograph of alternate light sources-enhanced fingerprint.

DISCUSSION QUESTIONS

1. How many photographs should be taken at a forensic scene?
2. What best describes an examination or evidence quality photograph?
3. Good composition will satisfy what two goals in crime scene photography?
4. When taking midrange shots, how should you position the subject and the fixed feature?
5. What is the basic purpose of crime scene photography?
6. Why should .tiff and .raw file formats be utilized for images that may be used for reconstruction?

Chapter 5

Crime Scene Sketching and Measurement

Chapter Outline

Learning Objectives

Upon completion of this chapter, the reader should be able to:

- evaluate and construct the particular type of sketch necessary for each type of crime scene,
- evaluate and utilize the proper measuring technique for sketch documentation of a crime scene and to place evidence in the sketch, and
- understand the value of a rough and final crime scene sketch.

PURPOSE AND METHOD

To effectively document a crime scene, the investigator needs to complete a sketch. This sketch will compliment the notes, video, and photographs already used as documentation components. The sketch is used to accurately depict the appearance of the crime scene and its physical evidence. The purpose of the sketch is to allow for any subsequent investigators, if needed, to place all items of evidentiary value back into their original positions as they were found at the scene. This accurate placement of evidence is critical for a crime scene reconstruction. It can also assist those who were not present at the scene to obtain an understanding of the scene's proportionality and size that cannot be achieved with just photography or videography. The sketch allows for selectivity of the evidence and structures at the scene. With the other two visual documentation techniques, the entirety of the scene is recorded. With the sketch, the investigator decides what is critical to include in addition to all of the evidence. It is impractical to draw every object. Major pieces of furniture, structures, and measuring points are some of the items that are significant at the scene and in the sketch. The sketch also allows for no spatial distortions because everything is measured accurately. Multiple sketches for large or complex scenes can be used to supplement the photography.

Each crime scene sketch should include some basic documentation information: the specific case identifier for the sketch and the location(s) of the sketch depiction. In order to allow subsequent individuals to orient themselves to the sketch, the use of a compass direction, generally north, is used. Historically a simple compass would be all that was needed. Now with smartphone and GPS technologies, other more advanced geolocation points can be obtained and recorded. The final two required items for a sketch are distance measurements to allow for the reconstruction and a legend to allow for the viewer to understand what is depicted in the sketch. Because the rough sketch is not drawn to scale, that information should be

The Crime Scene. https://doi.org/10.1016/B978-0-12-812960-9.00005-6

included on the sketch so as to allow for size inconsistencies. The rough sketch is done at the scene in sufficient detail so as to allow the final sketch to be constructed from its information. See Figs. 5.1 and 5.2.

The finished or final sketch contains the exact same information as the rough sketch; however, it is now cleaned, organized, and drawn to scale. If the final sketch is not drawn to scale, then measurements need to be added and are either included on the sketch or in a separate chart. If it is drawn to scale, then the scale used must be included. The investigator should always work with a scale that is reasonable. See Figs. 5.3 and 5.4.

There are three models of crime scene sketches utilizing the two perspectives generally observed in the sketch: from above or from the side. Looking from above the investigator draws the items of evidence and the important landmarks. This is a great sketch if all of the evidence and objects are located on the lowest level at the scene. This model is called the floor plan or bird's-eye view. See Fig. 5.5.

Documentation for Crime Scene Sketch

The crime scene sketch must include not only the measurements of the crime scene and the physical evidence but also other important documentation information. The information to be included in this portion of the sketch is as follows:

1. Agency case number.
2. Offense or incident type (death investigation, burglary, etc.).
3. Victim(s) name(s). Never place a suspect(s) name on the sketch.
4. Address or location.
5. Scene describer (interior of house, outdoor area of scene, Room 222, etc.), including weather and lighting conditions.
6. Date and time the sketch was begun.
7. Sketcher's name, assistant sketcher's name, or verifier's name.
8. Scale used (1 mm = 1 inch).
9. Legend (# = item of evidence) of physical evidence.

In reality, all the evidence at the scene is not on the floor. At many scenes, the evidence, such as blood spatter and bullet holes, are up off the ground and found in or on a wall. The floor plan or bird's-eye view does not allow for accurate depiction of the evidence in that above floor location.

The elevation sketch was developed to allow for vertical measurements. This type of sketch would be used in the scenario indicated above. It can also be utilized for in-ground excavation scenes or any time height or depth is required for the scene to be correctly documented. See Fig. 5.6.

The cross-projection or exploded view combines the best of the overview and the elevation sketches. This model allows for three or four dimensions to be displayed all in one plane. The best method for describing this type of sketch is to take the overview sketch, slice each corner, and lay the walls down. This type of sketch also allows for the ceiling to be recorded. The ceiling is added to a wall and laid out. For many situations this cross-projection sketch is the preferred model for sketching a crime scene. See Fig. 5.7.

CHALLENGES AND BARRIERS

One of the biggest challenges or barriers with investigators who create sketches is that often there are no measurements recorded or even taken. Without these measurements, the sketch is nothing more than a drawing, which will not allow for reconstruction. There are several tools that can be utilized to gather accurate measurements. These tools include steel measuring tape, sonic measuring devices, and laser measuring devices that include Total Stations.

A steel measuring tape is preferred over any other material, as it will not stretch and thus allows for accurate measurements. The sonic measurers operate by sending out sound waves, which bounce off the object and return to the device. These devices are very accurate. The lasers operate similarly; however, they utilize light waves. They are usually accurate to one thousandth of an inch. These lasers can be handheld or as with the Total Station, require a tripod. See Figs. 5.8 and 5.9.

The laser measurement devices gather the measurement data that is downloaded into a specific software program and will then create a computer-generated graphic sketch containing scale measurements. Whichever method of measurement acquisition is chosen, it cannot be overstated enough that every item of evidence be measured.

While it makes the task of gathering the measurements very accurate and quicker, many agencies do not have the financial capability of obtaining a Total Station. A quality tape measure can be purchased for less than five dollars and the handheld laser for a few hundred dollars.

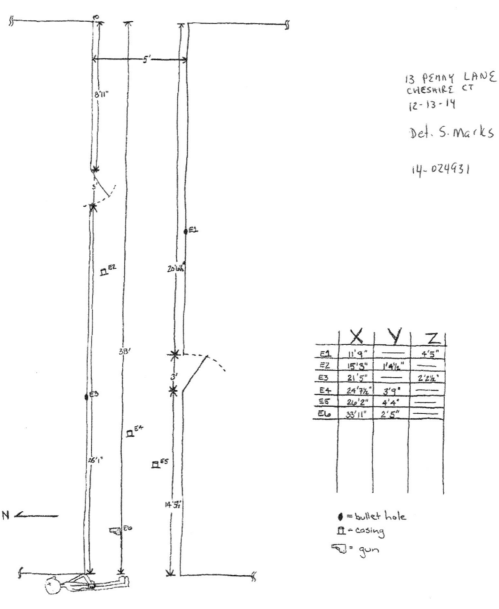

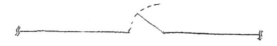

FIGURE 5.1 Rough sketch.

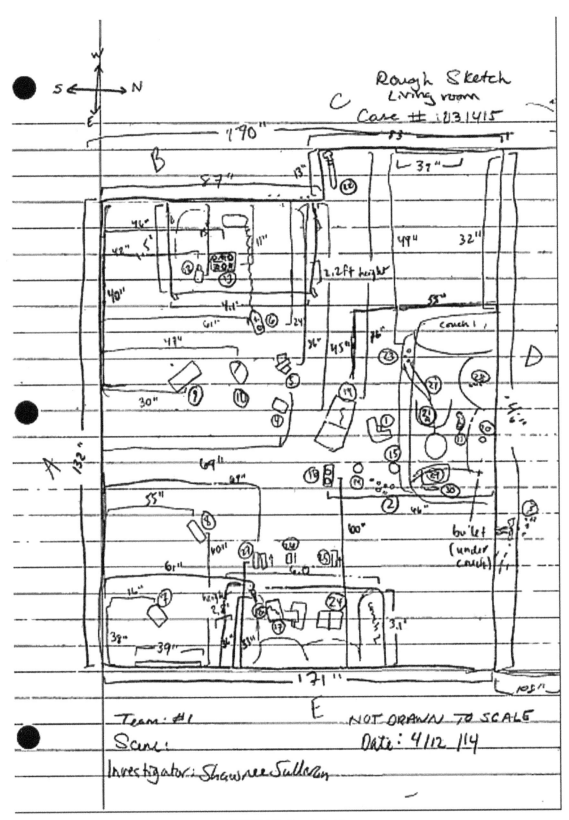

FIGURE 5.2 Rough sketch.

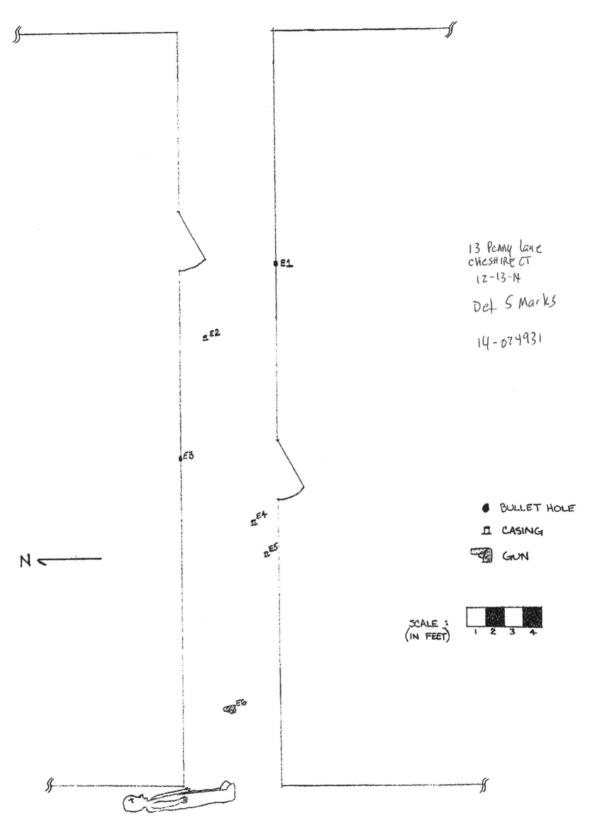

FIGURE 5.3 Finished sketch.

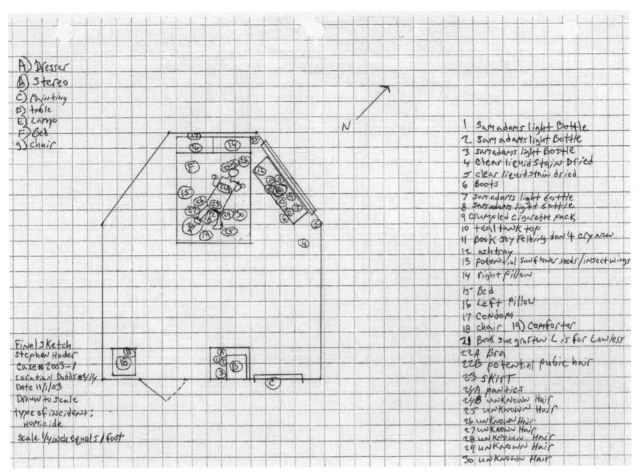

FIGURE 5.4   Finished sketch.

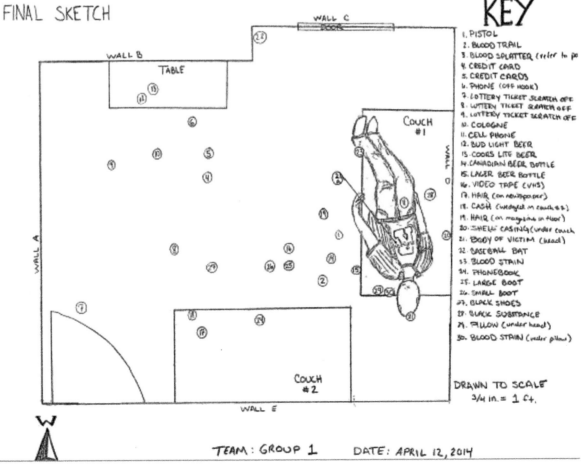

FIGURE 5.5   Floor plan or bird's-eye view sketch.

SKETCH OF WALL D

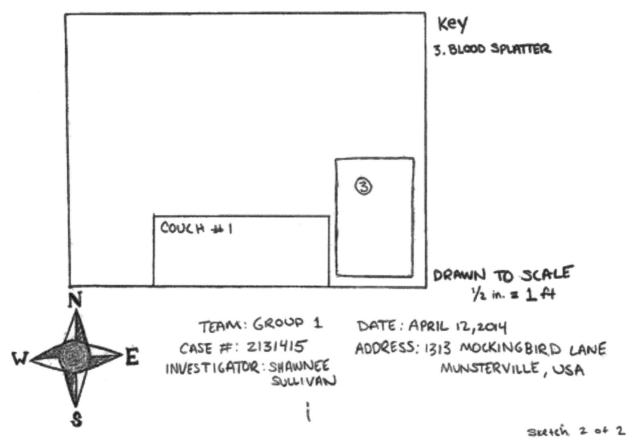

Key

3. BLOOD SPLATTER

③

COUCH #1

DRAWN TO SCALE
½ in. = 1 ft

N
W   E
S

TEAM: GROUP 1
CASE #: 2131415
INVESTIGATOR: SHAWNEE
SULLIVAN

DATE: APRIL 12, 2014
ADDRESS: 1313 MOCKINGBIRD LANE
MUNSTERVILLE, USA

i

sketch 2 of 2

FIGURE 5.6   Elevation sketch.

There are several techniques used to obtain accurate measurements of the evidence on the crime scene. The first is called triangulation. All measurements start from a fixed point. There are many fixed points available at any type of crime scene. These can be a curb; survey marker; utility pole; room corner; wall; or door frame. From this fixed point, a straight line in the same plane as the item of evidence is measured. A second fixed point is chosen and a second straight line in the same plane as the item of evidence is measured. If the rotational axis of the item of evidence is not critical (extremely long items of evidence), then the end point would be the center of the item of evidence. If rotational axis is critical, then the two lines would be the separate edges or ends of the item of evidence. This process can be repeated from different fixed points to ensure accuracy, if desired. See Fig. 5.10.

The second measurement technique is rectangulation. This is very similar to triangulation; however, instead of using a triangle for the points, this entails using right angle measurements that are taken from the two closest walls that abut each other, curb edging, or some other object that is at a 90-degree angle with reference to the item of evidence. One series of these two measurements are needed for each item of evidence. As mentioned above, the more measurement points, the more accurate the sketch. See Fig. 5.11.

The third measurement technique is called baseline or fixed line. This technique employs the placing of the tape measure along one side of a room, and each item of evidence is measured at a 90-degree angle with reference to this baseline. The major concern with this measurement technique is that the sketch will be lopsided with all evidence to one side of the baseline, thus creating a cluttered sketch with recording of the measurements often difficult to recover at a later time. See Fig. 5.12.

It is easier to decipher the measurement data if the scene width is divided in half and the tape measure baseline is laid out lengthwise. The items of evidence are now measured perpendicular to this, similar to rectangulation. This technique seems to "balance" the sketch. See Fig. 5.13.

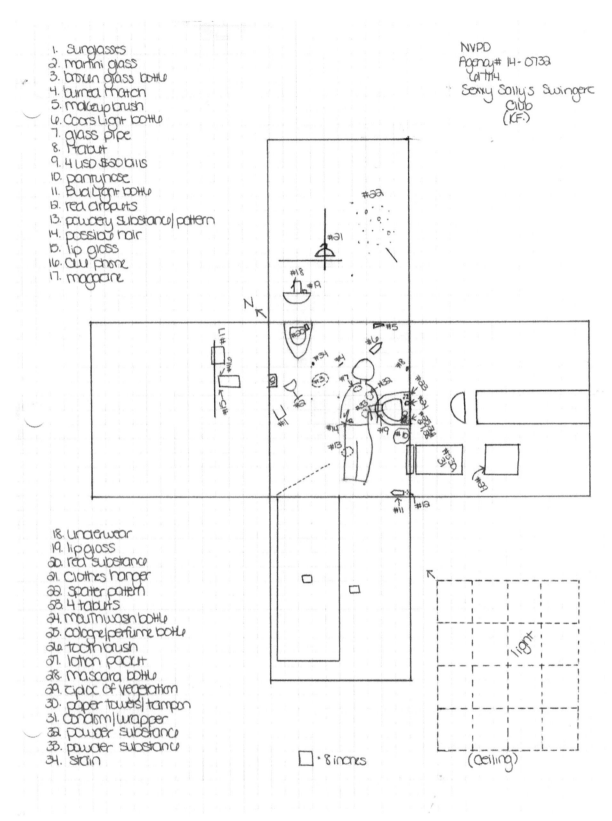

1. sunglasses
2. martini glass
3. broken glass bottle
4. burned match
5. makeup brush
6. Coors Light bottle
7. glass pipe
8. haircut
9. 4 USD $50 bills
10. pantyhose
11. Bud Light bottle
12. red droplets
13. powdery substance/pattern
14. possible hair
15. lip gloss
16. cell phone
17. magazine

NVPD
Agency # 14-0732
of 774
Sexxy Sally's Swingers
Club
(KF.)

18. underwear
19. lip gloss
20. red substance
21. clothes hanger
22. spatter pattern
23. 4 tablets
24. mouthwash bottle
25. cologne/perfume bottle
26. toothbrush
27. lotion packet
28. mascara bottle
29. ciploc of vegetation
30. paper towels/tampon
31. condom/wrapper
32. powder substance
33. powder substance
34. stain

□ = 8 inches

(ceiling)

FIGURE 5.7   Cross-projection or exploded sketch.

FIGURE 5.8 Handheld laser measure device.

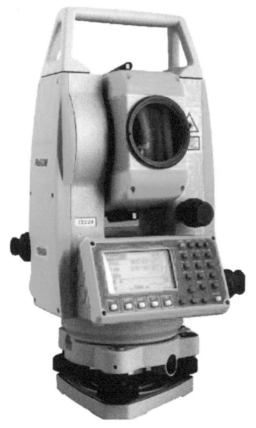

FIGURE 5.9 Total Station.

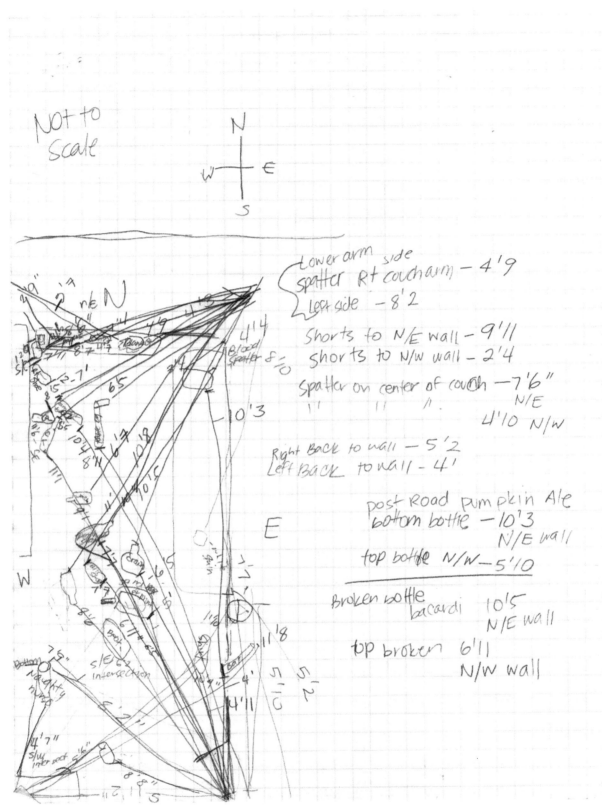

FIGURE 5.10   Triangulation measurement technique.

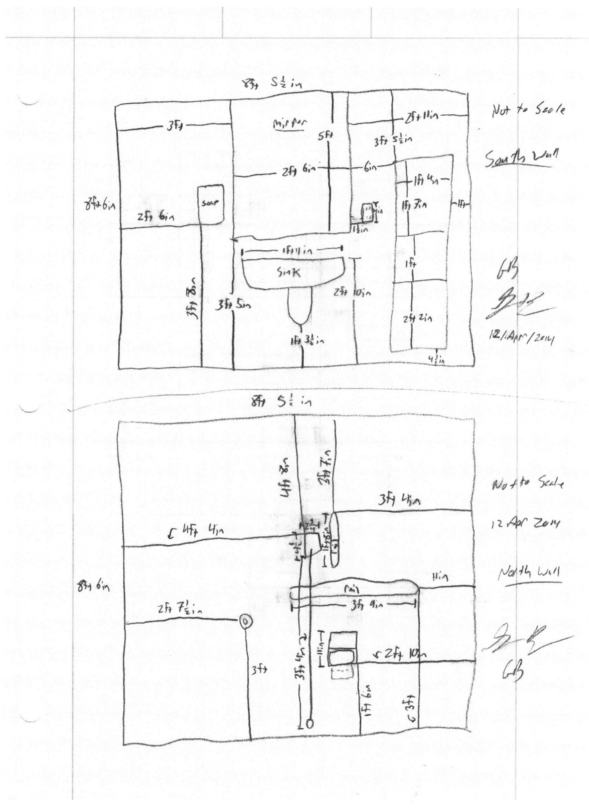

FIGURE 5.11   Rectangulation measurement technique.

FIGURE 5.12 Baseline measurement technique.

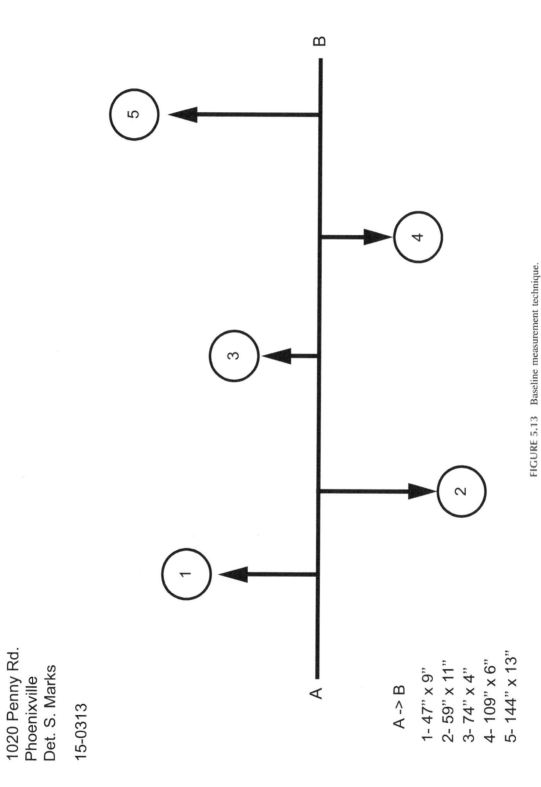

North ⟶

1020 Penny Rd.
Phoenixville
Det. S. Marks

15-0313

A -> B

1- 47" x 9"
2- 59" x 11"
3- 74" x 4"
4- 109" x 6"
5- 144" x 13"

FIGURE 5.13 Baseline measurement technique.

All of the above properly measured sketches would allow for subsequent placement of the evidentiary items by any individual at any given time.

CRIME SCENE DRAWINGS

The following examples of crime scenes are just crime scene drawings. See Figs. 5.14—5.17. They are missing many of the critical components as mentioned above.

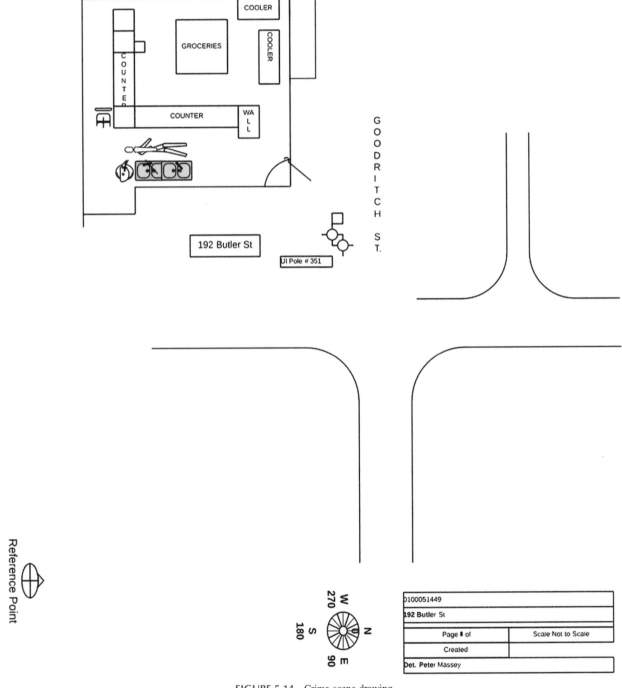

FIGURE 5.14 Crime scene drawing.

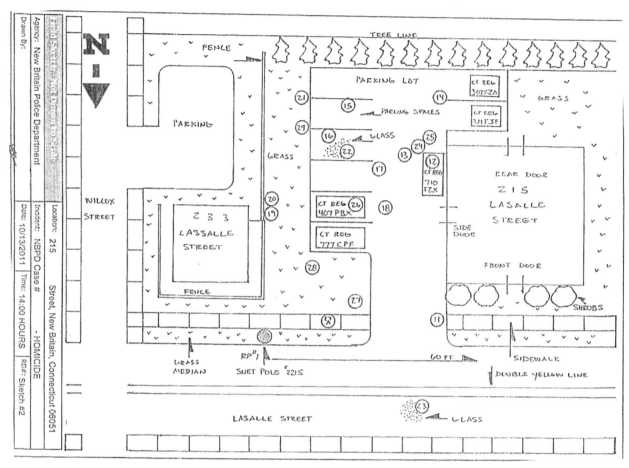

FIGURE 5.15   Crime scene drawing.

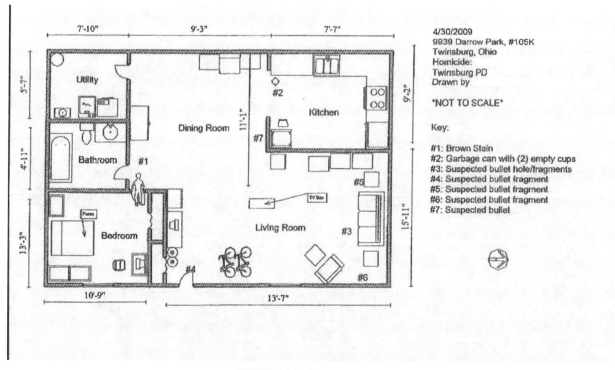

FIGURE 5.16   Crime scene drawing.

MAP #1 - LEGEND				Item	N-Wall	E-Wall
EXH #	N-Wall	E-Wall		Kit. table- NE corner	5'1"	9'
40	6'5"	3'9"		Kit. table- SE corner	7'1"	8'10"
41	5'11"	2'7"		Kit. table- NW corner	5'5"	12'6"
42	7'8"	5'2"		Kit. table- SW corner	7'5"	12'4"
43	4'6"	5'0"		A (Head)	5'10"	3'5"
				B (right hand)	3'1"	3'5"
				C (left hand)	6'10"	5'10"
				D (right foot)	3'5"	8'1"
				E (left foot)	6'1"	8'3"

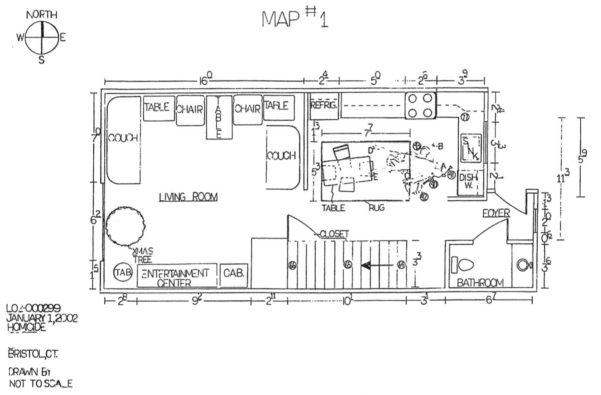

FIGURE 5.17 Crime scene drawing.

DISCUSSION QUESTIONS

1. Name the three most common types of crime scene sketches.
2. What are the three measurement techniques used for measuring evidence at the crime scene?
3. What type of sketch is best used for evidence located on the floor, ceiling, and walls?
4. What information should be included in every crime scene sketch?
5. What is the purpose of a crime scene sketch?

Chapter 6

Searching for Evidence

Chapter Outline

Learning Objectives

Upon completion of this chapter the reader should be able to:

- use areas at the crime scene that are of high probability for locating physical evidence,
- use physical geometric search patterns as a means for locating physical evidence at the crime scene, and
- identify and use lighting aids, chemical enhancement reagents, and portable instrumentation as a means for locating physical evidence at the crime scene based on the nature of the evidence.

INTRODUCTION

There is no doubt that the physical evidence is the associative link between the crime scene, the suspect, and the victim. While all the tasks of crime scene investigation can be learned, it should be an equally simple task to locate all the physical evidence, not just the obvious evidence found during the preliminary scene survey. The successful intensive search for all evidence can only occur when crime scene investigators understand the objectiveness of a crime scene search and rely on a systematic, science-based structured search process.

PHYSICAL SEARCHES—GENERAL CONCEPTS AND THEORY

Up until this point in a crime scene investigation all the evidence located has been obvious and identified during the preliminary scene survey. Something more must be done to find the less obvious evidence. See Photo 6.1 that shows obvious bloodstains but often it is the smaller bloodstains that are overlooked but important in determining the solution to the investigation.

PHOTO 6.1 Obvious bloodstain in a stairwell but the not so obvious bloodstains across the hall from the stairs.

FIGURE 6.1   Searching a crime scene.

In order to properly search a crime scene for all of its evidence, it is necessary to view the crime scene in its entirety. It is important to keep in mind areas that may require moving of objects in the scene and to look for evidence from different vantage points (See Fig. 6.1). It is extremely important to be cautious and take the time necessary for a methodical, systematic search. The intensive search should not be quick or an afterthought. This mindful approach to crime scene searching ensures that critical evidence will not be damaged or more importantly not overlooked.

AREAS OF HIGH PROBABILITY FOR FINDING PHYSICAL EVIDENCE

Useful crime scene searches are based on the "logic of the scene" that is based on the previous time spent at the crime scene (preliminary scene survey, documentation, etc.). Without risking the objectivity of searching for evidence, it is beneficial to deduce the types of evidence expected and potential locations of the evidence based upon the general type of crime committed and existing evidence. There are, however, areas present at the crime scene that have the best probability of producing evidence. Those areas are (1) point of entry; (2) point of exit; (3) paths of travel between the points of entry and exit; and (4) the target area of activity within the scene (see Fig. 6.2). These areas may not always be evident but are a good, objective starting point for the intensive search.

PHYSICAL SEARCHES—GEOMETRIC PATTERNS

There are no single correct crime scene search methods that are based on the specific type of crime scene. However, a fundamental way to begin the intensive search is to use a basic search pattern based on a geometric pattern. The most commonly used patterns are the line, grid, spiral, ray, zone, and link method. These patterns are simple and have a systematic nature once again, to insure that no physical evidence is overlooked. Note that some search methods are better suited for outdoor scenes while others work best for indoor crime scenes. It is a good idea to perform one search pattern and then opt for a second pattern as a double check. The members of the search team are not necessarily trained crime scene investigators, so they must be given explicit instructions before the search begins as how to search, what they are looking for, and instructed to stop, do not touch, and immediately notify one of the crime scene investigators if they find

FIGURE 6.2 Different points of access.

anything suspicious or valuable. Of course, any physical evidence found must be immediately documented using the techniques previously discussed.

Link Method

The link method is based on the four-way linkage theory, seeking to find associations between the scene, victim, suspect, and physical evidence. It is a systematic and logical fashion to gather physical evidence that can be linked to a particular crime, activity, or even type of evidence already identified in the preliminary scene survey. Although this method is not a geometric pattern, or easily definable, it is nonetheless a systematic approach that can supplement the other geometric pattern searches. For example, a victim with a gunshot wound leads to a firearm, to a projectile, to a casing, to gunshot residue (GSR), etc. See Fig. 6.3.

Line (Strip) Method

Outdoor crime scenes (parks, fields, yards, parking lots, highways, mass disasters, secondary crime scenes, etc.) are usually large and difficult to search because of vegetation, topography, water, and amount of area to cover. One of the easiest and efficient patterns to employ and be effective is the line method. This geometric pattern is the establishing of a series of predetermined lines or strips in the scene. Members of the search team are arranged at reasonable, uniform intervals and then proceed to search along straight lines. The searcher identifies any evidence in the path. See Fig. 6.4.

Grid Method

The grid method is a modified double-line search. With this search, a line search pattern as shown above is done, and subsequently, a second line pattern is done in the same area but at 90 degrees or perpendicular to the first line pattern. The advantages of this method are that the same area is searched twice and two different searchers search the same area. The time to search is longer, but the results are often better.

Zone Method

For this search method focusing within a defined area or zone in a systematic manner can very efficiently locate physical evidence. Indoor crime scenes are examples of such a scene; specific rooms can be assigned to searchers. Depending on the size of the scene, each zone may be subdivided as needed until it is of manageable size. As previously discussed, critical zones such as target areas, point of entry, and point of exit can be searched multiple times using this method. This pattern is also suited for mass disaster crime scenes where the area to be searched is "gridded off" into searchable zones. See Fig. 6.5.

Wheel/Ray Method

With the wheel method, the investigators start from a critical point and travel outward along many straight lines, or rays, from this point. This search pattern becomes increasingly difficult when searching larger areas and, therefore, is usually used only for special scene situations and with limited applications. This method can be successfully used on a smaller scale like searching a specific piece of evidence. See Fig. 6.6.

Spiral Method

The spiral method is used for larger scene searches, usually outdoors. There are two ways in which the spiral method is applied to scenes: an inward spiral and the outward spiral. Variations are the clockwise or counterclockwise direction. It may be beneficial to conduct the search twice, in opposing directions. Because of its dependency on navigational aids this search method is used by the military or other suitably equipped agencies for searching large areas like open water searches.

FIGURE 6.3 Link search—knife wounds leads to knife; bloody footwear impressions leads to bloody shoe.

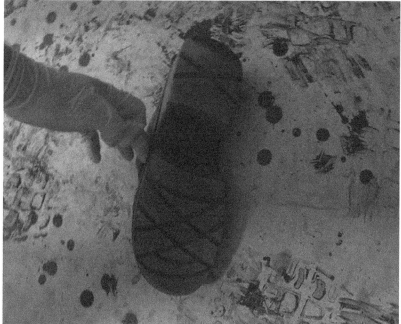

FIGURE 6.3 cont'd

FIGURE 6.4   Line search at night.

ENHANCEMENT AND VISUALIZATION

General Concepts and Theory

Just as discussed above there must be an attempt by every crime scene investigator to locate all evidence that may have been left at the crime scene. Searching areas of highest probability for evidence and searching while following a geometric pattern will greatly increase the likelihood of finding the evidence. However, physical evidence can be anything. It may be small or left in trace quantities. The physical methods for searching may not suffice. For this reason the use of optical or lighting methods can locate even the smallest of trace evidence. Knowledge about the chemical nature of the physical evidence is another process that can be used to make physical evidence visible and even enhanced, so it can be documented and collected.

Optical or Lighting Methods for Visualization and Enhancement

Any handheld flashlight held at a low angle or oblique angle will visualize physical evidence while physically searching a crime scene (see Fig. 6.7).

Unfortunately, a search for physical evidence using only visible wavelengths of light may not always visualize all the evidence present. Depending on the chemical makeup of the evidence and the surface upon which it has been deposited, the use of light sources with wavelengths beyond the visible spectrum can be used to visualize this evidence. The fluorescence, absorbance, reflectance, and luminescence of light by the physical evidence will occur when exposed to various wavelengths. Because this light is not visible, in order for the searcher to "see" or visualize the evidence's reaction, viewing while using barrier filters is needed. Most light sources with variable wavelengths are portable, powerful, and easy to use at the crime scenes. These light sources, alternate light sources (ALS), have a variety of wavelength capabilities for a variety of physical evidence to be found at the crime scene. See Table 6.1.

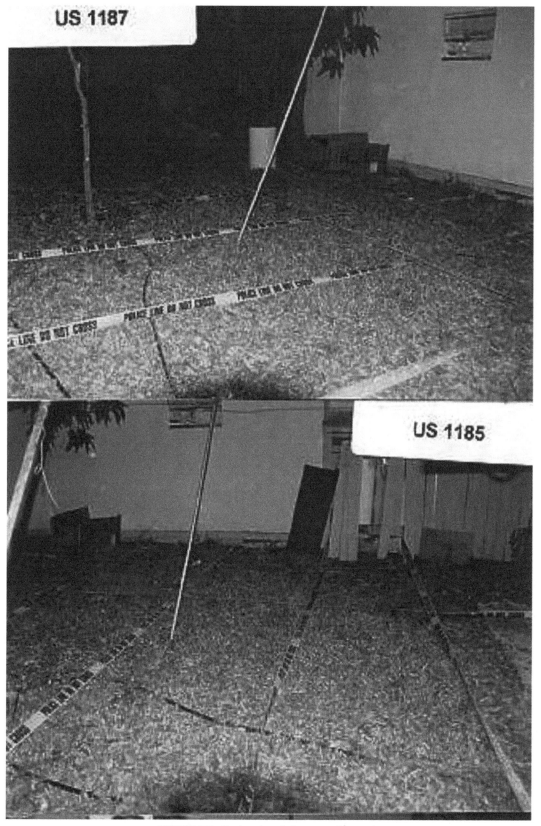

FIGURE 6.5   Backyard made into zones for search.

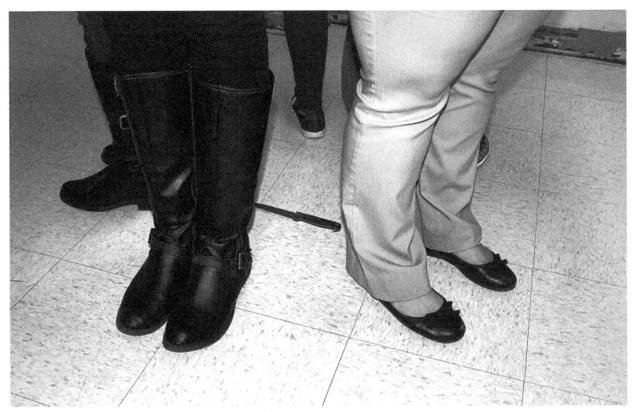

FIGURE 6.6   Wheel/ray search—not a good thing to start with so many shoes around the evidence at a crime scene.

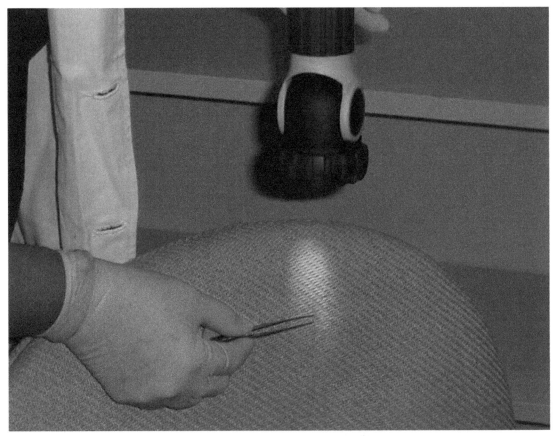

FIGURE 6.7   Oblique lighting to visualize evidence.

TABLE 6.1 Alternate Light Source (ALS) Wavelengths for Evidence Type

Evidence Type	ALS Wavelength	Barrier Filter Color
Bodily fluids	395 nm (UV), 455 nm	None, orange, yellow
Bone fragments	395 nm (UV), 455 nm	Orange, yellow
Bloodstains	395 nm (UV)	None
Latents in oils, grease	455 nm	Orange
Trace evidence on blue or green backgrounds	595 nm	Orange, yellow
Trace evidence	625 nm	None, yellow

UV, ultraviolet.

FIGURE 6.8   Using a blue alternate light sources.

Specific Evidence Types Using ALS

Latent Fingerprint Detection

Searching for latent fingerprints by use of the ALS with fluorescent enhancement is easily accomplished. This visualization by ALS for fingerprint detection works on highly textured, fluorescent, fragile, and contaminated surfaces. The most common ALS wavelengths used for the detection of latent fingerprints are 445–455 nm (blue light) with an orange barrier filter. See Fig. 6.8.

Body Fluids

Most body fluids, such as semen, saliva, and vaginal fluids, are inherently fluorescent by their chemical makeup. Therefore, the use of ALS is essential for visualization and enhancement. Ultraviolet (UV) lights are well established for the search for

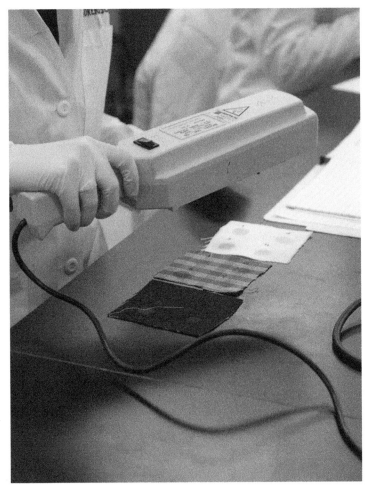

FIGURE 6.9 Searching using UV or black light.

body fluids. See Fig. 6.9 for use of a UV/black light. The problem is that many of the surfaces upon which the fluids are deposited will also fluoresce with UV light. Use of an ALS with longer wavelengths (540 nm or green) will eliminate the substrate background interference. Barrier filters of orange and yellow are needed.

Hairs and Fibers

The use of side lighting (oblique lighting) with a conventional visible white light like a flashlight is the best way to search for hairs and fibers at crime scenes. No barrier filters are necessary for white ALS searching. If background interference is encountered then the use of blue ALS with orange barrier filters can visualize this trace evidence. Chemically treated hair can be found with other wavelengths and corresponding filters.

Other Evidence Types

ALSs have a variety of applications for a variety of other evidence types not shown above. These other types of evidence include bruises, question documents, GSR, explosive residues, bone fragments, footwear patterns, drugs, etc. A portable, powerful ALS with a variety of wavelength options that can be used is an excellent crime scene search instrument.

Chemical Content and Reactions

Searching for physical evidence based on the chemical nature of the evidence will usually fall into two categories of evidence: biological or chemical evidence. For both categories the visualization and enhancement to assist in the search is based on the fundamental properties of all chemical reactions—a chemical reaction takes place when there is a color change, a temperature change, or a change in physical state. Evidence will be visualized or enhanced when:

- it changes color, usually colorless to colored, to enhance contrast of substance and background so as to now be seen;
- it gives off a gas, usually bubbles, to show presence but may be temporary; and
- it gives off light, usually luminesces or fluoresces, to improve visibility for documentation.

As an added bonus, the chemical reaction not only visualizes or enhances (like for enhancing patterns) but also serves as a preliminary test of identity for screening purposes at the crime scene.

Biological Evidence Visualization and Enhancement

Blood visualization and enhancement reagents fall into two basic groups depending on the chemical reactivity of the blood and the reagent chosen: hemoglobin (heme group) based or protein-reacting reagents.

Hemoglobin (Heme)-Based Visualization and Enhancement Reagents

These enhancement reagents are designed to detect minute traces of heme or heme-like derivatives. The iron heme in blood is easily oxidized (to carry the oxygen). The visualization and enhancement reagents are based on that reactivity and undergo an oxidation–reduction reaction. The oxidation reaction will convert a colorless, reduced form reagent to a colored by-product that is seen by the crime scene searcher.

The most commonly used heme-based reagents are phenolphthalein (Kastle-Meyer), ortho-tolidine, tetramethylbenzidine, leucocrystal violet, fluorescein, and luminol. Fluorescein has a positive result in the form of a product that fluoresces but must be visualized using an ALS. With luminol, a positive test is indicated by luminescence rather than a visual color formation. A positive reaction, as indicated by the formation of a colored or fluorescent or illuminating product, merely indicates the possibility of the presence of blood. There are many substances that will also catalyze this same reaction such as plant peroxidase or strong chemical oxidants. It is essential for the crime scene investigator to make sure that the testing reagents have been tested on known standards of blood prior to testing the suspected stains at the crime scene. The lack of a reaction on the unknown stain can be deemed as meaning that blood is absent and the searching can continue.

For large area or pattern searching at the crime scene, a sequential spraying process directly on the surfaces at the crime scene is the method of application. Any colored products are immediately documented. Because the colored products can fade or change over a short period of time, the documentation processes must be prepped and ready to go prior to spraying. Additional spraying can be done, but overspraying can wash away patterns and samples for collection (see Fig. 6.10A and B).

Protein-Based Visualization and Enhancement Reagents

There is a variety of biological protein-containing evidence present at a crime scene. Proteins are made of chemical units called amino acids, upon which the visualization and enhancement reagents are based. Proteins are components in many body tissues and fluids, including skin, tissue, blood, and milk. Proteins are also left by direct deposit of the body fluids, such as sweat, tears, blood, urine, semen, or saliva. A suspect or victim may deposit large or trace quantities of these substances at a crime scene by contact. Protein residues from latent fingerprints, palm prints, footprints, lip, and ear prints can be located by the use of a protein-reacting reagent, like ninhydrin or amido black. If blood is suspected, then a heme-based visualization and enhancement reagents could be used instead of the protein-based reagent. Most of the protein-based reagents are applied by spraying or by immersion. Many of the recently developed protein-based reagents require the use of ALS to assist visualization. As shown with the heme-based visualization and enhancement reagents, overspraying or background interference is seen (see Fig. 6.11).

CHEMICAL EVIDENCE VISUALIZATION AND ENHANCEMENT

Latent Fingerprints and Other Impressions

There are various methods for the visualization and enhancement of latent fingerprints and impression evidence (see Table 6.2). Special methods of visualization sometimes will combine the ALS with physical and chemical techniques.

(A)

(B)

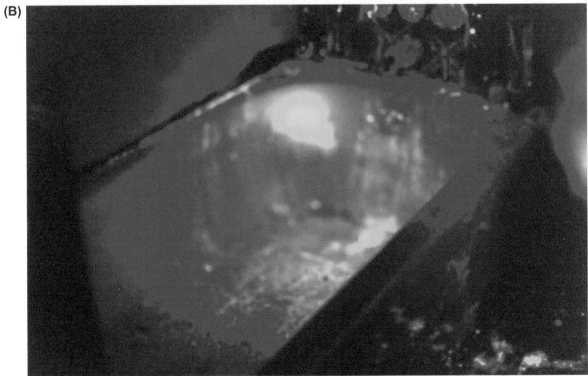

FIGURE 6.10 (A) Improper use of luminol overspray producing white residues. (B) Proper use of luminol.

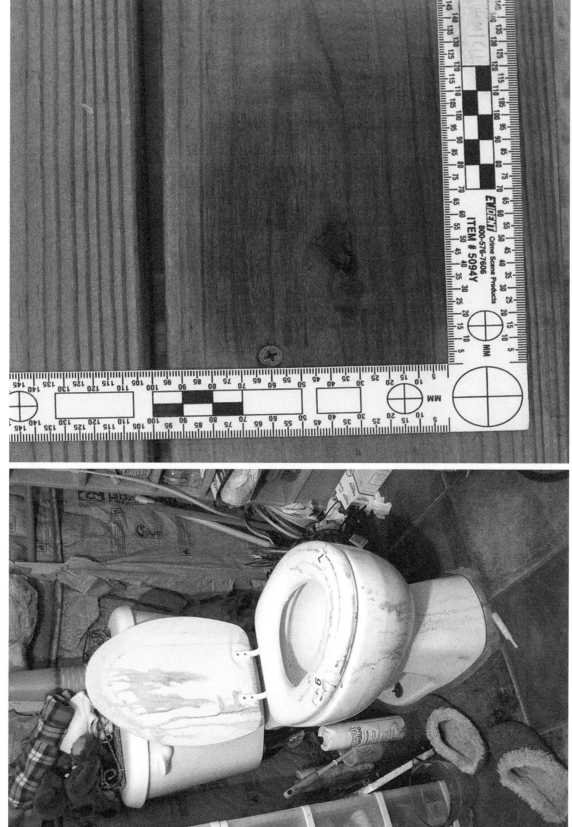

FIGURE 6.11 Proper use of protein-based reagents.

TABLE 6.2 Fingerprint and Impression Visualization and Enhancement

	Reagent Use
Blood enhancement	Amido black
	Coomassie blue
	Crowle's double stain
	Diaminobenzidine (DAB)
	Fluorescein
	Leucocrystal violet
	Luminol
Latent prints	Powder dusting
	Ninhydrin
	Superglue (hotshots, cyanow, and pouches)
	Sticky surface powder
	1,8-Diazafluoren-9-one (DFO)
	Small particle reagent
	Ardrox
	Rhodamine 6G

These combination methods are especially useful for latent fingerprints. The enhancement reagents are based on their chemical composition and the chemical reactions that occur when reacting with the various types of patterned impression evidence. The enhancement reagents for **latent fingerprint** enhancement react with chemicals found in the residues deposited on various surfaces by the finger.

- **Latent fingerprints on nonporous surfaces**: The secretions from the pores of the friction ridges on skin will contain water, salt, proteins, and oily substances. These secretions will be visible using oblique lighting methods followed by dusting with contrasting colored powders (black powder on light backgrounds or light powder on dark backgrounds). Magnetic and fluorescent powders are also used on this surface. Care must be taken not to "overdust" the surface.
- **Latent fingerprints on porous surfaces**: For this visualization a chemical reaction between the secretions and applied reagent occurs. It is a protein-based color reaction as discussed above. Ninhydrin remains the most successful reagent for this visualization method.
- **Latent fingerprints on sticky surfaces**: This visualization is easily seen with oblique lighting but can be enhanced using a solution of dusting powder in water with a couple drops of a surfactant (dish cleaning soap). Once brushed on the sticky surface a quick rinse with water will visualize the fingerprints or other impressions.
- **Latent fingerprints on a wet surface (porous and nonporous)**: This visualization and enhancement method is a chemical reaction of the wet surface reagent, small particle reagent, and the secretion chemicals. A black product is formed that visualizes the fingerprint pattern. The reagent is applied by spraying or immersion directly on to the wet surface. Overspraying is not a problem. See Fig. 6.12.
- **Superglue fuming:** For this visualization and enhancement technique, cyanoacrylate or superglue is used. It self-polymerizes upon exposure to the air. This polymer will coat the nonporous surface with the latent fingerprint so that it can be powder dusted. Portable fuming tanks can be transported to crime scenes for processing there or larger fixed tanks in laboratories are useful, too. It is possible to overfume the surface that will make dusting of the coated secretions impossible. Additionally, later collection for touch DNA cannot be done after superglue application. See Fig. 6.13.

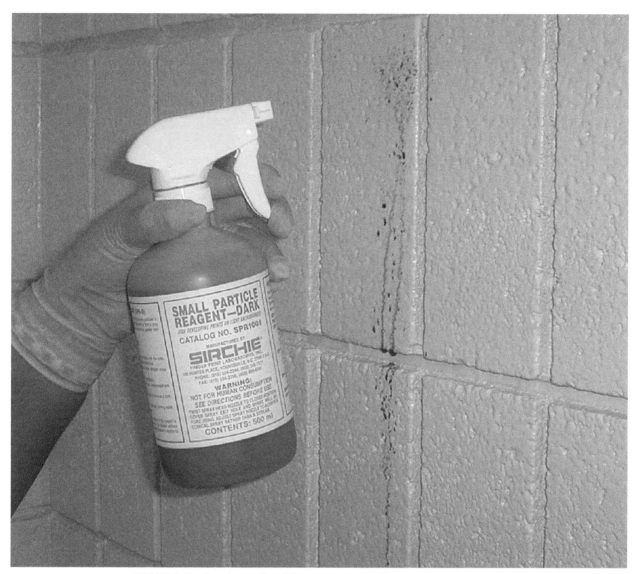

FIGURE 6.12   Spraying small particle reagent on wet surfaces—porous and nonporous.

Gunshot Residue

When a firearm is discharged, it creates gases, soot, and burned or partially burned gunpowder particles that are deposited on any and all surfaces at the crime scene, but especially on the shooter's hand and the intended target. GSR comes from detonation of the primer, gunpowder, lubricants, or components of the projectile. These materials are propelled forward with the projectile toward the target and many will fall on the surfaces of any nearby objects. Searching for GSR is done for two reasons: (1) to determine if an individual fired or handled a recently discharged firearm and (2) to analyze the pattern of GSR for the purpose of determining the muzzle-to-target distance. Any test designed to detect GSR must be used in a manner that minimizes the potential for damaging the GSR pattern. GSR is not evidence that will remain for a long period of time especially if it lands on a target that may move. For this reason the visualization and enhancement of GSR must be done within 2−4 h of firearm discharge. Documentation, preservation, and collection by correct methods should follow immediately. See Fig. 6.14.

These visualization and enhancement reagents react with nitrate and nitrite compounds in GSR, yielding a colored reaction or pattern. The modified Griess reagent, diphenylamine, and sodium rhodizonate reagents will produce colored products when reacting with GSR components. Reagents can be used as swabbed color tests or by a spraying application.

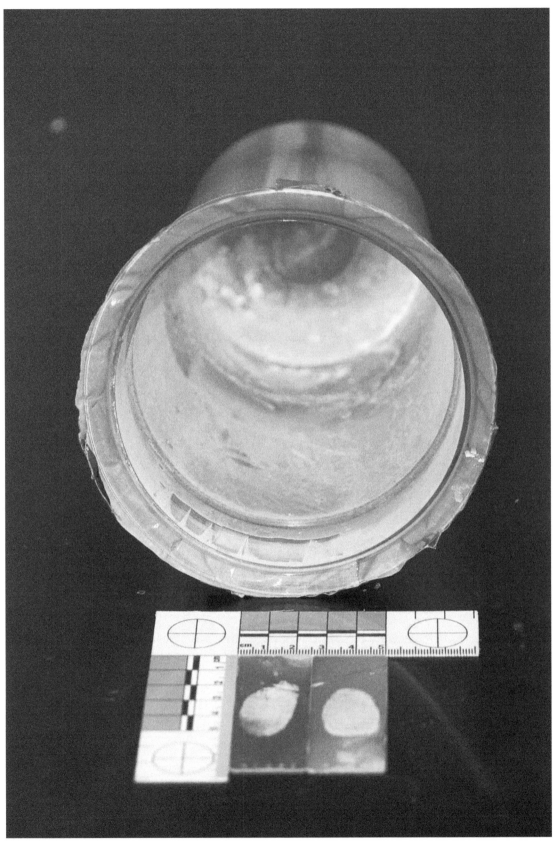

FIGURE 6.13   Too much superglue.

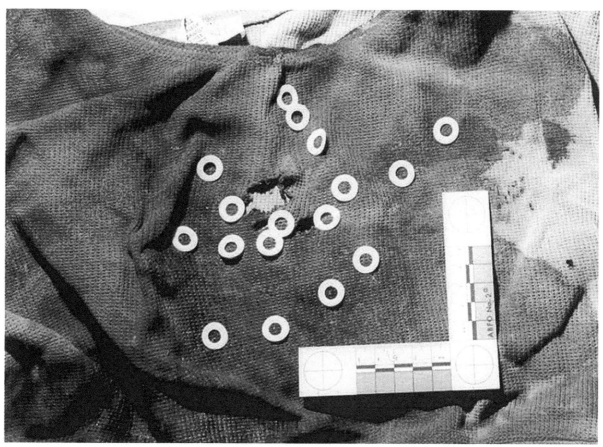

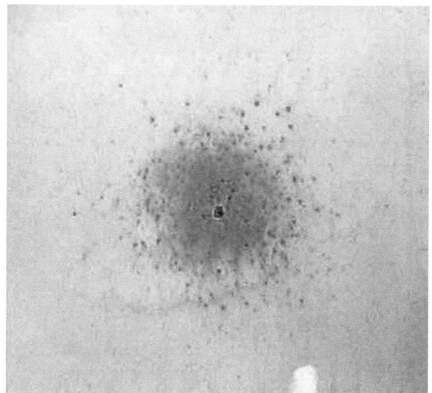

FIGURE 6.14   Gunshot residue on clothing and enhancement.

Attention to false positives from cigarette smoke, urine, and fertilizer is important to consider before interpretation is attempted.

Explosive Residues

Explosives are chemical substances, which are unstable in their natural form. When heated, shocked, or ignited, they are capable of rapid chemical reaction, producing an explosion by the liberation of large quantities of heat and gas often followed by fire. Explosive residues may be encountered in numerous forms at scene. Explosive residues may be located on the hands or clothes of a suspect, at storage or production scenes, and in vehicles or containers used to transport the explosive material. At postblast crime scenes there may be both unexploded explosive material and products of the explosion.

Searching for explosive residues can be done by portable hydrocarbon or ion "sniffers." Canine programs have reported significant success detecting minute amounts of explosive materials and remain as a popular searching tool. The visualization and enhancement of explosive residues is not usually done but using reagents as preliminary testing for screening purposes can be done. The color reagents that give characteristic colors are the same as the GSR reagents. These reagents react with nitrate and nitrite compounds found in all three categories of explosives to produce color reactions. As with the GSR these reagents can be used as swabbed color tests or by a spraying application. Positive reactions are only indicative and require collection for laboratory confirmation.

Controlled Substances and Drugs

Crime scenes are often part of drug investigations like clandestine labs or other crimes relating to drug cases. As such, crime scene investigators may be asked to search the scenes for controlled substances on a variety of surfaces. For these reasons, there is often a need for a quick screening test or field test to analyze a material suspected of being a drug or controlled substance. In many situations, this field test helps provide the necessary probable cause to substantiate an arrest for sale and/or possession of a controlled substance.

Certain drugs will react with selected chemical reagents to give characteristic color changes or precipitates. Easy-to-use kits with widespread use are commercially available which contain these reagents in convenient single-test vials. Some commonly used drug-screening reagents and their characteristic reactions are shown in Table 6.3.

Portable Instrumentation for Visualization and Enhancement

There are many different instruments that have moved out of the forensic laboratory and into the field and crime scenes. For many years the only instrument at the crime scene was the metal detector, but now it is common to find portable ground

TABLE 6.3 Screening Tests for Drug Substances

Reagent	Application	Result
Marquis	Large variety; general reagent	Opiates = purple PCP = colorless to light pink Phenethylamines = orange to brown LSD = orange/brown/purple Mescaline and psilocybin = orange
Mandelin	Variety; phenethylamines	Opiates = blue-gray Ampethamines = green LSD = orange/green/gray Psilocybin = green
Conc. nitric acid	Morphine versus heroin	Morphine = orange to red Heroin = yellow to green
Duquenois	Marihuana; THC	Marihuana, THC, and Hashish = blue-violet
Cobalt thiocyanate	Cocaine and derivatives	"Cocaines" = blue precipitate
Dille–Koppanyi	Barbiturates	Red-violet

FIGURE 6.15   Portable Fourier transform infrared spectrometer at scene.

penetrating radar, portable X-ray detectors, and a variety of classic lab instruments like Fourier transform infrared spectroscopy and Raman spectroscopy, even gas chromatography—mass spectroscopy. The negative for these portable instruments remains the availability of the scientist to get to the scene to operate the instrument. See Fig. 6.15.

DISCUSSION QUESTIONS

1. What was the crime scene investigator's first chance to identify physical evidence at the crime scene? Is all the evidence located at that time?
2. When is the next opportunity for searching the crime scene?
3. Is it acceptable to move objects at the scene in order to facilitate the intensive search? When is it not acceptable?
4. What types of lightning aids can be used to visualize and enhance evidence being searched for at the crime scene? What types of evidence are found using these lights?
5. Why is a barrier filter used with ALS?
6. If a crime scene is on the side of a mountain, what geometric search pattern would be best suited for this type of terrain? Why?
7. If the crime scene investigator has to search an industrial building what search pattern is best used in this situation?

8. Give the appropriate visualization and enhancement technique for the following types of evidence:
   a. Bloody footwear impression.
   b. Latent fingerprint on glass.
   c. Latent fingerprint on paper.
   d. GSR on the surface of a table.
   e. GSR on a T-shirt.
   f. Buried body.

Chapter 7

Collection and Preservation of Physical Evidence

Chapter Outline

Learning Objectives

Upon completion of this chapter, the reader should be able to

- Enhance, collect, and preserve latent, visual, and plastic fingerprints on a variety of surfaces.
- Understand the significance of and the collection/preservation of elimination prints and postmortem fingerprints.
- Define and collect impression evidence specifically imprints and indentations including bitemark evidence.
- Search for and collect trace evidence such as hair, fiber, paint, glass, and soil.
- Search for, collect, and preserve firearms evidence, gunshot residue, and toolmarks.
- Search for, collect, and preserve biological fluids including blood, seminal stains, and other body fluids.
- Search for, collect, and preserve chemical evidence including suspected drug or medicinal preparations, fire debris evidence, and suspected explosive materials.
- Properly collect and preserve questioned document evidence.

135

GENERAL CONSIDERATIONS

After the completion of the crime scene documentation and the systematic search of the crime scene for the physical evidence, the actual collection and preservation of each item of evidence can begin. Proper collection and packaging of the evidence will insure that no evidence has been lost, changed, altered, or contaminated. One person shall be designated as the evidence officer. This singular appointment as evidence officer will ensure that all evidence is collected, packaged, marked, sealed, and preserved in a consistent manner. The single collector assures that the relevancy, reliability, and validity of the physical evidence is maintained and not called into question at any stage of the investigation. There is no set order for the collection of evidence but some general considerations about collection should be mentioned. It is helpful to have a variety of collection, packaging, and marking materials nearby for easy access and convenience. Table 7.1 is an example of contents of an evidence collection kit.

Most physical evidence will be collected into a primary container or druggist's fold and placed into a secondary container or outer container. Druggist's folds are typically used for small trace evidence but are useful for protecting items of evidence of any size that may have other evidence associated with it that will need to be collected by the crime scene investigator at the scene or laboratory personnel at a later time. Outer containers are frequently envelopes, paper bags, packets, canisters, or specialty boxes. The outer containers are sealed with evidence tape and marked with documentation information about the item of evidence, identification of the collector, date, time and location collected, agency case number, and a brief description of the physical evidence with its location contained within the secondary container. It is a good idea to keep the item number the same number as the evidence marker (see Fig. 7.1 for consistency of numbering). As shown in Fig. 7.2, the evidence tape should completely cover any openings of the container and are marked minimally with the collector's initials, the time of collection, and the date of collection. A huge amount of packaging materials, sealing tape, and assorted items for marking packaging are commercially available.

Most items of physical evidence are solids and can easily be packaged, stored, and preserved in the above containers. If the physical evidence is volatile or easily lost due to evaporation, airtight containers such as metal paint cans, jars, and specially designed bags are to be used for packaging. Liquid items of physical evidence can be packaged and transported in unbreakable, leak-proof containers. Moist, wet, or biological evidence (blood, suspected marijuana plants, etc.) collected by methods to be described can temporarily be packaged as above and later, in a secure drying area, be allowed to air-dry and repackaged into nonairtight containers (see Fig. 7.3 for secure drying cabinet). The original packages must be retained and packaged with the evidence.

Each item of physical evidence must be collected and packaged separately to prevent any cross-contamination between items of evidence. The packages must also be closed and sealed at the time of collection. This procedure will insure that during transportation no intermingling of the physical evidence will occur.

While it is impossible to identify all possible types of evidence that could be found at the crime scene, the remainder of this chapter will address the various types of physical evidence that can be encountered at the crime scene. Each type of physical evidence will be discussed in terms of the collection techniques best suited for that evidence and then the proper packaging technique.

TABLE 7.1 Evidence Collection Kit Contents

Basic Components of Crime Scene Collection Kit	
• Variety of paper envelopes	• Metal paint cans
• Assorted sizes of pillboxes	• Sterile swabs and boxes
• New cardboard boxes	• Large butcher paper
• Strings	• Tamper-resistant tape
• Glassine paper	• Rape Kits
• Permanent markers	• Gun boxes
• Eye-droppers and bottles	• Gunshot residue (GSR) Kits

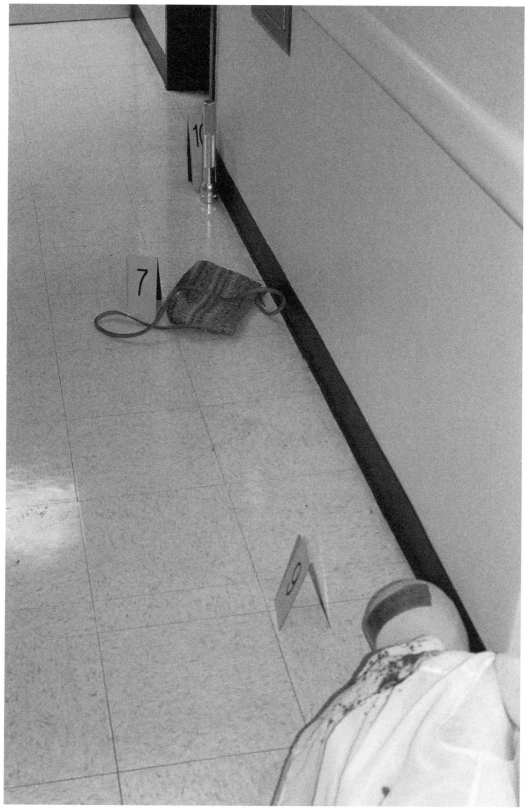

FIGURE 7.1   Use of evidence markers.

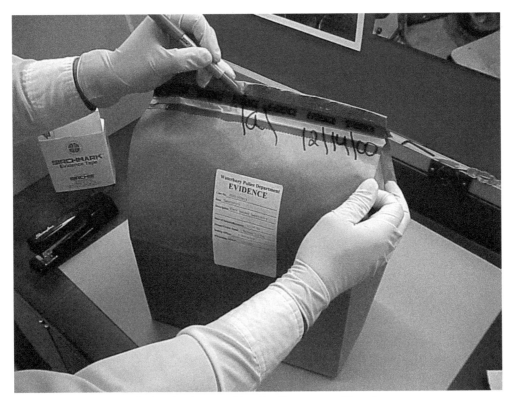

FIGURE 7.2   Proper marking of sealing tape on evidence bag.

FINGERPRINTS

Fingerprints constitute one of the oldest, widely used, expected, and accepted types of physical evidence for positive identification or individualization. Other types of impression evidence such as palm prints, bare footprints, lip prints, and even ear prints are also encountered and should be expected at crime scenes. Fingerprint evidence found at scenes can be in the form of latent, plastic, visible, wet, inverted, and elimination fingerprints. As shown in an earlier chapter, each type will require different searching and enhancement or visualization techniques at the crime scene dependent on the type of surface with the fingerprint. Likewise, the collection is dependent on the surface.

   If the fingerprint is found on an immovable or large object, field processing is warranted and the fingerprints should be collected (See Fig. 7.4 below). If the fingerprint is found on a small, movable object then the entire object can be packaged for collection and processed later.

Latent Prints

As has been shown latent prints once found at the crime scene are enhanced or visualized by physical, chemical, instrumental, or by combining methods. Physical methods are used for any dry, nonporous surfaces such as glass or plastic. These methods include the use of various colored powders and brushes. The physical methods for visualization can be greatly assisted by the use of cyanoacrylate (superglue) fuming before powder application and some protein, alternate light source (ALS) visible patterns. Fig. 7.5A and B illustrate the application of superglue techniques in crime scene and laboratory.

   Physical methods—Colored powders and magnetic powders are the most common powders used for nonporous surfaces. Once the latent prints have been visualized by the superglue and powder dusting techniques, they should be photographed again. Then the developed latents need to be lifted and placed on backing cards. The latent cards are documented by putting the case number, date and time of lifting, initials of person processing the evidence, and a sketch indicating the location of the lifted latent print on the back of the lift card, as shown in Fig. 7.6. The lift card is evidence and should be then placed in a secondary container. If the item containing the latent fingerprint is movable, then it must be marked as to the location of the lifted latent and packaged into a primary container followed by a secondary container that is appropriately marked.

FIGURE 7.3   Secure drying cabinet.

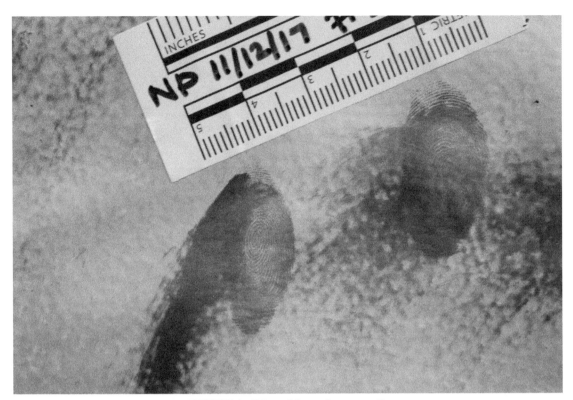

FIGURE 7.4   Enhanced fingerprints on a wall.

Chemical methods—Chemical processing methods for latent fingerprints can be used on dry and wet surfaces. Various dye staining techniques, such as gentian violet, fluorescent dyes, or other laser-excitable dyes, followed by searching with an ALS, then photography of the developed latent fingerprints work on dry surfaces. Most chemically visualized prints are not lifted and are simply photographed. The original object with the prints should be collected into primary and secondary containers if moveable. If the surface with the developed latents is immovable, then photography becomes the primary source of the latents' documentation and subsequent comparison.

Papers and other documents should be individually placed in nonairtight, window envelopes. See Fig. 7.7 for the use of window envelope below.

Visible Prints

Visible prints, finger, palm, or sole prints, generally result when friction ridges are coated with material that is transferred to another surface leaving the outline or impression of the friction ridge. Visible prints do not need to be dusted (occasionally they may need enhancement depending on the nature of the material transferred; see below), the visible prints should be photographed, and the object with the visible print should be packaged into primary and secondary containers and then collected. If the object cannot be collected then the photograph will become the evidence. A visible shoe print is shown in Fig. 7.8 below.

Plastic Prints

These types of prints are produced when the friction ridge on the finger, palm, or foot sole comes into contact with a softer surface and makes a three-dimensional impression or indentation into the receiving surface. Photographic documentation of impression evidence has already been discussed and those procedures applied. The photograph will represent the best evidence in this case and should be treated accordingly. Depending on the surface materials, some casing materials can be used for casting and collection. See Fig. 7.9 photo of plastic fingerprint below.

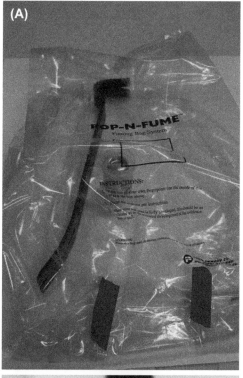

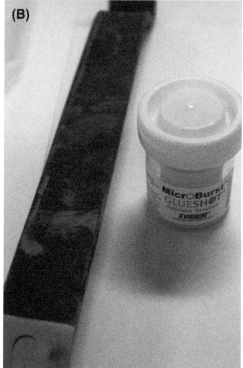

FIGURE 7.5   (A) Portable superglue fuming tank. (B) Result of superglue fuming.

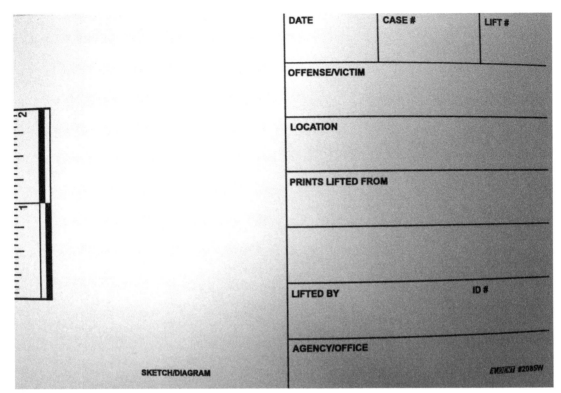

DATE	CASE #	LIFT #
OFFENSE/VICTIM		
LOCATION		
PRINTS LIFTED FROM		
LIFTED BY	ID #	
AGENCY/OFFICE		

SKETCH/DIAGRAM

EVIDENT #2085W

FIGURE 7.6 Latent lift backing card.

Elimination or Known Prints

For comparison purposes, the crime scene investigator must obtain known fingerprints (palm prints or sole prints) from every person who may have been in the scene. These known fingerprints are referred to as elimination fingerprints. Elimination fingerprints are inked prints onto ten-print fingerprint cards or scanned at the scene using portable scanning technology (see Chapter 9 on Emerging Technology).

Elimination fingerprints of deceased victims must be taken too. Postmortem elimination fingerprints and palm prints should be accomplished only after consultation from the medical examiner and only after trace evidence has been collected. The ink will need to be placed on the victim's fingers and the fingers rolled onto the fingerprint card. In some cases, this can easily be done. However, if the fingers are difficult to roll then a "spoon" apparatus is advisable to use (see Fig. 7.10). Portable scanning biometric devices are excellent for the collection of fingerprints from these victims.

Once the known inked prints are obtained, they should be marked and packaged into sealed envelopes and treated as evidence.

IMPRESSION EVIDENCE

Impression evidence is physical evidence commonly found at crime scenes. When properly recognized, documented, and interpreted, impression evidence can be extremely valuable in the investigation and subsequent reconstruction. Two types of impression evidence may be encountered at crime scenes: (1) two-dimensional impressions, sometimes called imprints and (2) three-dimensional impressions, sometimes called indentations. This type of impression is usually found at outdoor scenes deposited in softer receiving surfaces. Impression evidence when recognized at crime scenes should be properly documented and collected for further examination and possible comparison.

Fig. 7.11 shows a general procedure for the recording and collection of indentation impression evidence found at the crime scene by casting with dental stone. Standards or origins for comparison to the crime scene impression evidence must be collected too. Special care must be taken to prevent contamination or destruction of the impression evidence, to maintain its integrity, and to preserve the chain of custody.

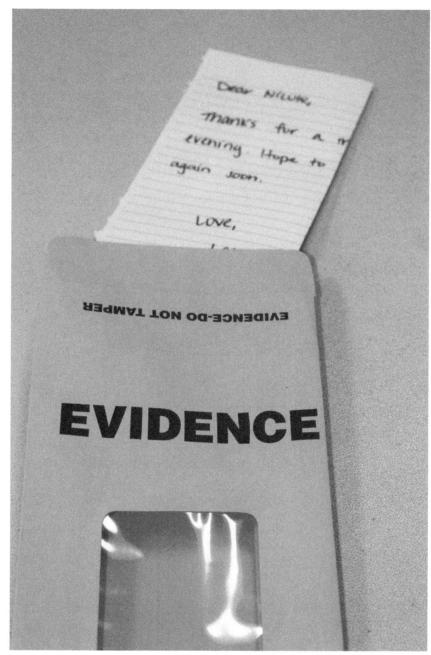

FIGURE 7.7   Window evidence envelope.

Imprints

Two-dimensional residue impressions are referred to as imprints. They are created at the crime scene when two surfaces come into contact. The material or residue from one surface is transferred to the second surface. Fingerprints, footwear, and tire tread impressions are the most common types of imprints found at crime scenes, but imprints can be made by any objects or surfaces, too. Collection techniques for residue imprints are similar to the fingerprint techniques discussed previously. The imprint evidence is searched for using various side-lighting sources (flashlights, ALSs, etc.). Once the imprint is located, it must be photographed as shown in Chapter 4 on photography. The collection of the residue imprint and the lifting techniques are dependent on the surface characteristics of the object with the imprint. See dust imprint on a dark surface in Fig. 7.12 below.

FIGURE 7.8   Visible imprint in blood.

FIGURE 7.9 Plastic fingerprint.

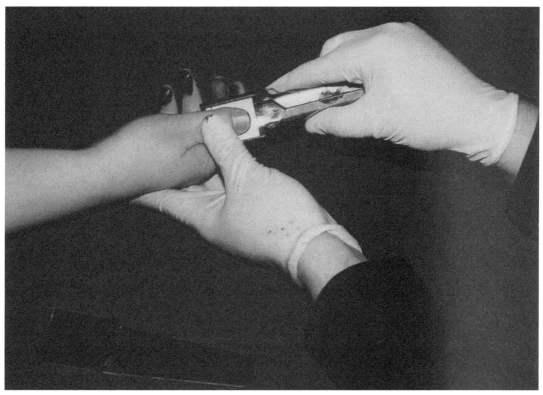

FIGURE 7.10 Spoon apparatus for obtaining inked fingerprints.

FIGURE 7.11 Dental stone casting of indentation.

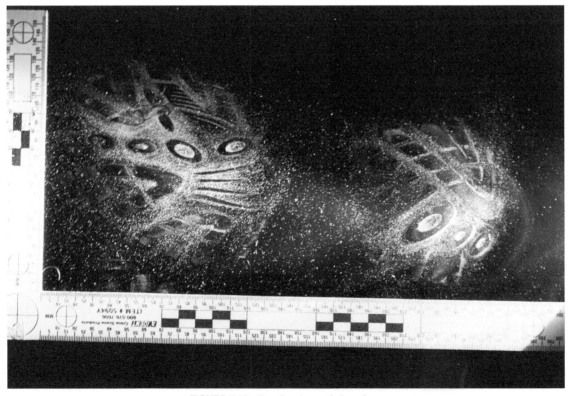

FIGURE 7.12 Dust imprint on dark surface.

Porous Surfaces

Imprint evidence on porous surfaces cannot be lifted using tape or other adhesive materials. Gel lifters are especially well suited for lifting residue imprints without lifting any of the porous surface's material (see Fig. 7.13 below). Gel lifters consist of three layers: the backing or carrier, the gelatin adhesive, and the protective cover sheet. The backing material is colored or transparent. The gel lifters are available in a range of sizes and can be cut to any size dependent on the size of the imprint. Once the imprint is lifted, it should be photographed without the cover sheet in place. The intact gel lifter should then be placed in an evidence bag or envelope for storage. Because the gelatin layer will melt at temperatures above 104°F, it must be stored at room temperature or below room temperature. The backing material must be marked with the case number, collector's initials, date, and time.

Electrostatic lifting can also be used as a technique for collection of residue imprints on both nonporous and porous surfaces (see Fig. 7.14 below). The unit consists of three basic components: a power supply, metal ground plate, and metalized lifting film. The power supply causes a high-voltage static charge on the lifting film that attracts the dust particles of the imprint thereby transferring the imprint to the film. The transferred dust print is then photographed and preserved between pieces of cardboard or poster board as the primary container and then placed in an outer secondary container with appropriate documentation.

Nonporous Surfaces

Gel lifters, electrostatic lifting, and strongly adhesive lifters are very well suited for the lifting, collection, and preservation of residue imprints on nonporous surfaces too. Once the imprints are lifted, those lifts should be packaged in plastic bags, envelopes, or other primary containers into secondary containers. The packaging should be marked and documented as previously described.

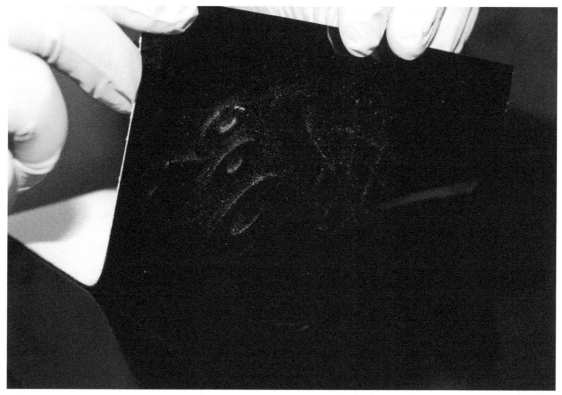

FIGURE 7.13   Gel lifter used to lift dust imprint.

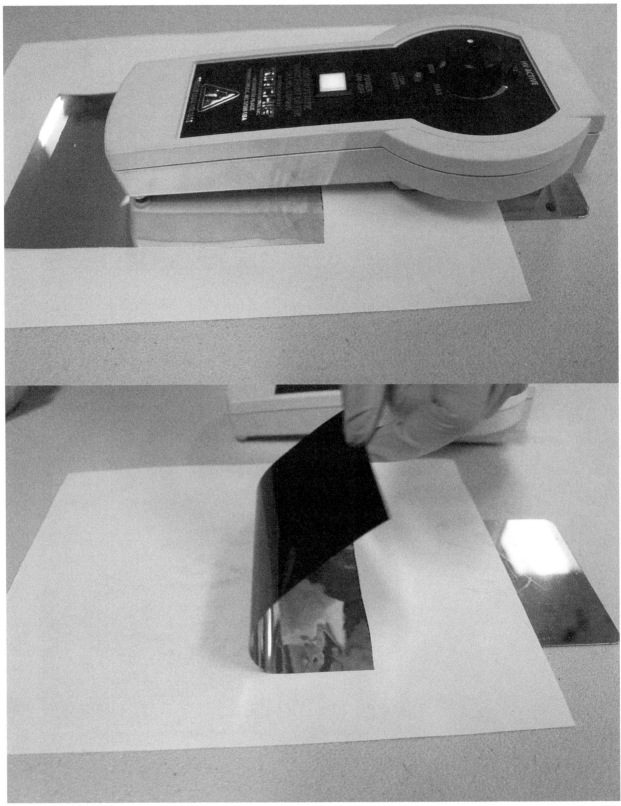

FIGURE 7.14 Use of electrostatic lifter for dust imprint.

Indentations

Three-dimensional impression evidence is produced like imprint evidence when two surfaces come into contact with one another. One of the surfaces is softer than the other surface, and the softer surface becomes "indented" with the shape, length, width, and depth of the harder item. The softer surface has an impression with a detailed replication of the pattern of the harder object.

As previously described, indentation evidence is properly photographed using oblique lighting that is raised slightly so as to cast shadows and illuminate various surfaces of the indentation with an attempt to view details of the indentation. Once the indentation is photographed, it should be cast so as to collect the impression evidence. The casting material is chosen based upon the type of surface containing the indentation. If the indented surface is a hard type of material, such as metal or painted hardwood, it may contain microscopic markings; thus, silicone rubber material is best suited for the casting. If the indented surface is softer, like dirt or snow, then a material like dental stone is the best casting material. The surfaces of the softer indentations must be prepared before casting is done. See Fig. 7.15 of dental stone casing results.

Table 7.2 provides the procedures to follow for casting indentations in various surfaces.

HAIR AND FIBER EVIDENCE

Hair Evidence

Hair evidence found at a crime scene can be used to identify racial origin and somatic origin of the source of the hair. If a root sheath is attached to a hair (such as, anagen or catagen hairs), then PCR-STR DNA typing can be used to identify the contributor of the hair. Mitochondrial DNA typing of hair shaft identification methods have also been used in many investigations.

Once the hairs have been found at the scene using the previously discussed methods, they are collecting by using tweezers or forceps and placed into a druggist's fold as a primary container. The primary container should then be placed into a secondary, outer container. The outer container can be plastic or glassine bags, envelopes, vials, or pillboxes. They should be properly documented, sealed, and marked.

FIGURE 7.15   Dental stone cast of indentation.

TABLE 7.2 Casting Procedures

Media	Casting Procedure
WET SOIL of a fine, even consistency will produce an impression with a high degree of detail.	1. Remove excess water by sprinkling a small amount of casting material over the impression. 2. Mix and pour as normal. 3. Accelerator may be needed. 4. Drying time: 45–60 min.
MUD of a fine, even consistency will produce an impression with a high degree of detail.	1. Mix and pour as normal. 2. Drying depends on how wet the mud is: 45–60 min.
DRY SOIL of a consistency of talcum powder will retain detail to a varying degree.	1. Spray impression with pump hair spray. 2. Mix and pour as normal. 3. Drying time: 20–30 min.
DRY SOIL with a hard packed consistency will retain detail to a varying degree.	1. Spray impression with pump hair spray. 2. Mix and pour as normal. 3. Drying time: 20–30 min.
SAND will vary in texture and consistency and will retain detail.	1. Spray impression with pump hair spray. 2. Mix and pour as normal. 3. Drying time: 20–30 min.
When impression is in water: WATER varies in texture and consistency. Detail depends on the amount of water and the amount of pressure applied to the ground. Time-consuming process.	1. Build form around the impression, if needed to control water and remove excess water if possible. 2. Sprinkle small amount of casting materials over impression until covered. 3. Mix and pour as normal. 4. Accelerator can be added. 5. Drying will vary from 60 to 120 s.
When water is in impression: WATER varies in texture and consistency. Detail depends on the amount of water and the amount of pressure applied to the impression by the water.	1. Remove excess water by pipetting. 2. Sprinkle small amount of casting materials over impression until covered. 3. Mix and pour as usual. 4. Accelerator can be added. 5. Drying time will vary form 60–90 min depending on amount of water.
When impression is in snow: SNOW varies in texture, cohesiveness, and detail retention with temperature. Excellent detail can be reproduced if careful.	1. Spray the impression with "Snow Print Wax". 2. Mix water with snow to lower the temperature of the water. 3. Add accelerator. 4. Pour as usual. 5. Drying time will be 60–90 min and may take longer due to the exterior temperatures.
Accelerator is potassium sulfate.	

Hairs from same locations may be packaged together. Indiscriminate vacuuming at the crime scene will produce a remixing effect of the "newly deposited" hair evidence and should be avoided in crime scene investigations. Vacuuming of small areas near bodies or primary crime scenes can be useful as a hair collection technique without remixing the newly deposited hair. Care should be taken to make sure that a new filter for the vacuum is used. The filter should be packaged separately into a druggist's fold and placed into an appropriately sealed and marked outer container. The use of tape lifts or gel lifters in small, distinctive areas at the crime scene is appropriate, too (see Fig. 7.16 for photo of vacuum filter and gel lifter for collection of hair evidence). If movable objects at the crime scene are suspected to contain hair evidence, they should be wrapped in a primary container and placed in a secondary, outer container (properly sealed and marked) and taken to a controlled environment or the entire object submitted to the forensic laboratory for searching of the hair evidence. Similarly, if a hair is attached or caught on an item of evidence, as in dried blood or a part of fabric, it should be left on the item and collected in its original condition. It should be packaged within a primary container and placed in an outer secondary container.

FIGURE 7.16   The use of vacuuming and gel lifters for hairs.

The collection of known or standard hairs from victims and/or suspects will be necessary for most criminal investigations. These known hairs should never be cut. A total of 25—50 pulled hairs should be collected from different regions of the area, packaged into a druggist's fold, placed in an outer container, properly sealed, and marked by the collector with their initials, the case number, the date, the time, and a brief description. Combings of the head or pubic areas are designed to remove loose hairs on those surfaces, and it is not a technique for collecting known standards. Any combings are to be considered as unknown or questioned samples.

Fiber Evidence

Fiber evidence is searched, collected, and packaged like hair evidence. The picking, vacuuming, tape lifting, and scraping techniques are used for the collection of fibers or threads. Where there is fiber evidence adhering to a movable object found at the crime scene, that object should be wrapped and packaged intact. It is useful for the crime scene investigator to remember that fabrics are easily caught or torn by broken windows, edges of ripped screens, and other damaged or sharp materials, so their collection and packaging should preserve the additional evidence. See Fig. 7.17 with a photograph of a piece of glass with attached fibers below.

Other fiber evidence, such as fabrics, thread, cordage, rope, or cloth may also be found at the crime scene. They should be collected as with fiber evidence. They should be photographed, packaged in primary containers, and placed in outer secondary containers that are sealed and marked as other evidence previously discussed. Knotted cordage evidence can be found at the crime scene. The knots should never be untied; they should be photographed intact. If removal of the knots and cordage is necessary for transportation, the cordage may be cut at a new location and marked by the person removing the cordage. Removal and cutting at new location must allow the knots to remain intact (see Fig. 7.18 below).

As with hair evidence, known standards of possible sources of the fiber evidence must be collected and packaged for subsequent comparison in the laboratory. If possible, the entire known source should be collected. If not possible, then a representative sample from the source should be obtained. Cuttings from carpets, fabrics, or other materials can be used as the known sample of the possible source. The knowns are packaged into primary containers, placed into outer secondary containers, and preserved as shown previously. See Fig. 7.19 below with a photograph of carpeting being sampled.

FIGURE 7.17 Glass with fiber evidence.

FIGURE 7.18 Identification of knots on ligatures.

FIGURE 7.19   Collection of known samples from carpeting.

OTHER TRACE EVIDENCE: GLASS, PAINT, AND SOIL

Glass Evidence

Glass as evidence is persistent and as typical for trace evidence is unknowingly transferred from one surface to another surface. Fig. 7.20 shows the securing and sometimes tricky documentation of glass evidence prior to collection.

As with hairs and fibers, any objects that are movable and may contain glass evidence should be wrapped or placed in a primary container to prevent loss of the glass evidence. They should then be placed in an outer secondary container that is sealed and marked properly for preservation purposes. For example, any objects that are contaminated with glass such as shoes (See Fig. 7.21 for a photo of glass on the sole of shoe) should be folded into a primary paper druggist fold and put into an outer secondary container with appropriate documentation. If the object to contain the glass evidence cannot be moved, then previously described collection methods of picking, tape lifting, scraping, or vacuuming can be done and placed into a primary container followed by an outer secondary container with proper documentation. Large pieces of glass should be placed between pieces of cardboard to prevent further breakage, wrapped in primary container material, and placed into an outer secondary container. Each large piece of glass should be numbered, sealed, and marked appropriately. The containers should also be marked that they contain sharp edges and careful handling is necessary.

Suspected sources of glass evidence should be collected using proper methods. Any frames holding the glass should be packaged and preserved intact with any broken glass particles. If the possible source of the glass is an exterior window, then be sure to label the source's exterior or interior surfaces. The edges of the fractured glass can be used to reconstruct the side to which force was applied to fracture marks on the glass. Pieces of broken glass may also be used to reconstruct windows by direct-edge matching. See Fig. 7.22 below for glass window reconstruction.

Paint Evidence

Suspected paint evidence exists as intact paint chips or as paint smears or scrapings. Intact paint chips must be carefully collected and preserved. Paint chips are packaged into druggist's folds as primary containers and placed in outer stiff secondary containers such as pill vials, pillboxes, or coin envelopes. Paint scrapings are often found in specific locations at

FIGURE 7.20   Documenting glass evidence can be difficult. Do not forget avoid reflections.

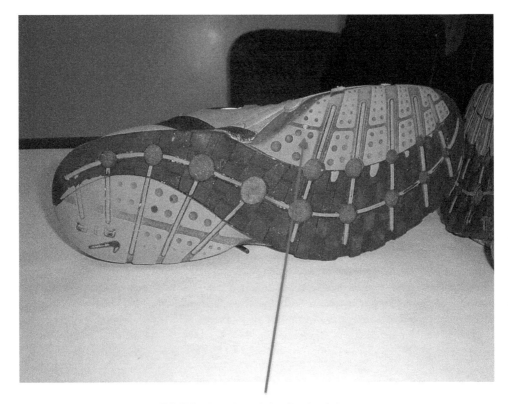

FIGURE 7.21   Piece of glass in sole of shoe.

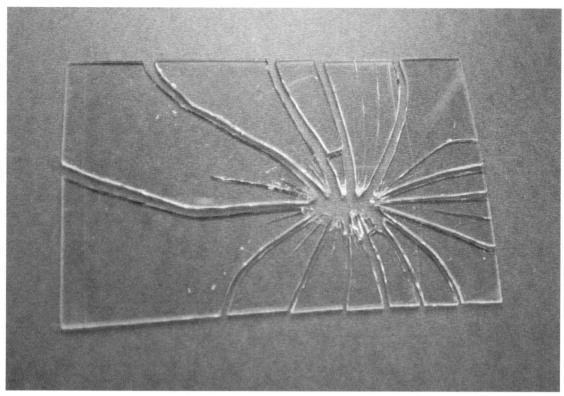

FIGURE 7.22   Window glass reconstruction.

crime scenes or on vehicles. Care should be taken to document locations, specifically heights of paint scrapings on poles, road abutments, or on damaged vehicles.

As shown with other trace evidence from crime scenes, representative samples of possible known sources for the paint evidence need to be collected and preserved by use of the primary and secondary container procedures with proper documentation (Fig. 7.23).

FIREARMS, TOOLMARKS, AND GUNSHOT RESIDUE

Firearms Evidence

Firearms, spent casings, and fired projectiles are frequently found at crime scenes. Firearms are documented by notes, photography, videography, and sketching as discussed in an earlier chapter. Searches for firearms are a commonplace occurrence in criminal investigations. The collection, packaging, and preservation of firearms evidence require some additional documentation. Besides make/model/caliber/serial number additional information about location, condition (loaded or unloaded), time of discovery, and identification of other physical evidence present on the firearm should be recorded. If the firearm needs to be moved to determine this information, then it should be carefully handled to avoid disturbing any potential fingerprints or blood spatters that may be deposited on the firearm. The firearm may be picked up or touched on the textured grips without altering or damaging existing fingerprints. Never stick anything in the barrel of the firearm to move it; this may alter or change the rifling in the barrel.

Firearms should never be collected or packaged in a loaded condition. Before the firearm is unloaded, if the firearm is a revolver, then the cylinder needs to be diagrammed (as shown in Fig. 7.24 below). If it is a semiautomatic pistol, then the condition of the slide mechanism, the number of live rounds in the magazine, and the presence of any chambered rounds need to be recorded. Any unused ammunition must be collected with the weapon, packaged, marked, and described as to its location near or in the firearm.

The firearm should be packaged in a primary container or wrapping and placed in a secondary container such as a paper bag, envelope, or cardboard box specific for firearms. Never clean the barrel, chamber, or cylinder of the firearm. Do not

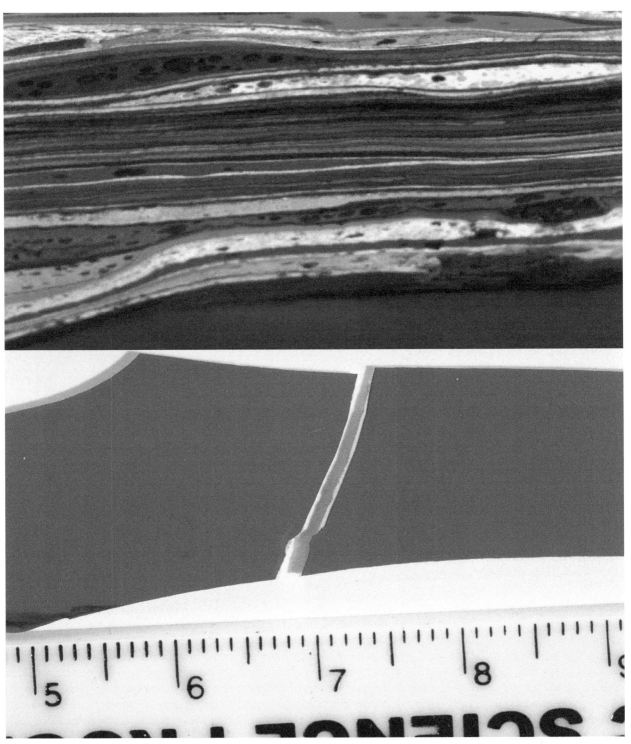

FIGURE 7.23 Paint evidence.

take the handguns, rifles, or shotguns apart before submission to the forensic laboratory. The live ammunition found in the firearm should be similarly packaged but in a separate container and submitted with the firearm. Any additional live ammunition or boxes of ammunition found at the crime scene should also be collected and packaged properly and submitted with the firearm (see Fig. 7.25 below).

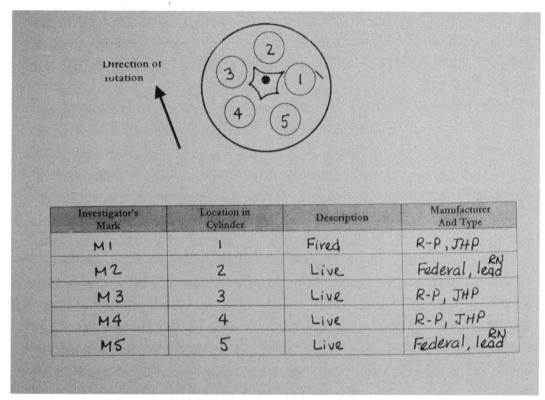

Investigator's Mark	Location in Cylinder	Description	Manufacturer And Type
M 1	1	Fired	R-P, JHP
M 2	2	Live	Federal, lead ^{RN}
M 3	3	Live	R-P, JHP
M 4	4	Live	R-P, JHP
M S	5	Live	Federal, lead ^{RN}

FIGURE 7.24 Diagrammed cylinder of revolver.

FIGURE 7.25 Secure firearms collecting box.

Projectiles

Projectiles found at the crime scene should never be marked or scored in any way. They should be wrapped in soft paper as the primary container and packaged in a secondary container with clear documentation of where the projectile was recovered. Do not attempt to clean the projectiles. If the projectiles are coated in blood or other biological fluids, then they should be allowed to air-dry, wrapped in paper, and placed in an outer secondary pillbox with a detailed description included on the pillbox (see Fig. 7.26 below).

Spent Cartridges

Spent cartridges found at the crime scene should be wrapped with soft paper as primary containers, packaged separately, and placed in outer containers such as pillboxes or coin envelopes (as shown in Fig. 7.27 below). The metal spent casings should not be marked. Spent shotgun casings may be marked on the plastic shell material. As with projectiles, all spent casings recovered at the scene must be submitted to the forensic laboratory.

Toolmarks

Toolmarks found at the crime scene are static indentations or dynamic indentations called striations. Indentations are discussed above with regard to collection, packaging, and preservation. Careful packaging of suspected tools or implements must occur. Suspect or known tools should be secured in a box to protect the tool's unique markings. Under absolutely no condition should the suspected tool be placed or fitted into the toolmark found at the scene. A reminder that collection after proper documentation is best done by collecting the toolmark intact on moveable surfaces. Immoveable objects with toolmarks will require casting with silicon rubber materials (many commercially available products and delivering modes are available; see Fig. 7.28).

Gunshot Residue

Gunshot residue (GSR) found at the crime scene is very fragile and therefore should be collected as soon as possible after firearm discharge. Collection of GSR on live subjects can be done by the use of laboratory supplied kits or commercial kits.

FIGURE 7.26 Projectile collection pillbox.

FIGURE 7.27   Cartridge cases in pillbox.

FIGURE 7.28   Toolmark collection by Mikrosil casting.

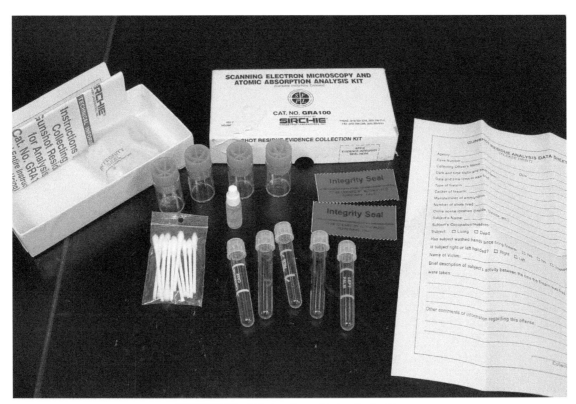

FIGURE 7.29   GSR (gunshot residue) collection kit.

Currently, there are the two commonly used techniques for GSR collection: the SEM disc lifting method and atomic absorption (AA) swabbing methods (as shown in Fig. 7.29 below). Investigators should consult with their local forensic laboratory as to which test the laboratory performs. The collection of the GSR must be done within 6 hours on live subjects, and they should not be allowed to wash their hands or extensively contact their hands with other surfaces in case they loosen the GSR particles. If a body is to be sampled for GSR, the sampling must be done before the body is moved. If no sampling can be done at the scene, then bagging the hands with paper bags should be done.

GSR on clothing can oftentimes be useful in the determination of range of fire for reconstruction purposes. The clothing must be carefully packaged so as not to dislodge any GSR particles. The packaging technique that best accomplishes this is to place clean wrapping paper on each layer of the clothing. Clothing should be placed in a box, and folding avoided as much as possible. For GSR pattern determination of the range of fire, the firearm and matching ammunition must be submitted to the laboratory (as shown in Fig. 7.30 below).

BIOLOGICAL EVIDENCE: BLOOD, BODY FLUIDS, AND TISSUE

Blood

General Considerations

The collection, packaging, and preservation of blood evidence at the crime scene should never take place until the investigator has taken extra care to make sure that the bloodstain patterns have been extensively documented for possible reconstruction to be discussed in Chapter 8.

Recent advances in DNA typing techniques allow for older and smaller bloodstains to be analyzed. The collection of even the smallest of bloodstain samples at the crime scene may significantly add to an investigation. For example, small bloodstains belonging to the victim found on a suspect's clothes or shoes can be the only link between the victim and a suspect. New research on DNA in criminal investigations has raised the possibilities of microchip DNA "on-scene" analysis. With the advent of artificial intelligence systems, such as CODIS (Fig. 7.31), in the near future a crime scene investigator may be able to identify the donor of a bloodstain by on-scene DNA database search.

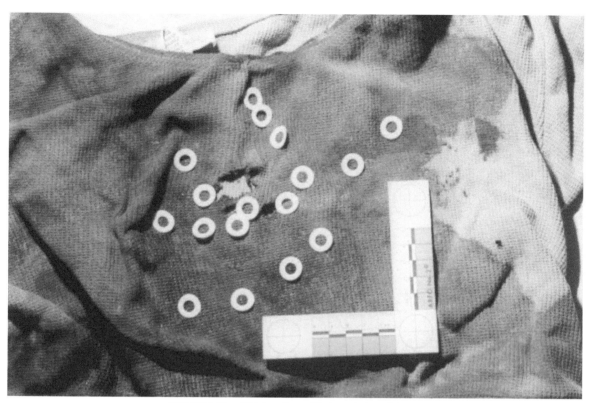

FIGURE 7.30 GSR (gunshot residue) on clothes of victim.

FIGURE 7.31 DNA analyst at work.

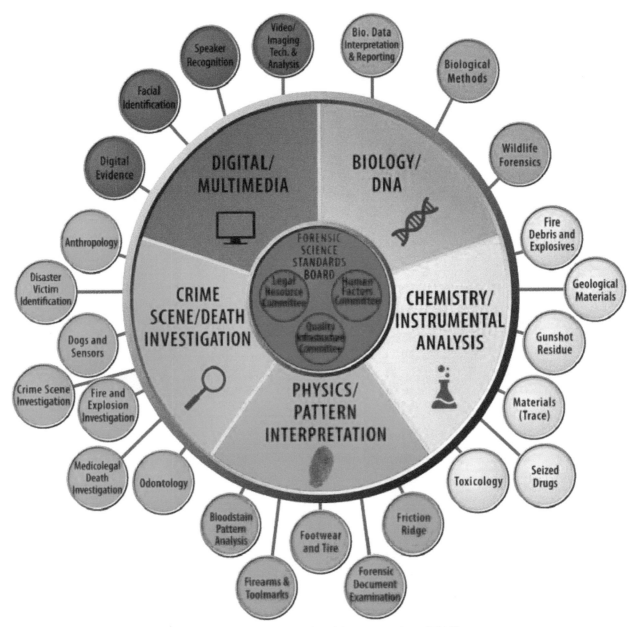

FIGURE 7.32 Organization of specialty area committees (OSAC).

The advances in the identification and individualization of bloodstains and the successful court presentation and resolution of an investigation with bloodstain evidence cannot be accomplished *unless the correct procedures are followed for collection, packaging, and preservation of the blood evidence.* The Scientific Working Group for DNA Analysis and Methods (SWGDAM) and the DNA Subcommittee of the Organization of Specialty Committees (OSAC) have suggested some best practices for the collection of blood found at crime scenes (Fig. 7.32).

After documentation of the blood evidence at the crime scene, the collection can begin. Generally, the most easily lost blood must be collected first. These are bloodstains that may be located in high volume traffic areas of the scene; bloodstains that are in doorways, hallways, or roadsides; or blood that may be present at outdoor crime scenes. Bloodstains that are found on movable objects can be protected by temporarily moving the object to a safer location until the stain or object may be collected. See Fig. 7.33 below.

FIGURE 7.33   Suspected bloodstains at point of entry.

Blood at crime scenes will be found either as a dried stain or in a liquid state. Generally, if blood at the crime scene is liquid, then let it air-dry! If the object with the bloodstain is *movable*, then collect the entire object! The packaging of blood and bloody objects will follow the same packaging principles that have been discussed throughout this chapter for all physical evidence. Place blood and bloodstained objects in a primary container (druggist's folds or blood swab box) followed by packaging in an outer secondary container (envelopes or paper bags), as shown in Fig. 7.34 below. Blood and bloodstained evidence should never be placed in airtight containers.

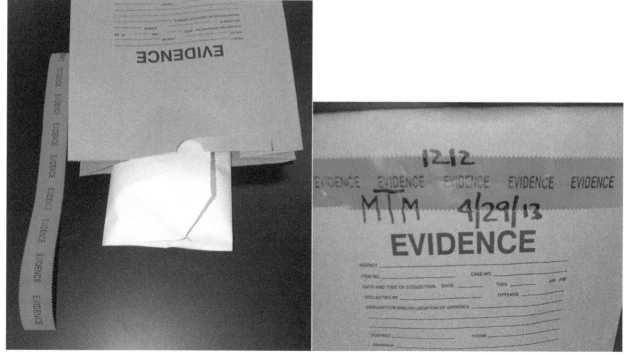

FIGURE 7.34   Sealing of evidence bags.

The secondary container should be sealed with evidence tape, marked appropriately, and placed in a secure location. Bloodstained evidence frequently will have other trace evidence present. If the blood loosely holds the trace evidence, then it is proper to collect that trace evidence at the crime scene (with techniques previously described). However, if a dried bloodstain holds the trace evidence tightly, do not attempt to collect the trace evidence. Carefully cover or protect the trace evidence while packaging the bloodstain. Bloodstained items should always be packaged separately to prevent cross-contamination.

Dried Bloodstains

As described above, if the object with the dried bloodstain is small and movable, then the entire object should be wrapped in a primary container and placed in an outer, nonairtight secondary container with proper markings. Whenever possible this is the preferred collection technique; however, dried bloodstains are frequently encountered on objects that are large or bulky and cannot be collected intact. In those situations the following procedures for collection should be followed:

- *Absorbing the bloodstain.* According to standards, dried bloodstains can be absorbed on to sterile cotton swabs. Moisten the swab with distilled water. Carefully swab the bloodstain with the swab. Absorb all the stain with a minimum of area consumed. Insert the swab into the swab-drying box. Allow the swab to dry once the stain has been collected. Seal the box and label all the necessary information. A suggested collection process is shown in Fig. 7.35.
- *Cut out the bloodstain.* If the bloodstain is located on a surface that can easily be removed, then cut an area around the bloodstain including the stain. If the surface material is fragile or easily broken, care should be taken to secure the cutout section to prevent breakage of the sample. Wrapping in a druggist's fold made of gauze or sterile swatch material works well (as shown in Fig. 7.36).
- *Obtaining reference standards.* Substrate and unstained controls should also be swabbed as above and collected with proper packaging.

Liquid Blood Samples

If the wet blood is small, then it should be collected with sterilized cotton swabs and then be allowed to air-dry. The stain can be collected by the procedure discussed above for dried bloodstains.

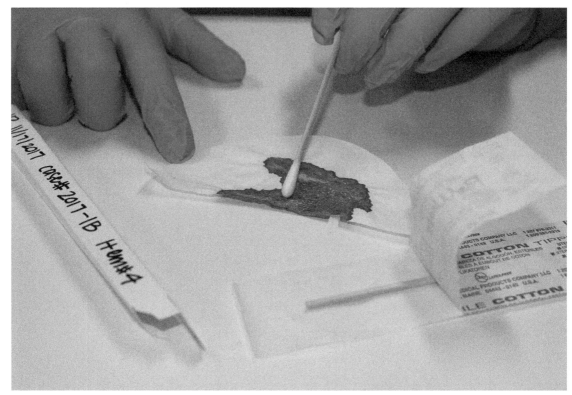

FIGURE 7.35   Swabbing for collection of suspected blood.

FIGURE 7.36 Cutting out suspected bloodstains from wall.

If the liquid bloodstain is large, then it may be collected by the following choices of collection procedures:

- Absorb the liquid blood sample onto sterile cotton swabs. Allow the swab to dry. The cotton swab is inserted into a swab box and placed in an outer secondary container sealed with evidence tape.
- If the large wet bloodstain is located on a movable object, for example, clothes or bedsheets, then wait until the bloodstain dries. Then place paper in-between layers of the clothing and collect the item carefully to avoid transfer or alteration of the bloodstain pattern. At the secure location, the object should be unwrapped and laid out for continued air-drying (as shown in Fig. 7.37). The original packaging should be maintained and used again for repackaging if possible. If new wrappings and packaging are used, then the old materials must be saved as evidence. The bloodstained object should be carefully photographed with scales and without before packaging. Sometimes, the heavily blood-stained object, such as bloodstained mattresses, must be cut to remove the bloodstain from the scene; *do not* cut through the bloodstains. Proper primary and secondary containers with proper marking should be used even if temporary.

Known Blood Samples

The appropriate known or standard DNA sample is collected from all individuals in the investigation. The accepted method for the collection of known DNA samples is now the use of epithelial cells from the inside of the source's mouth (see Fig. 7.38 below). There are a variety of collection devices commercially available for this collection. Minimally sterile swabs or buccal swabs are used and packaged like dried bloodstains.

Seminal Stains

Seminal stains in crime scene investigations are usually found in the form of hospital specimens taken from victims of sexual assault or in the form of dried stains on objects at the scene. The dried stains at the crime scene are collected, packaged, and preserved in a similar way to bloodstains as discussed above.

In sexual assault investigations the crime scene investigation will also include the collection of evidence from the victim at the hospital. The victim of a sexual assault should be taken to the hospital for examination as soon as possible. A doctor assisted by a forensic nurse will usually conduct the examination and collect evidence. Forensic training for nurses is available nationwide and should be encouraged for hospital staff. Commercially available or forensic laboratory-prepared sexual assault collection kits are used for the collection of the hospital specimens. These kits will include swabs, microscope slides, and various containers for the collection of a variety of evidence from the victim (see Fig. 7.39 below).

At the crime scene, dried seminal stains may be present on movable and immovable surfaces. Once the possible stains have been found and documented, collection can occur. As with dried bloodstains, absorbing samples onto sterile swabs is used, but because of the nature of seminal stains, minimize handling of suspected stains. The collected evidence should be placed in a primary container—swab box or druggist's fold—followed by an outer, secondary container that is not airtight. The container is sealed with evidence tape, marked appropriately, and preserved by refrigeration if possible.

Saliva, Urine, Perspiration Stains

The above biological fluid stains are collected, packaged, and preserved in a similar way to the methods and techniques described for blood and seminal stains. Liquid saliva samples should be collected with the sterile cotton swab method. Saliva stains or bitemarks can be collected with a moistened swab. Swab the area with a single swab and concentrate it in a limited area. The saliva standard is collected by use of sterile swabs, air-drying, and the use of swab boxes into outer secondary containers with proper labeling.

FIRE DEBRIS EVIDENCE: FIRE DEBRIS AND IGNITABLE FLUIDS

The collection, packaging, and preservation of suspected ignitable liquids at a fire scene should be done as soon as possible. However, the safety and security of the scene should be considered before any attempts of collection are done. Flammable fluids can be present at the fire scene in various forms. They may be absorbed into numerous materials or exist as liquids. The collection method is dependant on the form of accelerant found—absorbed or liquid. Regardless of the form, accelerants are volatile and will evaporate if not properly packaged into airtight containers.

FIGURE 7.37 Secure drying cabinets.

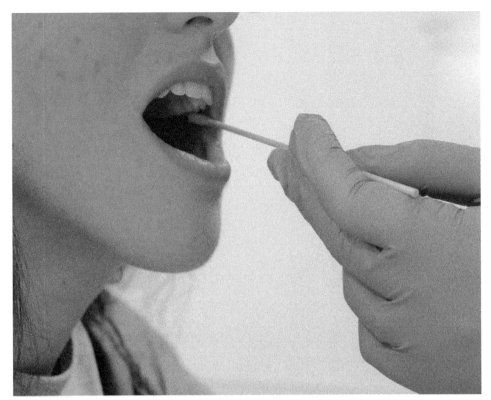

FIGURE 7.38 Buccal swabs.

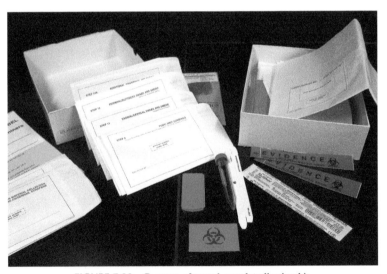

FIGURE 7.39 Contents of sexual assault collection kit.

Liquid Samples

Liquid samples of suspected ignitable fluids are found as pools mixed with water or in other containers at the scene (gasoline cans, plastic jugs, etc.) should be placed in an airtight container. Unused, lined metal paint cans are best suited for this collection. Glass jars can be used as a last resort if paint cans are not available, but the sample should be transferred as soon as possible. Absorbing the liquids to clean cloth material can be done. The absorbed samples should then be placed in airtight containers—paint cans or KAPAK bags—as soon as possible. The airtight container should have a piece of evidence tape placed over the opening and marked properly. Owing to the nature of arson investigations, the labels placed on possible accelerant evidence must have details about the location where the evidence was found. There are commercially available absorptive pads that have gained widespread use for the safe collection of suspected accelerant materials followed by successful laboratory separations and identifications.

Fire Debris and Absorbed Ignitable Samples

Burned and unburned carpeting, padding, furniture, bedding, flooring, wood, and walls at fire scenes are examples of materials that may have absorbed ignitable fluids that have been used to start a fire. The forensic laboratory will be able to separate the fire debris and water from the accelerant used. As with suspected liquid ignitable fluids, the absorbed fluids must be packaged into an airtight container. However, the size and location of the absorbing materials may preclude its intact collection. If the object with the absorbed ignitable fluid can be packaged into the paint cans or KAPAK bag in its original condition, then it should be collected intact. If the item is too large or difficult to remove from the scene, then a representative sample containing the ignitable fluid should be collected and placed in the airtight paint can as described above. The fire debris and ignitable fluid should approximately fill only two-thirds of the can's volume. *Do not fill the paint can.* The can (a primary container) should be sealed with tape and detailed descriptions shown (see Fig. 7.40 below).

EXPLOSIVE MATERIAL

Bomb scenes are characterized by mass destruction and unsafe conditions and as such makes the collection, packaging, and preservation of the physical evidence a difficult task. Generally, physical evidence at bomb scenes consists of explosives, fallout, timers, fuses, and bomb parts. Some of those items can be fragmented. The small size of evidence means that it is often overlooked or missed while searching and collecting. Most guidelines for the collection of evidence at the bomb scene suggest collecting everything. See Fig. 7.41 for collection of all bomb parts.

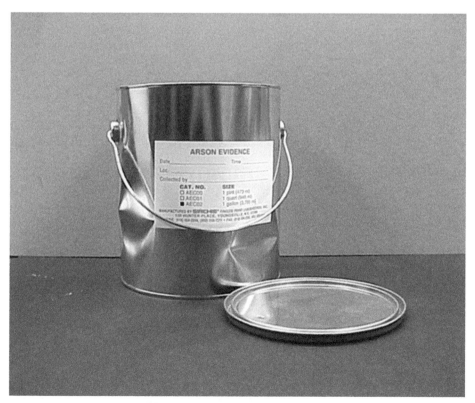

FIGURE 7.40 Fire debris collection paint can.

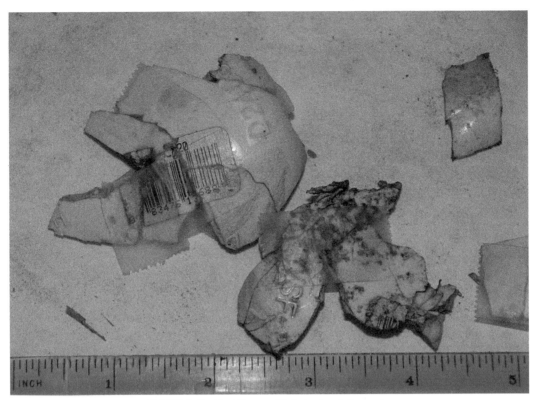

FIGURE 7.41   Partially assembled pipe bomb fragments.

QUESTIONED DOCUMENTS

A questioned document is a document whose origin or authenticity is unknown or is uncertain. Any written material found at the crime scene that falls into this category of physical evidence must be collected. The document in question should never be directly marked, folded, or defaced in any manner. Handling of the document should be kept to a minimum. Gloves and forceps should be used for all handling of the document, as illustrated in Fig. 7.42. The document should be packaged into a clear plastic bag or envelopes with clear windows on one side.

Exemplars

Various exemplars or standards for comparison purposes are often collected in this type of investigation. There are two types of exemplars for questioned document examinations: requested writings and nonrequested writings.

- Requested writings are standards that are obtained when the conditions for writing are exactly the same as in the questioned document. For example, the same type of ink, pen, paper, and content of a letter are used. The conditions should minimize stress. The requested writing should be repeated at least 10 to 12 times.
- Nonrequested writings are exemplars that are obtained from the normal writing activities of the suspected writer. Examples of nonrequested writings include canceled checks, journals, letters, etc. Any written document from the normal course of living is considered a nonrequested exemplar. Photo 6.35 consists of three pages of ransom notes found on the staircase in the house. The writing on this note consists of discarded printing. Similar exemplars should be collected for comparison.

Exemplars from mechanical writings are those documents that may be typewritten, printed, or produced by copy machines. The machine suspected to have been used to make the questioned document should be collected. However, if it is not available, then numerous samples from each machine should be collected. If typewritten or computer printer documents are to be examined, then the ribbon on the typewriter or printer must also be collected. The collected questioned document (QD) evidence should be properly packaged and shown above with appropriate documentation as to the source of the evidence (see Fig. 7.43 below).

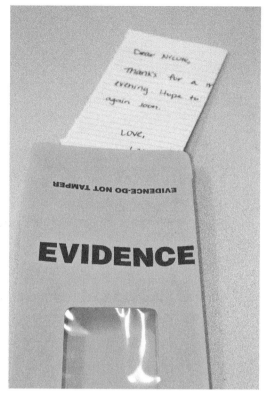

FIGURE 7.42   Packaging of questioned documents.

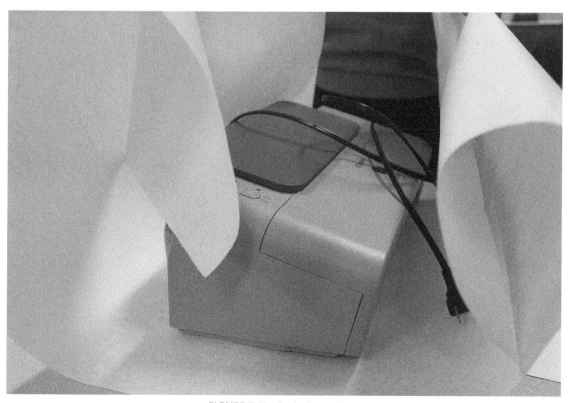

FIGURE 7.43   Packaging a printer.

DRUG EVIDENCE

General crime scene processing procedures should be followed with the collection, packaging, and preservation of drug evidence. At the present time, many criminal investigations will involve some aspect of suspected drug evidence. For example, a homicide investigation may indirectly involve the investigation of illicit drug activity of victims and/or suspects. As such, suspected drug evidence will be found and therefore must be properly collected, packaged, and preserved. The suspected drug evidence will fall into two basic categories: illegal controlled substances or medicinal preparations. Both types of drug evidence must be collected, packaged, and preserved as physical evidence by use of primary and outer secondary containers with proper markings.

Controlled Substances

All suspected controlled substances should be collected intact, properly packaged in sealed containers, and preserved for laboratory analysis. If the controlled substance is biological in nature, then it should be packaged in nonairtight containers. Never package the live plants in airtight containers! (See Fig. 7.44 below.) All tablets and capsules should be carefully described in the notes especially counts prior to collection or packaging. The forensic laboratory will sample and test a representative sample from the submitted drug evidence.

Frequently, paraphernalia and other items will be present at a crime scene, as shown in Fig. 7.45. These items may have residue coatings and trace quantities of drugs on their surfaces. For this reason, every attempt should be made to preserve these residues on the items from the crime scene. Many times it will be necessary to collect the residue from the items

FIGURE 7.44   Growing marijuana plants.

FIGURE 7.45   Containers with possible drug residue.

before it is collected and packaged. The scraping or rinsing of these items must be packaged separately from the item itself. If the department procedures prohibit the crime scene investigator to isolate the residue prior to laboratory submission, then the investigator must follow the department procedure. Do not attempt to process the items for fingerprints or other trace evidence if the residual drug substance is present.

Clandestine laboratories can produce a variety of illicit substances. Different types of laboratories or processes may be located at a single location. Yet, of all the clandestine laboratories seized in the United States during the past 10 years over 80% have been associated with the production of methamphetamine. Some processes are designed to extract an illicit substance from raw (plant) material, such as morphine from opium. Other laboratories synthesize the illicit substance using combinations of raw materials and/or chemicals. Many of the chemicals used in synthesis are inherently hazardous, and even more so when used and disposed of improperly. Chemicals are rarely labeled, are seldom in original containers, and may be mixed with other chemicals. Some chemicals are common household chemicals, which individually may not be hazardous, but when mixed together or used in the clandestine laboratory processes can be extremely dangerous thusly requiring the scene investigator to use caution. Apparatus may be improperly constructed or used. Further, the site may have been intentionally abandoned in a hazardous condition or booby-trapped. The following general precautions should be taken when seizing a clandestine drug laboratory, under the supervision of trained chemists or clandestine laboratory personnel. Once these precautions are implemented, the clandestine laboratory site should be treated as any other crime scene when identifying, collecting, and preserving other types of physical evidence. Evidence such as fingerprints, documents, money, records, computers, and supplies could be extremely important for further investigation. Samples of all chemicals should be seized and maintained for further analysis (see Fig. 7.46 below).

FIGURE 7.46   Unsafe conditions in clandestine methamphetamine laboratory.

Medicinal Preparations

In investigations where prescription vials are found, the labels on the vials provide useful information that can be used in the investigation. The vial labels will often identify the user of the pharmaceutical, the identity of the preparation, the quantity prescribed, and when the preparation was filled, and the vial can be easily processed for fingerprints (see Fig. 7.47 below). The contents of the vial can always be compared with the label, too. The vial and its contents should be collected, packaged, and preserved in an intact condition using procedures discussed previously in this chapter.

BITEMARK EVIDENCE

When bitemark evidence is discovered at a crime scene, it will need to be preserved as soon as possible. This type of evidence is both biological and impression evidence. The crime scene investigator should consult with a forensic odontologist as soon as possible. Trace quantities of saliva may be present on the bitemark and should be collected and preserved using the swab techniques discussed above. If the bitemark has been found on a live subject, then photographs taken several days after the bite incident may produce bruising that is best suited for subsequent comparison testing.

DIGITAL EVIDENCE

Digital evidence whether part of a "seen" crime scene or "unseen" electronic crime scene as part of a computer at the crime scene should be carefully documented. All the cords or peripherals attached to the computer should be labeled and corresponding labels placed on the computer. The safest way for any crime scene investigator to collect and preserve digital evidence is to have a computer forensics expert on scene to assist and advise.

Collection with the use of proper primary and secondary containers with detailed markings is appropriate for any electronic equipment found. Collection of all peripherals and software found at the crime scene should accompany the hardware to the laboratory.

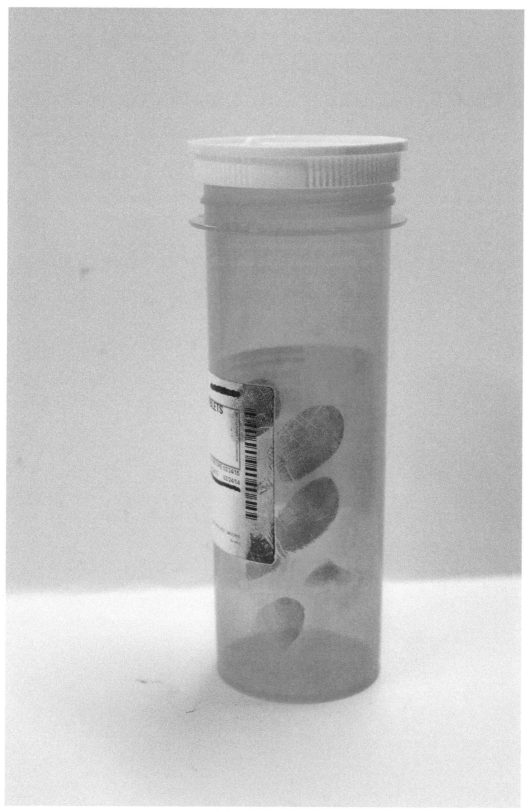

FIGURE 7.47   Prescription vial with latents and label information.

DISCUSSION QUESTIONS

1. What are some general guidelines for the collection, preservation, and packaging for physical evidence found at crime scenes?
2. What are the three methods for the collection and preservation of latent fingerprints? What determines which method to follow?
3. How are indentation impressions collected? Are footwear impressions in sand collected differently compared with toolmarks?
4. Gel lifters are especially well suited for the collection of what impression evidence?
5. What are general collection guidelines for trace evidence such as hair, fibers, or paint?
6. Firearms can be collected and packaged using special boxes, what should be done to the firearm before it is packaged (there are at least two things)?
7. Body fluids such as blood and semen are collected, preserved, and packaged according to what group's guidelines? What are their guidelines?
8. How are accelerants collected, preserved, and packaged at scenes of fires?
9. What are the two types of exemplars commonly collected with questioned documents?
10. Entomological evidence found at the crime scene can be used for what purposes as part of the crime scene investigation? How should insect evidence be collected, preserved, and packaged?

Part III

Concluding Processes

Chapter 8

Reconstruction Activities

Chapter Outline

Learning Objectives

Upon completion of this chapter the reader should be able to:

- define crime scene reconstruction and its importance;
- identify the components necessary for crime scene reconstruction;
- identify and discuss the types of crime scene reconstructions; and
- identify and explain reconstruction for common types of physical evidence found at scenes, including impression evidence, bloodstain patterns, glass fracturing, burn patterns at fire scenes.

INTRODUCTION AND REQUIREMENTS

Crime scene reconstruction is the determination of what happened or did not happen at the crime scene. The reconstruction is accomplished by the examination of patterned evidence at the scene, its location and position at the crime scene, and the laboratory examination of the physical evidence found on scene. Crime scene reconstruction is also the use of an individual's life experiences, reasoning or simple logic, and even, common sense.

The need to reconstruct the crime is one major reason for maintaining the integrity of a crime scene. The determination of what happened at a crime scene is significant to prosecutors for filing charges (and ultimately sentencing), and the juries for cases will likewise want to know what happened at the crime scene in their deliberations.

Once the necessary components for crime scene reconstruction have been obtained, there are five stages used by the crime scene reconstructionist for gathering the facts of the investigation working toward a reconstruction finding (see Table 8.1).

179

TABLE 8.1 Stages of Crime Scene Reconstruction for Gathering Facts of Investigation

Stage Number	Title	Description
1	*Data collection*	**All** investigative information (from victim, suspect, or witnesses) and documentation obtained at the crime scene (condition, patterns, location, etc.). Data are reviewed, organized, and studied.
2	*Preliminary thought identification*	Before any detailed analysis of the evidence is obtained, a possible explanation or conjecture of the events involved in a criminal act may be done, but it **must not** become the only explanation being considered at this stage. It is only a possibility as there may be several more possible explanations, too.
3	Hypothesis formation	Synthesis of data is based on the examination of the physical evidence and the continuing investigation. Scene examination and inspection of the physical evidence must be done. Scene and evidence examination can include interpretation of patterned evidence (bloodstain and impression patterns, gunshot patterns, fingerprint evidence, etc.) and analysis of other evidence. This process leads to the formulation of an educated guess as to the probable course of events.
4	*Testing or experimentation*	Once a hypothesis is formulated, additional experimentation or testing must be done to confirm or disprove the overall interpretation or specific aspects of the reconstruction hypothesis. This stage includes comparisons of samples collected at the scene with known standards and alibi samples, chemical, and microscopic testing usually done by the crime laboratory. Controlled testing or experimentation of possible physical activity must be done to collaborate the reconstruction hypothesis.
5	*Reconstruction findings*	Information may be acquired during the investigation about the condition of the victim or suspect, the activities of the individuals involved, accuracy of witness accounts, and other information about the circumstances surrounding the event. All the verifiable investigative information, physical evidence analysis and interpretation, and experimental results must be considered in testing and attempting to verify the hypothesis. Once the testing has been verified, when it has been thoroughly tested and verified, it can be considered a reconstruction finding.

CHALLENGES AND BARRIERS

As the reconstructionist works toward a finding of what happened at the crime scene, there may be some challenges and/or barriers encountered. The first of these barriers may occur when identifying the reconstruction type. What may start as a complete scene reconstruction may only lead to a limited reconstruction because forensic testing of evidence is incomplete or has provided no information about the possible source of the evidence or actions that created the evidence in the first place. The different types of crime scene reconstructions are shown here:

Specific type of incident reconstruction:

1. Accident reconstruction: traffic accidents, other transportation accidents, and industrial accidents.
2. Specific crime reconstruction: homicides, arsons, sexual assaults, white-collar crimes, etc.
3. Specific events reconstructions: sequences, directional, position, relational, conditional, and identify.
4. Degree of involvement reconstruction: total case, partial case, limited event, and specific pattern reconstruction.
5. Specific type of physical evidence reconstruction: impression evidence, firearm or shooting investigation, glass facture patterns, and bloodstain pattern evidence.
6. Special areas or determinations in reconstruction: criminal profiling—including modus operandi (MO), motive, and psychological determinations, or organized or disorganized crime scene determination and scene profiling—primary scene or secondary scene determination, etc.

CRIME SCENE RECONSTRUCTIONS BY TYPE OF EVIDENCE

For the purposes of this text, crime scene reconstruction will be based on the specific type of physical evidence found at the crime scene. This reconstruction process will follow the "information gathering process" as shown above. The conclusion will be the reconstruction theory—what happened at the crime scene! The reconstruction theory incorporates all the previously discussed processes of scientific crime scene investigation to find the physical evidence along with the investigator's knowledge of the value and use of forensic testing methods. The physical evidence resulting from the crime and found at the crime scene to be discussed with regard to reconstruction will be a variety of **patterned evidence and shooting investigation evidence**.

PATTERNED EVIDENCE IN RECONSTRUCTIONS

Pattern evidence is created by the contact of two surfaces (persons, vehicles, or objects). It results in the formation of impression evidence: imprints, indentations, or striation markings. These impressions may be from stationary contact or moving contact. They may be two-dimensional or three-dimensional. The contact may be a transfer of material from one surface to another resulting in pattern evidence in the form of a stain or deposit—imprints. Indentation impressions are the result of a hard surface contacting a softer surface. The following is a list of commonly found patterned evidence at different crime scenes well suited for reconstruction purposes:

1. Bloodstain patterns
2. Glass fracture patterns
3. Injury or wound patterns
4. Fire burn patterns
5. Footwear track/trail and tire/skid mark patterns
6. Clothing article damage or position patterns
7. Modus operandi and crime scene profile patterns

From the above list, this chapter will examine 1 through 6 only. The seventh type of patterned evidence is better suited for forensic psychologists or well-experienced law enforcement officers.

Bloodstain Patterns

Bloodstain pattern analysis is the use of the bloodstain size, shape, and distribution patterns found at a crime scene in order to determine the bloodshed event(s). Bloodstain patterns reveal not "who" but "what and how" with regard to the bloodshed event. The bloodstain patterns at a crime can be used for the following reconstruction purposes:

- Type of bloodstain patterns present.
- Direction of travel of the blood drops.
- Distance of the blood source to the target surface.
- Determination of directionality: direction of travel (from where a blood drop originated) and angle of impact of blood drop.
- Determination of blood trails, their direction, and the relative speed of their horizontal motion.
- Nature of the force and the object used to cause bloodshed, the number of blows involved, and relative location of persons/objects near bloodshed.
- Interpretation of contact or transfer patterns.

Basic Bloodstain Patterns

Blood is a mixture of cellular material, proteins, and ions suspended in a liquid or serum. It is a fluid that does not break up in flight unless given extra outside force and it deposits as a single stain. Bloodstain patterns found at crime scenes will fall into three broad categories: passive drop bloodstain patterns, spatter patterns, and special bloodstain configuration patterns. See Fig. 8.1 for examples of each pattern. Bloodstain pattern analysis is complex; therefore additional reading, careful

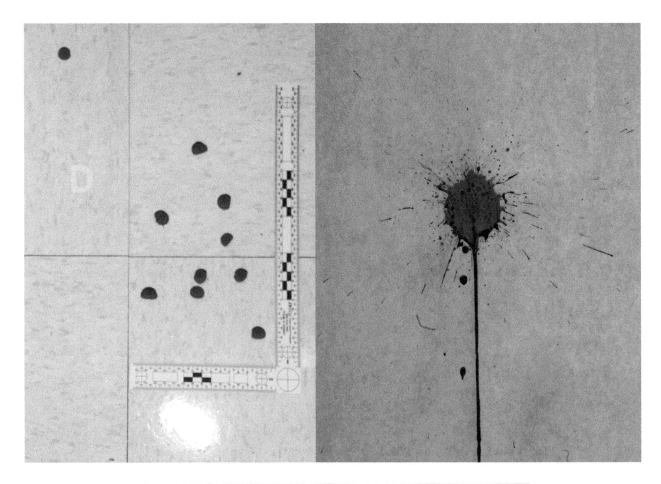

FIGURE 8.1 Passive drop patterns, spatter patterns, and special patterns.

study, controlled experiments, and significant practice must be undertaken for proper bloodstain pattern analysis. Each category of pattern will be briefly examined to get basic information about that bloodstain pattern and how it is used for reconstruction purposes.

Passive Bloodstain Patterns

The fluid dynamics of dropping blood are responsible for the stains or patterns produced. The surface tension of the liquid blood causes the blood drops produced from a blood source to be spherically shaped. Blood drops are much more viscous than water and it possesses an adhesive quality that provides for small amounts of blood to adhere to most surfaces and begin drying upon contact.

Many factors will influence the size and shape of a bloodstain once the drop reaches a target surface. A falling drop of blood when it impacts a surface directly below will generally produce circular-shaped patterns. The diameter of a bloodstain will increase as the distance that the blood drop falls increases until the acceleration of the drop remains constant and terminal velocity is reached. At terminal velocity the resulting stain size remains constant. For reconstruction purposes that means that by examining the diameters of the bloodstain it is possible to determine if a bleeding source was standing or near the ground or vise versa (Fig. 8.2).

The texture of the target surface upon which a drop of blood falls affects the size and shape of the bloodstain pattern. Hard, nonporous surfaces will produce circular stain patterns that have smooth edges, but softer, porous surfaces will produce spatter stains that are scalloped or have rough edges. See Fig. 8.3.

The resulting shape of a bloodstain is changed when the angle at which a blood drop impacts a surface is changed. As the angle of impact is made smaller or more acute, the bloodstain pattern will become more elongated, elliptical, or oval in shape. The resulting bloodstain's shape will indicate the direction of travel for that stain and thus, the origin of the drop of blood. The "tail" or wave castoff of the bloodstain generally points to the direction of travel of the blood drop. The direction of travel and the angle of impact are referred to as the *directionality* of a bloodstain pattern. The directionality of a bloodstain will be used for reconstructing where the bloodshed occurred. The *angle of impact* of the drop of blood can be determined from measurements of the length (the extra tail of the bloodstain represents additional force or a bounce effect and is not part of the original drop of blood, so it should not be measured) and the width of bloodstain. The trigonometric relationship between the ratio of the long axis (length) versus the short axis (width) of a bloodstain can be measured. See Fig. 8.4.

Trails of blood are frequently found at crime scenes. Careful examination and analysis of the trail pattern will provide information about direction of travel and the relative traveling speed of the bleeding source—the reconstruction. As the speed of the bleeding source in a horizontal motion is increased, the more elongated shape of the individual stains will result and the distance between bloodstains will be increased in the blood trail. See Fig. 8.5.

Contact bloodstain patterns occur when blood on the surface of an object or body is transferred onto a new location or surface. The contact pattern retains the shape of the original bloody object due to a stationary transfer, a type of mirror image. Therefore, the original bloody object can be identified and a reconstruction of activity at the crime scene accomplished. See Fig. 8.6.

Contact patterns can be formed due to folded bloody surfaces. Two similar bloody imprints may result from the same object, or one image from the other bloody image, hence a "butterfly" or mirror image of the original stain is created. Contact patterns can often be created through dynamic motions. When an unstained object moves through a bloody surface or an existing bloodstain the resulting pattern is called a *wipe pattern*. Examination of the wipe can often show motion of the original unstained object. A swipe pattern is also produced when a moving bloody object contacts an unstained surface. See Fig. 8.7.

Spatter Bloodstain Patterns

The second basic category of bloodstains is "spatter." Spatter bloodstain patterns are blood patterns produced as a result of having received additional force or motion than gravity. It has more force than passive drops/drips.

Impacted bloodstain patterns have received more energy (force) than gravity and are called impacted bloodstains. The force added to the blood causes the blood to break into smaller sized spheres of blood or spatters. The smaller sized blood spatters are relative to the amount of force or energy involved. The greater the added force then smaller the size of the resulting spatter. Though the spatter may be smaller than passive drops, the blood drops' directionality property remains unchanged. See Fig. 8.8.

FIGURE 8.2   Passive drops of blood with changing diameters.

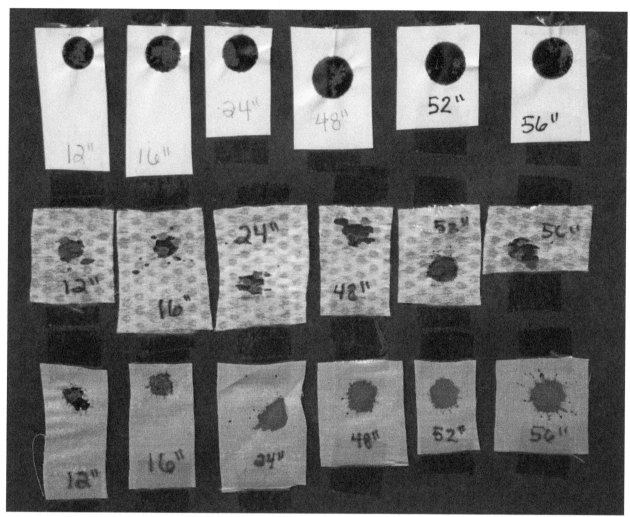

FIGURE 8.3   Effects of surface texture.

This spatter behavior will be used to determine the origin of the impact or where bloodshed occurred. Generally, impacted blood spatter falls into two types: (1) medium-force and (2) high-force impact spatter. See Fig. 8.8. Medium-force impact spatter is produced by a force associated with beatings and blunt or sharp force trauma. The size of this spatter is much smaller than passive drops. High-force impact spatter is almost always associated with the use of firearms (explosions or high-speed collisions can produce similar patterns). The spatter has a mistlike appearance. It is difficult to see, easily overlooked, and can be altered or lost without careful handling of the physical evidence. See Fig. 8.9.

When bloodshed occurs it is not uncommon for that bleeding source to continue to bleed out. This bleeding will cause blood to drip into an increasing pool of blood that will cause secondary spatters to be produced. These secondary spatters basically bounce and make for smaller stains around the pool of blood. If sufficient blood drips and time passes, a blood pool is created that obliterates the smaller spatter. The repetitive dripping pattern into a pool shows no motion but with motion can create a cluster pattern of passive drops. See Fig. 8.10.

When there is a sudden release of an increased quantity of blood from a severed artery the resulting stain is called a *projected bloodstain pattern.* This bloodstain pattern is commonly associated with major injuries with open wounds usually to an artery. This pattern has sharp, spinous edges and can easily show movement. For this reason, these patterns

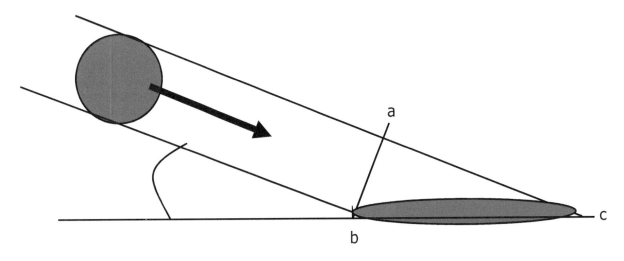

arcsin *i* = distance ab/distance bc

FIGURE 8.4   Directionality of a bloodstain.

FIGURE 8.5   Blood trail showing speed and direction.

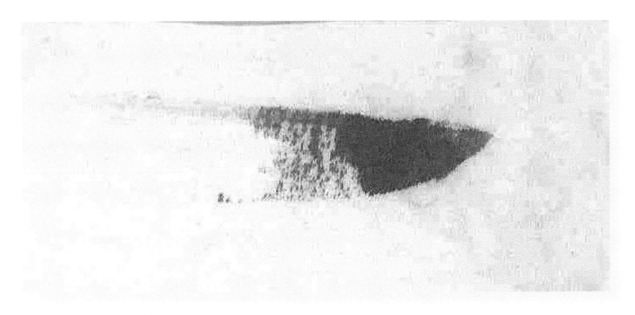

FIGURE 8.6   Contact bloodstain pattern of knife blade.

FIGURE 8.7   Wipe pattern showing movement.

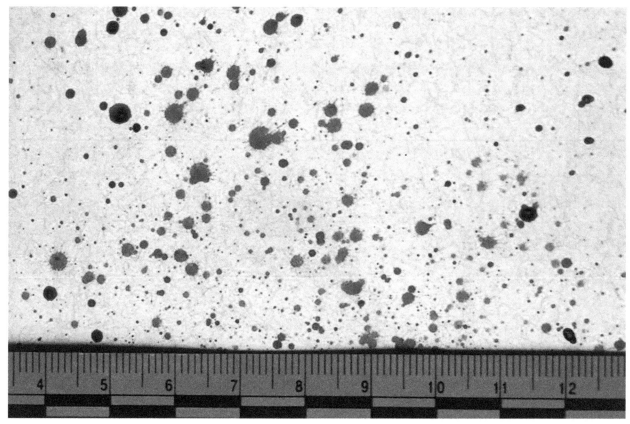

FIGURE 8.8   Impact bloodstain spatter smaller than passive bloodstains showing added force.

FIGURE 8.9   High-force impact spatter from gunshot wound.

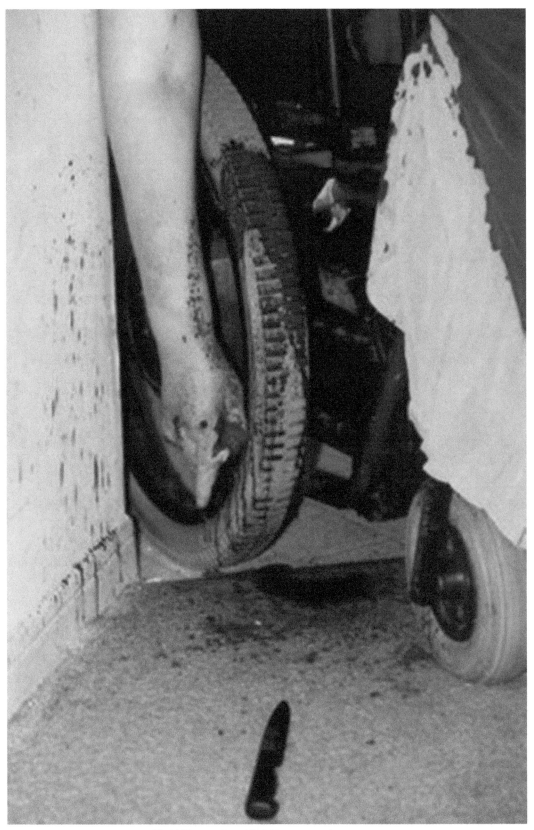

FIGURE 8.10 Repetitive drips on to various targets.

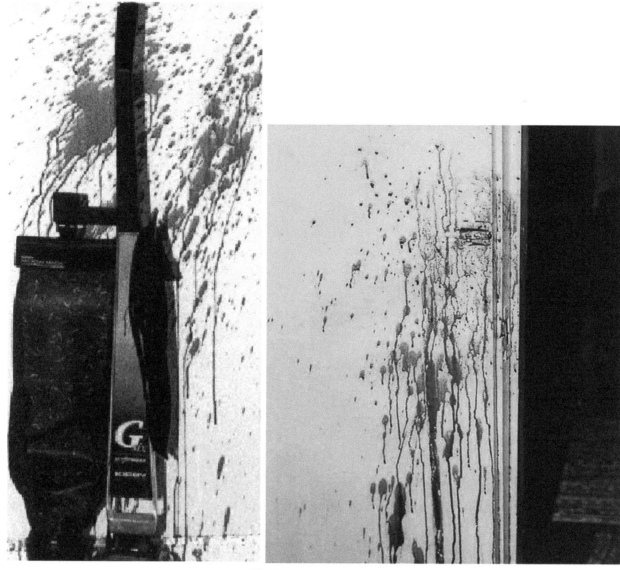

FIGURE 8.11 Arterial gushes.

are useful for reconstruction purposes. If larger quantity of blood is deposited on a vertical surface, the blood will flow downward as it is acted upon by gravity and produce a *flow pattern* of the blood. Arterial gushes deposited on horizontal surfaces show the projection and the increased volume of blood into pools. See Fig. 8.11 for arterial gushes.

When a bloodshed event occurs as when blood impacted, the blood will be broken into smaller sized blood spatter with directionality. Impacted spatter travels out in all directions. Therefore, at a crime scene when impacted bloodstains are found and after documentation, those bloodstains can be used to determine where the impact occurred using directionality of the individual stains in the overall pattern as part of reconstruction activities.

A two-step process determines the area of origin of bloodshed from an impact mechanism. First, representative samples of individual blood spatter in the impact pattern are selected. Their **direction of travel** is marked by placing a line through the center of each stain and drawn back to the direction of their origin. The lines will converge in an area called the "point of convergence." See Fig. 8.12. The second step will use the impact angle of each individual spatter and add a third dimension to the reconstruction. The impact angle of each line is calculated. By using a protractor to "lift" the lines to the correct angles, the lines form the "area of origin" of the impacted bloodshed event. See Fig. 8.13.

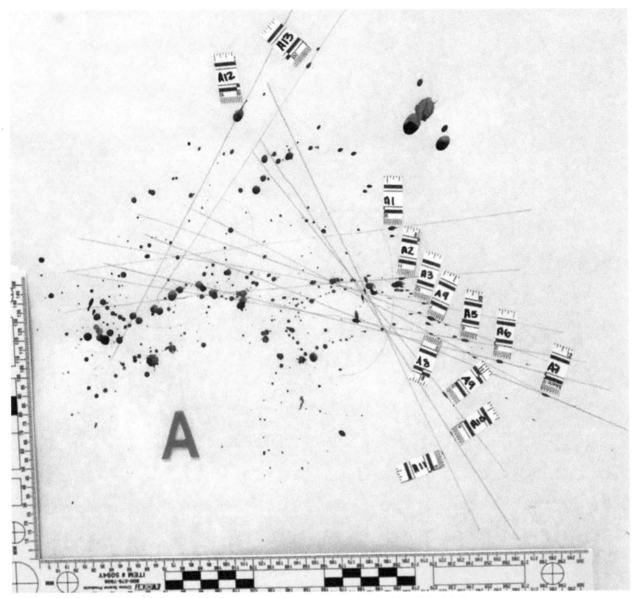

FIGURE 8.12   Area of convergence and area of origin of bloodshed.

It is a good practice to use more individual spatters than fewer spatters. The area of origin of bloodshed or area of impact determinations will allow the reconstruction of the nature of the force used, the sequence of events, and the relative position of persons or objects near the impacted source.

Glass Fracture Patterns

Broken glass at crime scenes can sometimes aid in reconstruction and providing information about the events that took place involving the breaking of glass—like broken or shot out windows. Glass fracture patterns can be present at a wide variety of crime scenes ranging from minor to capital cases. The reconstruction information that can be obtained by studying glass fracture patterns are (1) the determination of the direction of impact force that broke the glass (for example, was the window broken from the inside to outside or outside to inside) and (2) the determination of the sequence of firing, direction of firing, and the type of firearm for the projectile holes present. The use of glass fracture patterns in crime scene reconstruction relies on careful recognition, documentation, and examination of radial, stress, and concentric glass fracture markings found on the glass' surface.

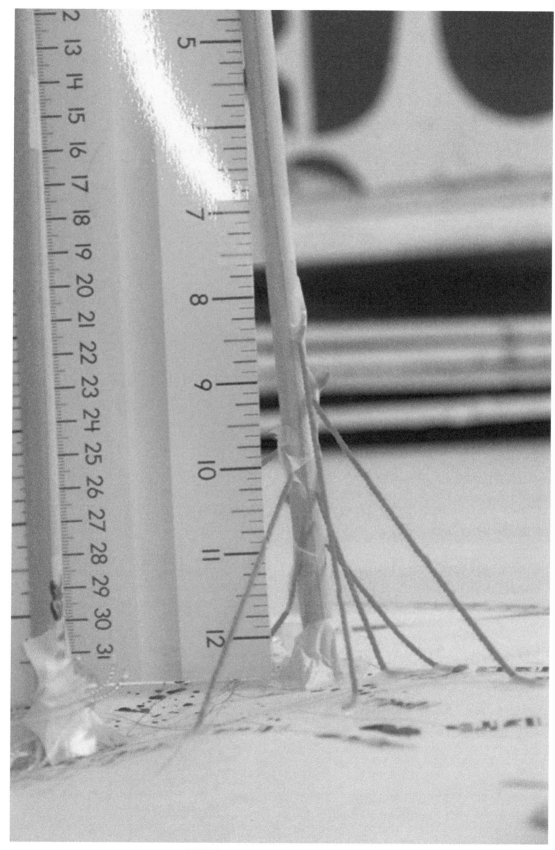

FIGURE 8.13 Area of origin of bloodshed.

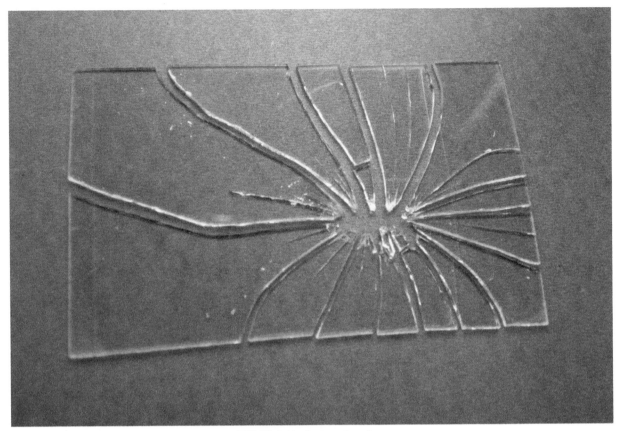

FIGURE 8.14   Broken plate glass.

To conduct even a basic reconstruction based on glass fracture evidence, investigators should be familiar with the different categories of glass. There are three general classes of glass: plate (window glass), tempered, and safety. Each type of class has certain characteristics, will fracture differently, and may change a reconstruction theory.

Plate glass is a common variety of glass used to make windows and mirrors. When plate glass is exposed to a force significant enough to break the surface tension and thus, the glass, characteristic pie-shaped glass shards are formed. If broken glass remains in the frame the observed fracture pattern will consist of a center point, where the force contacted the windowpane, with radiating (radial) fracture lines going out from the center point. See Fig. 8.14.

Fig. 8.15 shows the inside edge of a piece of a radial glass fracture. By examining a broken edge of a piece of glass along a radial line, you can determine the direction of force. This analysis is helpful in determining from which side of the glass the force was applied causing the window to be broken.

When the force is applied to the surface of a piece of glass, the glass begins to bend. As sufficient force is applied the surface of the plate glass opposite of the force breaks first. The result is the formation of the radial cracks. By looking at the inside edge of the radial crack, curved markings are shown. They start on one side and then curve to the opposite side. The curve that is closed to 90 degrees was the side of the glass that broke first and the force was applied to the opposite surface. See Fig. 8.16. That result means that by observing the marking on the radial cracks a reconstruction of the glass breaking can be done. The curved marks will reflect the side to which the force was applied.

Safety glass is found in automobile windshields. Safety glass is two separate panes of plate glass adhered together with a clear laminated layer between them. While this glass fractures in a similar way to plate glass, it remains intact after breaking due to the laminate layer. Safety glass was designed to reduce injuries to passengers should they have an accident. Caution must be exercised when interpreting safety glass fracture patterns in that there are two separate panes of glass, which will have independent radial fractures.

Since safety glass remains intact it can provide valuable information in reconstruction shooting incidents. The direction of each gunshot can be determined by locating the crater, which is located on the side of glass opposite the impacting force. Also, if more than one bullet penetrates the windshield it is possible to sequence the shots if the bullet holes are close

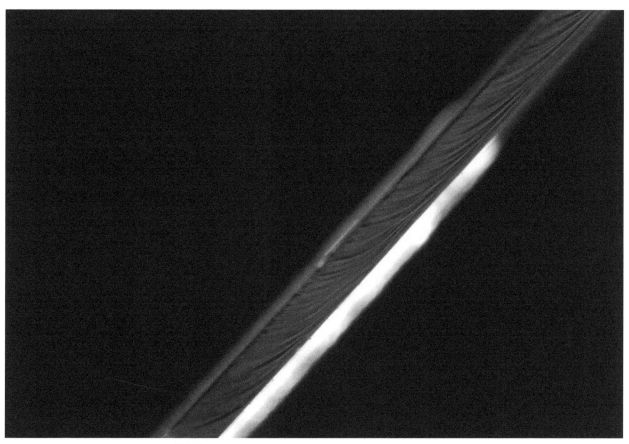

FIGURE 8.15   Inside edge of a radial crack of broken plate glass.

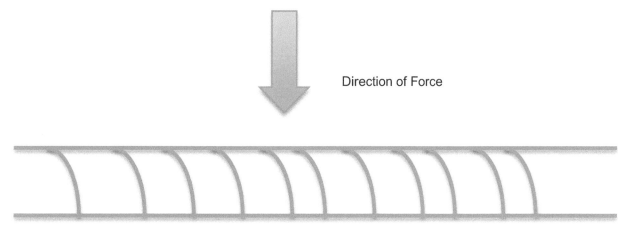

Direction of Force

This side broke first--marks at 90 degrees

FIGURE 8.16   Radial crack marks to determine direction of force.

enough together that their separate radial fracture lines converge. The subsequent bullet hole can be determined because radial lines from that bullet hole terminate where they meet the existing radial line from the prior fracture. See Fig. 8.17.

Wound Dynamics

Wounds, wound dynamics, and wound causes are the responsibility of the forensic pathologist or medical examiner as part of a criminal investigation. The crime scene reconstructionist must work with the medical examiner to use the type of

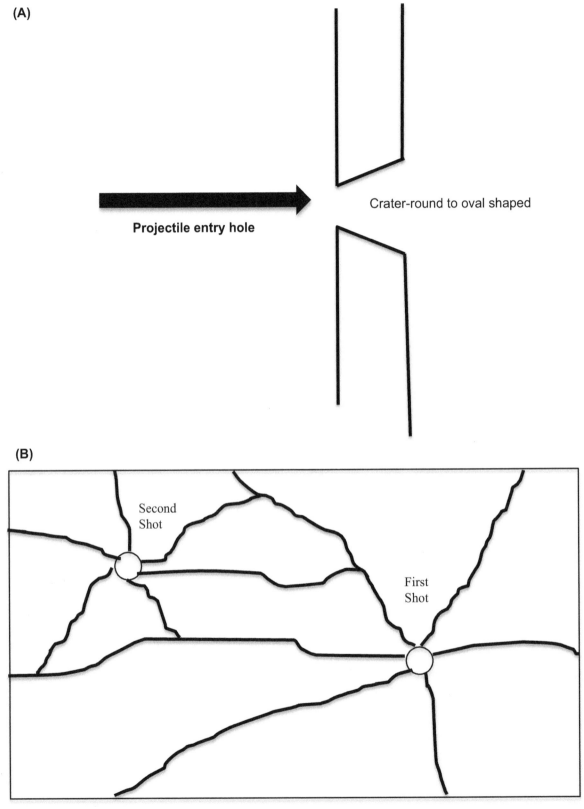

FIGURE 8.17 Glass fracturing by projectiles. (A) Crater shape and location and (B) sequence of firing.

wound to help determine the causes the wounds found on the body. Many wounds are distinctive. For this reason wounds often may indicate a specific mechanism and type of instrument or weapon used. It is possible for wounds to exhibit more than one character but with experience the reconstructionist can identify wound types and possible mechanisms of cause. The broad categories of wound types are firearm, sharp force, blunt force, asphyxia, burns/chemical, poisoning, explosion, and electrical. See Fig. 8.18 for some examples of these wounds.

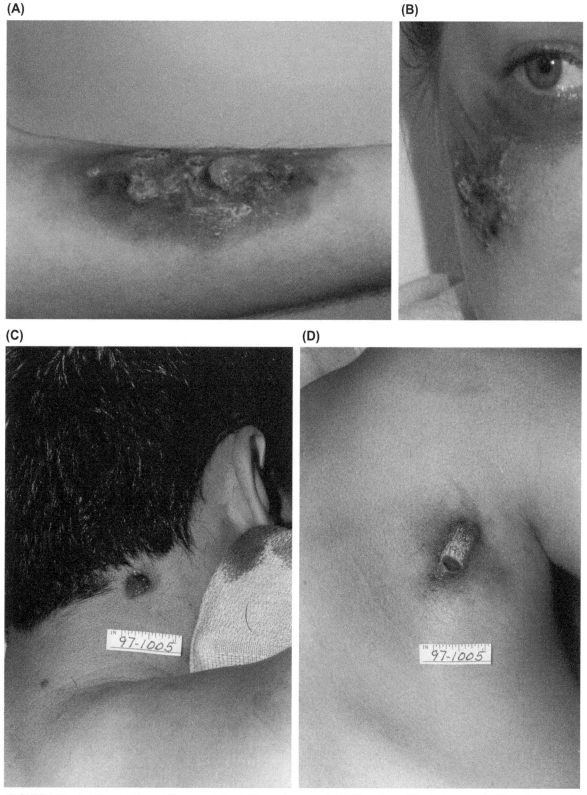

(A)

(B)

(C)

(D)

FIGURE 8.18 (A) Chemical burn; (B) scrape; (C) and (D) gunshot wounds; (E) blunt force; (F) stabbing wounds; (G) incised wound.

(E)

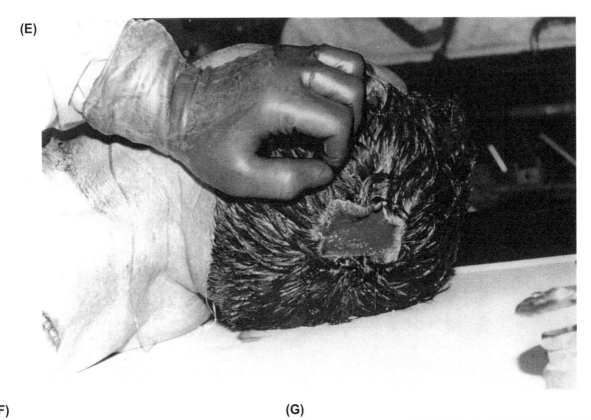

(F)   **(G)**

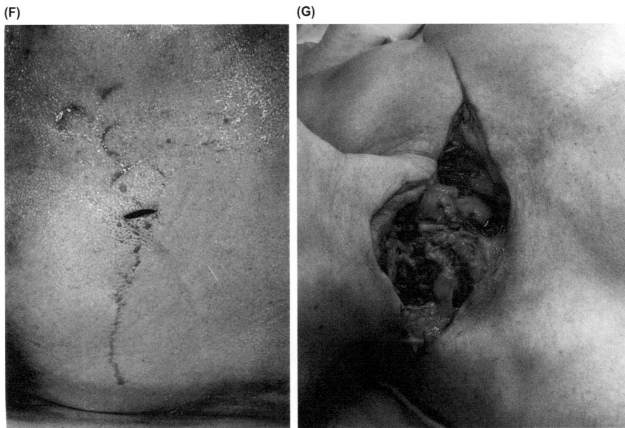

FIGURE 8.18 cont'd

Fire Burn Patterns

Fire burn patterns often provide information on the various factors that led to or caused a fire. Depending on the jurisdiction, most suspected arson or suspicious fires are investigated by the fire marshal. Reconstruction of a fire can be especially useful in categorizing a fire as an arson. Identification of the burn patterns generally helps in determining the point of fire origin (a site with possible ignitable fluids), the direction of fire travel, and the degree of damage of a fire, which may contain clues for arson investigations. The following is a partial list of common patterns found at fire scenes:

- Inverted cone or "V" pattern
- Multiple points of origin burn patterns
- Low-burn pattern configurations
- Depth of charring patterns or alligator patterns
- Trailer patterns
- Smoke stain pattern
- Melted material patterns
- Concrete spalling patterns

Every fire forms a pattern that is determined by the configuration of the structure, the availability of combustible material (an accelerant), and the type and intensity of the fire. From a study of the fire patterns, and a determination of any deviations from normal or expected patterns, an experienced fire investigator can reconstruct a fire scene. See Fig. 8.19(A−C).

Footwear Trails and Tire Mark Patterns

Occasionally, track-trail patterns are encountered at crime scenes. Visualization and enhancement of tracks can yield information about how many persons were present at a scene, whether they were moving about, the nature of the movement (walking, running) and the direction of travel, and whether heavy objects were being carried or dragged. See Fig. 8.20. Track-trail patterns can provide information or data about the individuals present at the scene, such as shoe size, stride length, sex, weight, or any abnormalities in movement or gait.

Tire or skid mark patterns are often seen at out-door crime scenes and can provide important reconstruction information for the crime scene investigator. The value of skid mark patterns in traffic accident reconstructions is well known and documented. However, the use of these patterns in crime scene investigation and reconstruction is often neglected. These markings can yield information about the number and types of vehicles involved, the possible speed of travel, direction of travel, whether or not brakes were applied, and whether turns were made. Figs. 8.21 and 8.22 show some of the tire and footwear marks found at a crime scene.

Clothing Damage or Position Patterns

This type of pattern evidence can be both subtle and obvious, yet useful for reconstructions. It is important for the scene investigators to keep detailed observations, measurements, documentation, and correct interpretation of these patterns. Some examples of reconstructions that can be obtained from these patterns are whether a suspect ransacked a scene, proof or disproof of an alibi, direction and route taken by a suspect, physical contact between persons, persons and vehicles, or between vehicles, disturbances of expected patterns at the crime scene, and possible information about the sequence of events. Fig. 8.23A and B shows two different scenarios of how an item of clothing was damaged.

Shooting Scene Reconstruction

Reconstruction of shooting scenes is often necessary to determine several factors critical to the investigation. Determination of homicide, suicide, or accidental discharge may be impossible without a reconstruction. Shooting reconstruction provides information as to the relative location(s) of the shooter(s) and victim. A shooting reconstruction can determine the muzzle-to-target distance, oftentimes useful for distinguishing between homicide, accidental discharge, or suicide. Also, trajectory reconstructions can be performed to provide valuable information that can in many cases prove or disprove suspect, victim, or witness accounts of shooting scenarios. A reconstruction in shooting cases is highly dependent upon the quality of crime scene documentation, searching, and the collection and preservation of all relevant evidence. A lot of the physical evidence used in shooting scene reconstructions, like gunshot residue (GSR) or finding projectiles, are easily lost

(A)

(B)

FIGURE 8.19   (A) Burn pattern on exterior of house fire. (B) Burn pattern at front door. (C) Burn pattern at accelerant placement.

(C)

FIGURE 8.19 cont'd

or overlooked. For this reason good crime scene methodology, good searches, and successful visualization or enhancements need to be done to insure locating all relevant evidence (Fig. 8.24).

GSRs for Shooting Incident Investigations

GSR analysis can be of great value in helping determine who may have been involved in the shooting and approximate muzzle-to-target distances. However, GSR can be easily lost if not properly collected and protected. In most cases it is advisable to swab the hands of the victim and any potential shooter for the presence of GSR as soon as possible. GSR can be collected by swabbing with 5% nitric acid solution and/or collected on SEM collection disks. See Fig. 8.25 for collection of GSR. Collection should be done as soon as possible as GSR will dissipate over a relatively short period of time.

A gunshot victim's clothing should be preserved, as a GSR distribution pattern can assist in distance determinations. The clothing must be carefully removed, not folded, and allowed to dry. Clothing from both victim and potential shooters should be seized as it may contain GSR, blood spatter, glass fragments, other forms of trace or transfer evidence, or tears, damage, or soil patterns that may be useful for reconstruction purposes. The presence of trace evidence or damage to the clothing may be used to corroborate a statement regarding movement or events during and after the shooting incident. Documentation of possible GSR (and other evidence) on clothing is best accomplished at the crime scene before packaging.

Role of Markings on Projectiles

Projectiles found during autopsy show the trajectories into and out of the bodies. These projectiles and any others found at the crime scenes can be examined by forensic laboratories and provide valuable information that can be used in the reconstruction process. See Fig. 8.26A and B. Firearms examination by the forensic laboratory can provide information about the type of firearms used in the investigation, such as the caliber of the firearm, type of ammunition used, and rifling characteristics that may provide a list of possible manufacturers and models. Microscopic examination of the projectile may also provide information about the types of surfaces contacted by the projectile after firing.

FIGURE 8.20 Bloody footwear track-trail.

FIGURE 8.21   Tire marks on road into crime scene.

Postmuzzle Markings and Trace Evidence

Useful markings placed on a projectile after it leaves a barrel can be used for reconstruction. These markings used for reconstruction can be attributed to intermediate target impacts and the final impact surface or terminal trajectory marking. If the projectile passes through the intermediate target, then a pathway of direction will be made and used for reconstruction. Some additional useful types of trace evidence from intermediate targets for reconstruction are GSRs on hands and clothing and patterns of cylinder and muzzle flash. The size and shape of the terminal trajectory surface marking and the markings on the projectile are useful for the reconstruction. See Figs. 8.27 and 8.28.

Muzzle-to-Target Distance Determinations

Generally, distance determinations involve a comparison of GSR distribution patterns found on the item collected at the crime scene to laboratory-prepared GSR patterns acquired at various distances using the actual firearm and any collected ammunition from the crime scene. The actual comparison is it can be done by the medical examiner or by forensic laboratory personnel, but the crime scene investigator will often assist. The results of the distance study or range of fire will absolutely be used for the shooting reconstruction. Each step in the preparation, detection, and comparison of the GSR should be carefully documented (Fig. 8.29).

Methods for Trajectory Determinations

Although two points can be used to establish a projectile trajectory, this is insufficient if deflections have possibly taken place. It is for this reason that the least amount of points is three or more for relatively accurate trajectory reconstructions. In addition, an assessment of the likelihood and possible degree of deflection is necessary for a reconstruction that is

FIGURE 8.22 Footwear marks going into front door of crime scene.

scientific in nature. Well-designed controlled experimentation may be indicated. The experimentation should include a range of deflection scenarios and test firings of the weapon, if available, to determine its variability.

The crime scene investigator can use two geometric methods for trajectory determinations. One method of trajectory reconstruction is based on physical methods (probes, rods, and strings) and the other method is based on optical projection methods (visual sightings and the use of low-power lasers). Whichever method is chosen, careful documentation of the entire reconstruction process should be accomplished.

Physical Projection Methods

1. *Entry hole geometry*: The shape of projectile entry and exit holes in target surfaces can be measured and an estimated angle of entry can be calculated. Most projectile holes are elliptical shaped and by the use of trigonometry (cosine of the ratio of the width to the length of the hole) the angle of impact can be determined.
2. *Probes and rods*: Probes are useful for establishing projectile trajectories if the projectile holes are close together and there is no access to the blind side of one of the projectile holes. Be careful to avoid altering or damaging projectile holes when inserting the probe. Wooden rods, solid metal rods, or hollow metal tubes are useful for this reconstruction method. Use a rod in width close to the approximate diameter of the hole; however, do not use a rod so thick that you have to force the rod into the hole. See Figs. 8.30–8.34.

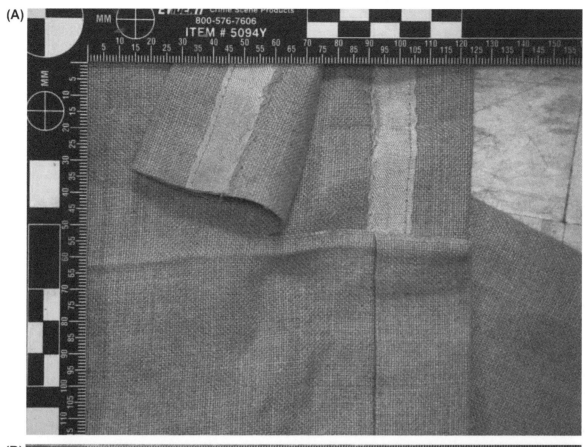

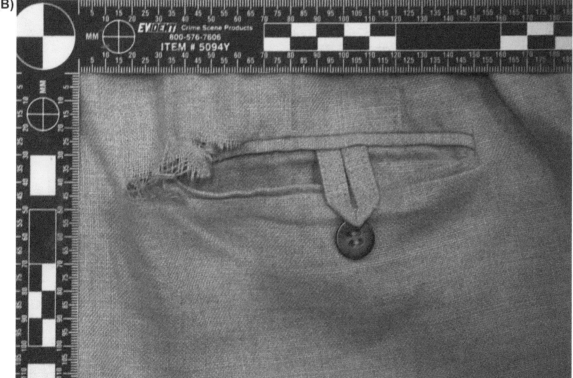

FIGURE 8.23 (A) Clothing cut; (B) clothing torn.

FIGURE 8.24 Firearm discharge producing gunshot residue, projectiles, and casings to be used for reconstruction purposes.

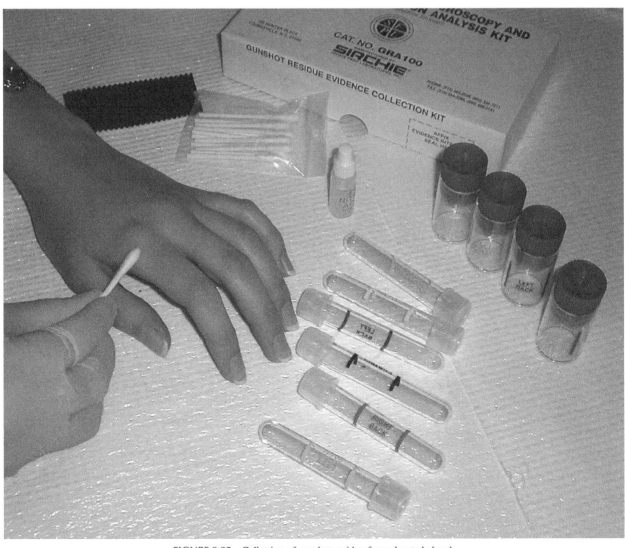

FIGURE 8.25 Collection of gunshot residue from shooter's hand.

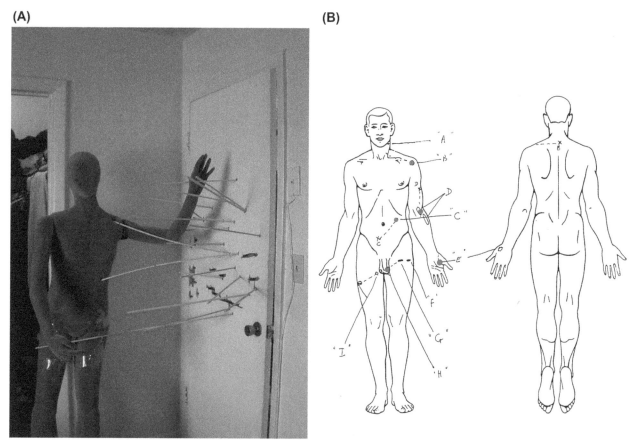

FIGURE 8.26 (A) and (B) Projectiles and trajectories from autopsy.

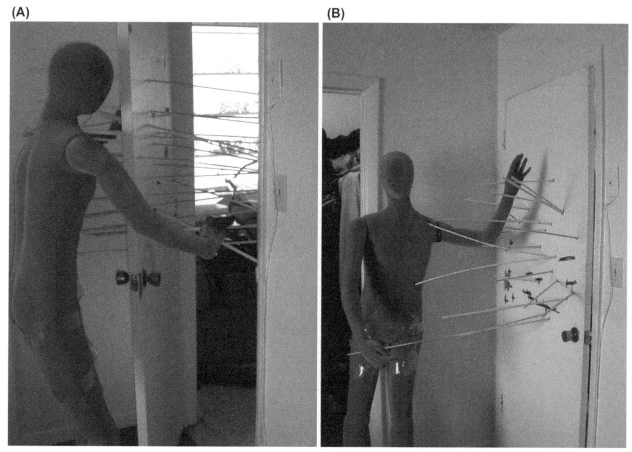

FIGURE 8.27 (A) and (B) Which actually happened? Use the autopsy information, trajectories, and trace evidence on the bullets.

FIGURE 8.28 Bullet impact mark indicates the bullet trajectory.

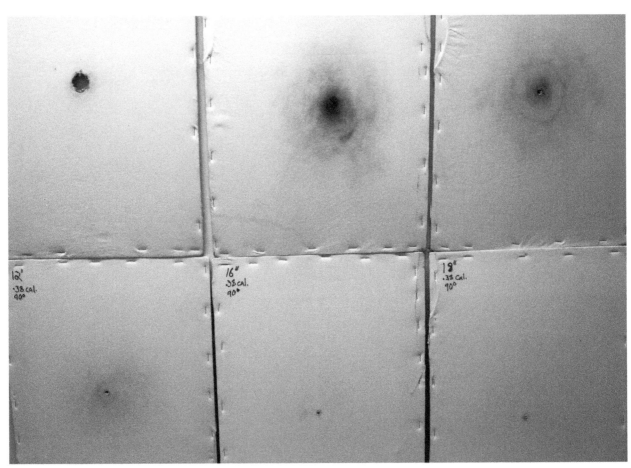

FIGURE 8.29 Distance study for range of fire determinations.

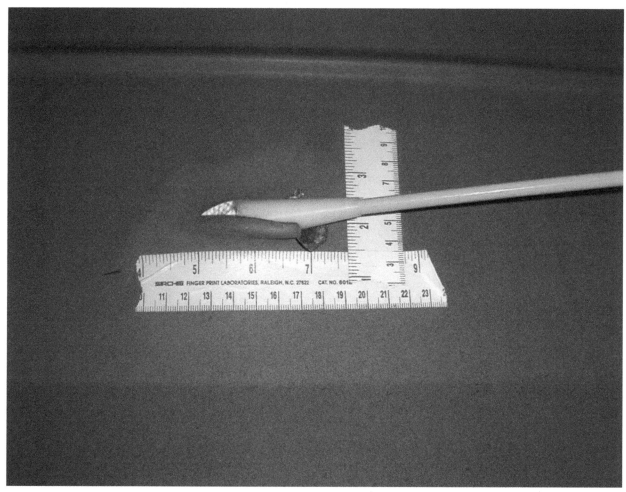

FIGURE 8.30   Trajectory rod for a through and through shot.

Optical Projection Methods

1. *Optical sighting*: An easy method for sighting a trajectory is to simply look. The alignment achieved is only preliminary and lacks precise direction. Photographing the trajectory reconstruction alignment through one projectile hole to the other hole should be attempted.
2. *Low-power lasers*: The laser is useful for aligning projectile holes over simple optical sighting because it is capable of defining a straight line over a longer distance. Very long distance laser trajectories determination must be carefully applied. Bullet trajectories can curve while the laser will not. This difference may affect the reconstruction. See Fig. 8.35 for use of red and green lasers for trajectories.
3. *Documentation of laser beam*: Documentation (video and photographic) should be continuous, but at least done when the laser beam is aligned with two or more projectile holes. Visualization of the laser beam path is enhanced by the addition of smoke or dust or some fogging material. See Fig. 8.36 for photographing laser trajectories.
4. *Positioning stages*: Commercially manufactured positioning platforms for lasers are available to facilitate the positioning of the laser. The laser head is mounted on a multiaxis stage with appropriate scales for calculations and documentation purposes.
5. *Angle information from the aligned laser beam*: Protractors and tape measures can be used to establish the orientation and document the location of the projectile holes in relation to fixed points at the crime scene. Plumb bobs, inclinometers, and levels are useful for further insuring correct measurements of angles. After a projectile trajectory has been obtained and documented, a second determination of trajectory should be done. See Fig. 8.37 for use of inclinometer.
6. *Placement of intermediate targets in the laser beam*: Using a laser beam allows for easy interposing of objects or people in the laser so as to check reconstruction scenarios. In the case of soft intermediate targets (mattresses, pillows, cushions, etc.), hollow probes or fiber probes can have fiber optic properties for ease of documentation.
7. There are many commercially available products for trajectory reconstructions in daylight or low-light conditions.

FIGURE 8.31   The impact site after Figure 8.30.

Shell Casing Ejection Patterns

Shell casings located at a crime scene can provide valuable information. The forensic laboratory can use the casings for subsequent comparisons to suspect guns for the purpose of determining if they fired the particular cartridges. If no weapon is found, the cartridge case can be entered into a firearms database, such as Drugfire, Integrated Ballistics Identification System (IBIS), or National Integrated Ballistic Information Network (NIBIN), and compared to a database of cartridge cases.

The location of the shell casings may be useful in determining the approximate location of the shooter in reference to the ejected shell casing. A majority of semiautomatic or automatic firearms eject to the right, but before forming a reconstruction theory about the location of a shooter, it is best for experimentation to be conducted with the actual weapon used, or a similar make and model, to determine the ejection pattern of that particular gun. When test firing a weapon to determine the ejection pattern, several factors must be considered as they can influence the ejection pattern. These factors include type of ammunition, shooter's hand-hold and body position, whether the shooter was stationary or in motion during the ejection, the ground surface that the ejected casings land on, and environmental factors such as rain and wind. See Fig. 8.38 illustrating that the way in which a firearm is held could affect the ejection pattern.

In addition to considering these factors, caution must be exercised in reaching conclusions regarding shell casing ejection patterns in that the observed location of one or more of the casings may not be the true ejection location—the casing may have been stepped on, kicked, or moved by anyone on the crime scene after being ejected. See Fig. 8.39 for a huge crime scene with many casings that could be easily moved.

For documentation purposes it is better to "grid-off" a scene to preserve the location of spent casings as soon as possible. See Fig. 8.40.

FIGURE 8.32   Longer trajectory rod for reconstruction.

WRITING A RECONSTRUCTION REPORT

Reenactment Versus Reconstruction

Crime scene reconstruction is different from "reenactment," "recreation," or "criminal profiling." Reenactment in general refers to having the victim, suspect, witness, or other individual reenact the event that produced the crime scene or the physical evidence based on their "eyewitness" knowledge of the crime. Recreation is to return to the crime scene where the evidence will be replaced by the use of the original crime scene documentation. Criminal profiling is a process based upon the psychological and statistical analysis of the crime scene. It is used to determine the general personal characteristics of the most likely suspect for the crime. Each of these types of analysis may be helpful for certain aspects of a criminal investigation. However, these types of analysis are rarely useful in the solution of a crime. Crime scene reconstruction is based on the ability to make observations at the scene, the scientific ability to examine physical evidence, and the use of logical approaches to theory formulations.

Report of Findings

Crime scene reconstruction is based on scientific experimentation and on past personal and professional experiences. Crime scene reconstruction is a process that uses "the present" at the crime scene with its evidence, to reach conclusions about "the past," how the crime scene came to be when found by the first responders and started the whole process.

Theoretically, crime scene reconstruction is the use of the crime scene as investigated with its physical evidence, the results of the laboratory testing of the physical evidence, life's experiences, and reasoning (common sense). Practically,

FIGURE 8.33 Be careful of sag with longer trajectories.

crime scene reconstruction is using crime scene reports, crime scene photographs, crime scene sketches, autopsy reports (injury reports), all forensic laboratory reports, and sworn statements of victims, suspects, or eyewitnesses. Putting all the relied-upon information is a report format as follows:

- Purpose, scope, or intent of report—good to restate how crime scene reconstruction defined or used
- List of material reviewed, scenes visited or observed, and any physical evidence examined or viewed
  - Charts and tables work well
  - Insert and refer to photographs
- Conclusions reached
  - Group areas or locations together
  - Insert and refer to photographs

Other general guidelines are to have report and case materials peer reviewed to prevent any Daubert issues. Do not overcommit or too narrowly limit your conclusions and observations with careful wording (consistent with, similar to, inconsistent with available data or facts, inconclusive, cannot be determined with the available information, etc.). As with any scientific methodology keep an open, objective mind.

Finally, the process of information gathering and its use in crime scene reconstruction show the scientific nature of crime scene reconstruction and will allow for its successful use by investigators.

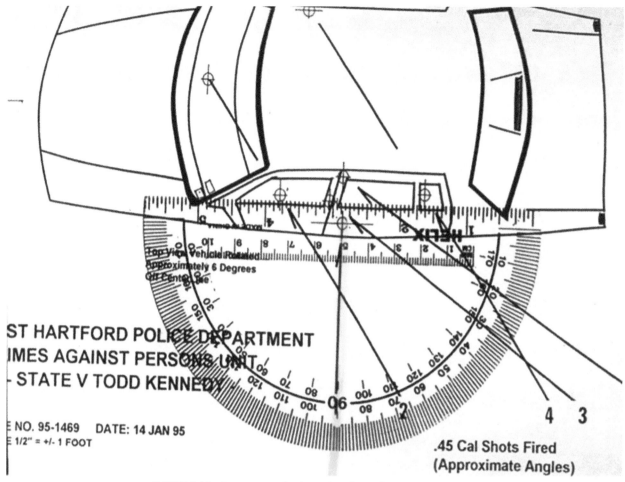

FIGURE 8.34 Protractor overlay for angles of entry for multiple trajectories.

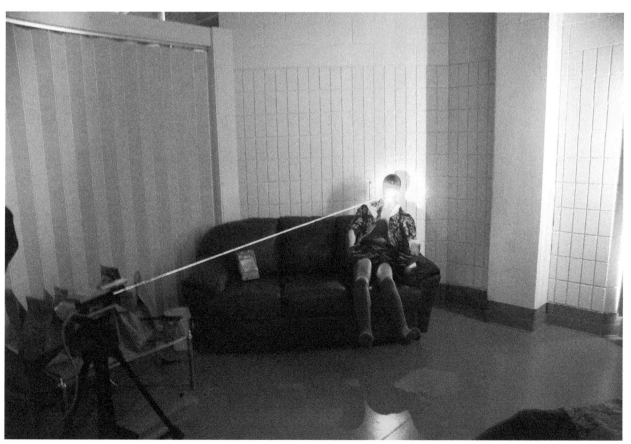

FIGURE 8.35 Red and green laser trajectory determinations.

FIGURE 8.36   Use of fogging agent for photographing laser trajectory.

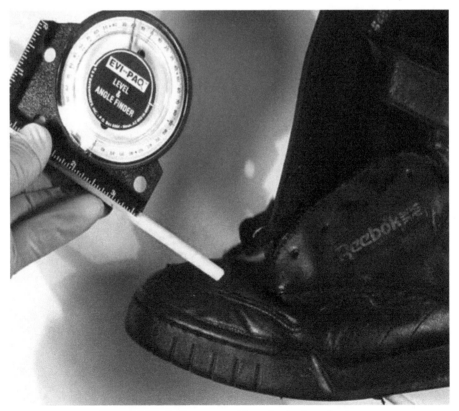

FIGURE 8.37   Inclinometer used for trajectory determination.

FIGURE 8.38 A right ejection pattern could change by rotating to the left.

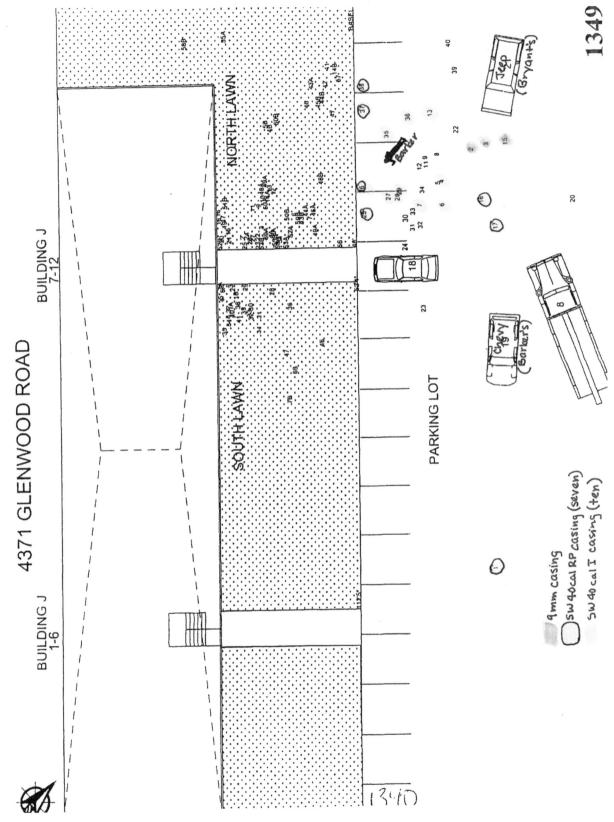

FIGURE 8.39 Many spent casings found at the crimes that could be easily moved, lost, or altered.

FIGURE 8.40 Spent casings in designated grid pattern.

DISCUSSION QUESTIONS

1. Define crime scene reconstruction and why is it important in the criminal justice system?
2. What are the four components necessary for a crime scene reconstruction? Explain each one.
3. Given the broken windowpane shown below, what is the order of fire or the reconstruction of this window?

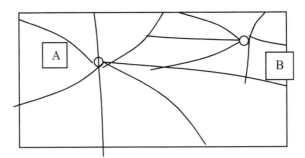

4. Using an arrow to indicate, what is the direction of force applied to the broken window below? You are looking at the markings on a radial crack side.

5. What is bloodstain pattern analysis? What are the three major categories of bloodstain patterns and give an example of each?
6. What is the area of convergence and the area of origin of bloodshed?
7. Fill in the missing labels from the diagram below that forms the geometric basis for the calculation of impact angle: Impact Angle = arcsin (width/length).

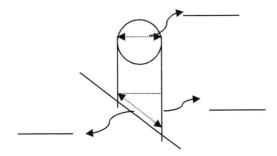

8. How is impact spatter distinguished from an arterial gush?
9. What are two reconstruction activities for which gunshot residue can be used?
10. Trace evidence and postmuzzle markings will assist in what kinds of reconstructions?
11. What sources of error may be encountered in shooting reconstructions?
12. What case and crime scene materials are essential for crime scene reconstructions after a scene has been released?

Sample Crime Scene Reconstruction Report

Address of Writer
Date of Report
Senior Assistant Attorney General
New Hampshire Department of Justice
33 Capitol Street
Concord, NH 03301-6397

RE: **Report of Findings**
 State of NH v. John Smith
 NHSP Case No. MC-0X-XXXX

Dear Sr Assistant Attorney General:

I have examined the following list of materials in this investigation from August 2009 to the present date:

- Digital Format Materials:
  - Crime scene photos by Officer on 6/13/2008
  - Photographs of Suspect on 7/3/2008
  - Crime scene video on 6/13/2008
  - Compact disc #14, of laboratory images of latent prints, footwear patterns, and toolmark examinations.
  - Compact discs #15 & #16 of bloodstain patterns at crime scene by Forensic Scientist on 6/14/2008.
  - Autopsy photographs by CMEO.
  - Compact disc #18 of photographs and negative scans.
  - Compact disc of photographs of the victim's pants.
- New Hampshire State Police Materials:
  - Five (5) finished sketches.
  - Overview Crime Scene Report of 6/13/2008.
  - Continuation Report of MEO at the crime scene 6/13/2008.
  - Continuation Report of evidence collection at the crime scene on 6/13/2008.
  - Continuation Report of evidence collection at morgue, 7/3/2008.
  - Continuation Report of collection of postmortem fingerprints.
  - Continuation Report of taking autopsy photographs on 6/14/2008.
  - Continuation Report of Witness A interview on 6/13/2008.
  - Continuation Report of Witness B interview on 6/16/2008, with assorted legal documentation.
  - Continuation Report of Sgt X of case timeline, written 6/27/2008.
  - Continuation Report of Sgt Y of the interview of suspect on 6/18/2008.
  - Transcript of the interview of Witness Z on 6/16/2008 by Sgt G.
  - Transcript of the interview of Witness W by Sgt Estabrook on 6/14/2008.
- Report of Laboratory Examination, assorted bench notes, and corresponding request for evidence examinations:
  - Latent prints, 6/19/2008
  - Serology, 6/24/2008
  - Footwear and footprint impressions, 6/25/2008
  - Bloody impressions, 7/11/2008
  - Serology, 8/12/2008

- Latent prints, 8/14/2008
- Serology, 8/19/2008 (two reports)
- Serology, 1/28/2009
- Footwear impressions, 3/6/2009
- Latents and footprint, 3/10/2009 and 4/16/2009
- Serology, 4/27/2009
- Bloodstain Pattern Analysis, 4/27/2009
- Toolmarks, 5/15/2009
- DNA Analysis, 6/29/2009.
- Other materials:
  - Cause of Death Report with Death Certificate of Victim, 6/14/2008.
  - Autopsy Report of Victim, CS#192-08, by Medical Examiner, MD on 6/14/2008.
  - Neuropathology Report of Victim by Neurologist, MD on 7/24/2008.
  - Toxicology Report of Victim by NMS Labs on 7/15/2008.
  - Danville Police Department Report, #08-1003-OF.

Crime Scene Reconstruction

I was asked to perform a crime scene reconstruction in the above matter. Scene reconstruction is the use of physical evidence found at a scene—its appearance, its condition, and its location—along with results of forensic testing, reasoning, and experience in order to determine the activities that occurred to create the physical evidence found at the crime scene. Crime scene reconstruction done properly is an applied science that can be conducted in a manner consistent with the scientific method. Patterned physical evidence is especially well suited for reconstruction, as it is physical evidence that is reproducible and predictable with regards to its creation. Bloodstain patterns, wound dynamics, and most impression evidence are common types of patterned evidence used in reconstruction activities.

All of the reviewed case materials are necessary to assist me in my reconstruction of the events that occurred at 164 King Road, Anyville, New Hampshire on June 11–13, 2008. Additionally, I have asked to personally examine the residence in Anyville at a time convenient to my schedule and prior to trial. I am preparing this report without that on-scene viewing based on all the materials listed above and should any substantive evidence or information be obtained at that future date I will render a supplemental reconstruction report.

The wound dynamics of the victim and the location of bloodstain pattern evidence show that the assault on the victim occurred initially in the area of the hallway between the kitchen and the dining room. The presence of a recently made indentation in the wall adjacent to the kitchen along with the castoff and impact bloodstain patterns supports this conclusion (see Sketch 8.1 and Photos 8.1 and 8.2).

The oval shape, size, and height above the floor of the indentation is consistent with a shoulder impacting the wall as opposed to a head or a knee in contact with the wall. Intact, impact blood spatter found within the indentation show that a bloodshed event occurred after the indentation was made in

Continued

Sample Crime Scene Reconstruction Report—cont'd

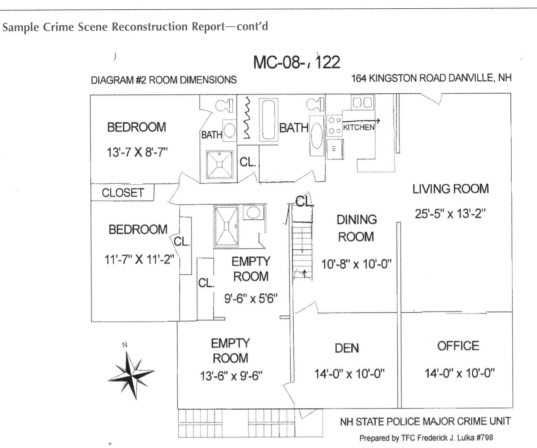

MC-08-, 122

DIAGRAM #2 ROOM DIMENSIONS

164 KINGSTON ROAD DANVILLE, NH

BEDROOM
13'-7 X 8'-7"

BATH

BATH

KITCHEN

CL.

CLOSET

CL.

BEDROOM
11'-7" X 11'-2"

CL.

CL.

EMPTY
ROOM
9'-6" x 5'6"

CL.

DINING
ROOM
10'-8" x 10'-0"

LIVING ROOM
25'-5" x 13'-2"

N

EMPTY
ROOM
13'-6" x 9'-6"

DEN
14'-0" x 10'-0"

OFFICE
14'-0" x 10'-0"

NH STATE POLICE MAJOR CRIME UNIT
Prepared by TFC Frederick J. Lulka #798

SKETCH 8.1   Homicide scene.

PHOTO 8.1   Hallway between kitchen and dining room.

Sample Crime Scene Reconstruction Report—cont'd

PHOTO 8.2   Indentation in wall.

this location. The assault and bloodshed events occurring in this area was such that none of the items on the counter were disturbed. Thus, most of the assault and struggle occurred closer to the hallway and not the living room.

Subsequently, the struggle and bloodshed events continued further into the hallway, moved to the area adjacent to the empty room area, and ended in the doorway to the bathroom of that room (see Sketch 8.2).

The assault in the hallway and adjacent to the empty room's bathroom occurred with the victim at various heights. However, most of the assault to the victim in the doorway of the bathroom occurred while the victim was on the floor. Given the wounds of the victim as shown in the autopsy and the bloodstain patterns in this area, the assault ended in this location with a large number of blows given to the victim in this face down, prone position (see Photos 8.3—8.6). A number of impact toolmarks were also found in this location, thus, supporting the reconstruction that the victim was down while receiving the blunt force trauma to his body and head.

A large amount of the blunt force trauma to the victim occurred while he was face down on the floor. This mechanism of bloodshed is additionally demonstrated by the lack of blood flow patterns and elongated bloodstains on his pants. The pants are covered with contact/transfer bloodstain patterns, passive drops, and circular impact blood spatter. See Photos 8.7 and 8.8.

In my opinion one weapon was used to inflict this blunt force trauma. It would have been difficult to continue the intense nature of the struggle and assault on the victim with one weapon and then switch to another weapon while struggling. Therefore, it is more likely that one weapon with both a flatten blade head and a circular head was used for the assault.

After the victim had been murdered, the suspect moved victim's body to the basement area. Due to the lack of drag bloodstain patterns in the areas from the bathroom doorway to the top of the stairs to the basement, the suspect had to have been able to stem the flow of the victim's blood by some undetermined means. However, at the top of the stairs the victim's blood produced the bloody drag marks on the floor molding and jam. Additional bloody drag marks, passive blood drops, and contact/transfer patterns on the floor and on objects in the basement confirm the movement of the victim from upstairs to the basement (see Photos 8.9—8.12).

Once the victim's body had been deposited in the basement, the suspect attempted to clean up the crime scene as evidenced by the various cleaning solutions and supplies found near the body and in the basement.

Interview of the Suspect

One of the primary uses for physical evidence in a criminal investigation is to substantiate or refute statements given by eyewitnesses, victims, and suspects. In this case, I was asked to review the transcribed interview of the suspect by Detective Sgt A and Detective Sgt G of the NH State Police on June 18, 2008 in Vermont and identify physical evidence that refutes the statement. I have divided the interview/statement of the suspect into the following areas: (1) The spontaneous nature of the assault; and (2) Other areas of interest.

Continued

Sample Crime Scene Reconstruction Report—cont'd

MC-08-, 122

DIAGRAM #2 ROOM DIMENSIONS   164 KINGSTON ROAD DANVILLE, NH

NH STATE POLICE MAJOR CRIME UNIT
Prepared by TFC Frederick J. Lulka #798

SKETCH 8.2   Homicide scene.

PHOTO 8.3   Area adjacent to empty room from hallway.

Sample Crime Scene Reconstruction Report—cont'd

PHOTO 8.4   Area adjacent to empty room from room.

PHOTO 8.5   Doorway to bathroom.

Continued

Sample Crime Scene Reconstruction Report—cont'd

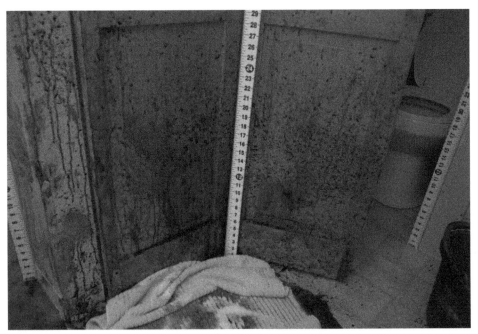

PHOTO 8.6   Doorway of bathroom, floor level.

PHOTO 8.7   Front of pants.

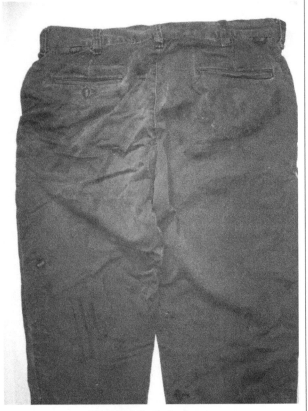

PHOTO 8.8   Back of pants.

Sample Crime Scene Reconstruction Report—cont'd

PHOTO 8.9   Top of stairs to basement.

PHOTO 8.10   Bloody drag marks.

Continued

Sample Crime Scene Reconstruction Report—cont'd

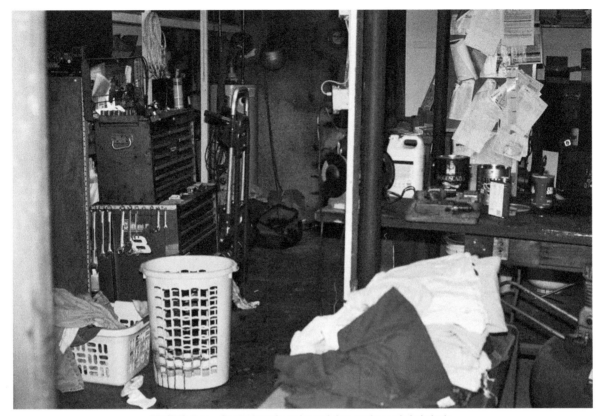

PHOTO 8.11   Contact/transfer stains and drag marks to victim's body.

PHOTO 8.12   Tarp covered victim's body.

Sample Crime Scene Reconstruction Report—cont'd

Spontaneous Assault   According to his interview the suspect asserted that the victim awakened him as he was sitting in the recliner in the living room. Then he "snapped" and spontaneously reacted by assaulting the victim by slamming the victim's head into the wall and otherwise hitting him. There are no impact marks from the victim's head at any location in the crime scene. The wound dynamics of the victim are consistent with a weapon that produced chopping wounds and circular blunt force trauma. The victim was assaulted with a weapon with a wide blade head and a circular head as stated above. According to his interview/statement, the suspect only admits to assaulting the victim with his fists and not a weapon. The spontaneity of the assault is further refuted by the fact that no construction tools of any kind were found anywhere in the upstairs of the residence. The only tools were downstairs which would have required the suspect to have already retrieved the tool prior to the assault.

The wounds administered on the victim would have required the suspect to pursue the victim from the living room to the hallway area between the kitchen and the dining room. The distance from the living room to the point of original bloodshed is approximately 15 feet. This pursuit and assault is persistent and not spontaneous.

The spontaneous and panicked reaction by the suspect is refuted by two of his actions after the victim died. With forethought he wrapped the victim by some means to stop the blood loss of the victim as he attempted to put the victim in the basement garage. Also, the suspect attempted to clean-up the crime scene, which requires some planning and non-spontaneous actions.

Other Areas of Interest   The suspect states that both he and the victim were drinking heavily on the evening in question and prior to the death of the victim. This alcohol consumption is not possible and refuted by the toxicology report on the victim. The toxicology report shows no alcohol to be present in the blood of the victim taken at autopsy. No physical evidence of any alcohol was found in the residence on June 13, 2008 by the New Hampshire State Police crime scene investigators.

The suspect stated that the victim swung a fork or some other object at him during the assault. The object cut his finger. No such object was found at the crime scene. The suspect asserts that during the assault at some point he blacked out. He would have disrupted the bloodstains on the floor and created some obvious contact transfer bloodstains consistent with his body. No such bloodstain patterns were found at the crime scene.

If any additional materials become available before trial, please make them accessible to me.

Respectfully submitted,

Signature

Crime Scene Reconstructionist

Emerging Technologies

Chapter Outline

Learning Objectives

Upon completion of this chapter the reader should be able to:

- Explain and utilize the newest types of technology to assist the crime scene investigator.
- Identify new technologies to assist with the documentation and measurement of evidence and crime scene.
- Identify the emerging technologies that bring scientific instrumentation to the crime scene and out of the forensic laboratory.

DOCUMENTATION

The use of technology to record forensic scenes has also evolved with the low cost and availability of tablet computers and lightweight laptop computers. The apps related to forensic scene management, measuring and sketching, photography, and tracking continues to grow. A major advantage for using this type of technology is that multiple investigators can access the recorded information in real time. If there is more than one forensic scene to a particular incident, all can be updated and accessed quickly. Lastly, once mastered, the time that it would take to properly document a crime scene would be reduced while maintaining proper documentation methodology. See Figs. 9.1–9.4 for examples of the use of the CrimePad app.

MEASUREMENT

As discussed in the chapter on measuring and sketching forensic scenes and the physical evidence contained in the scene, the use of laser measurers including Total Stations to assist in measuring and diagramming crime scenes can save time and create better accuracy. There have been great advances in the use of lasers primarily by having the lasers scan the forensic scenes. The time of flight or reflectance of the laser creates an electronic distance- or size-based image of the scene. These laser scanners then will digitally photograph the scene. Software programs supplied by the scanner manufacturers will then integrate the distance data with the digital images to produce accurately sized images, animated drawings, and videolike "fly-throughs" of the scene (see Figs. 9.5–9.7 below).

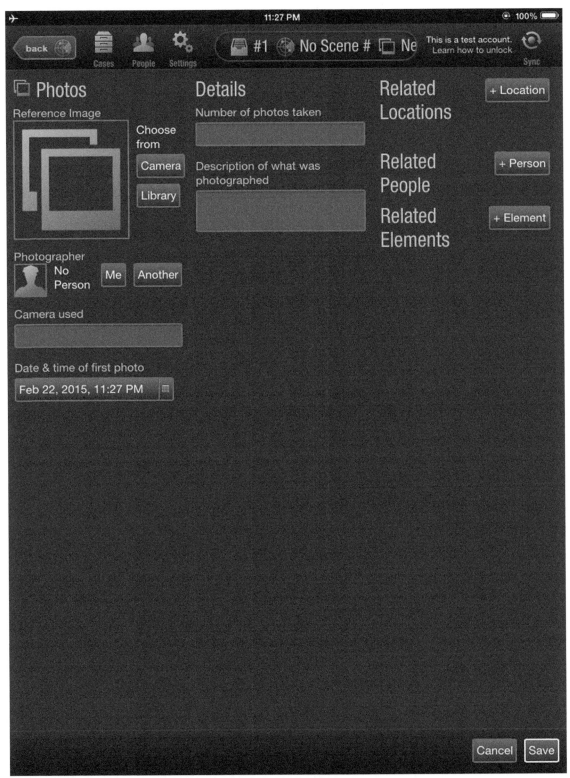

FIGURE 9.1 CrimePad app.

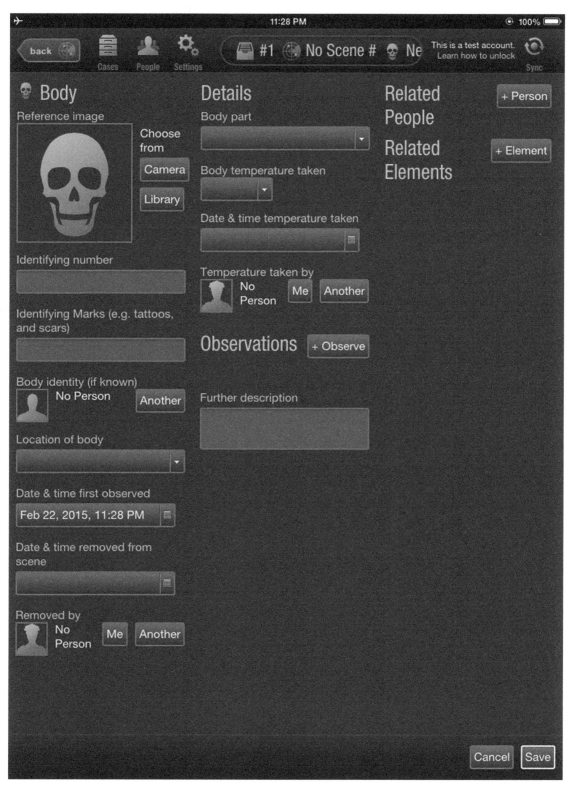

FIGURE 9.2   CrimePad app.

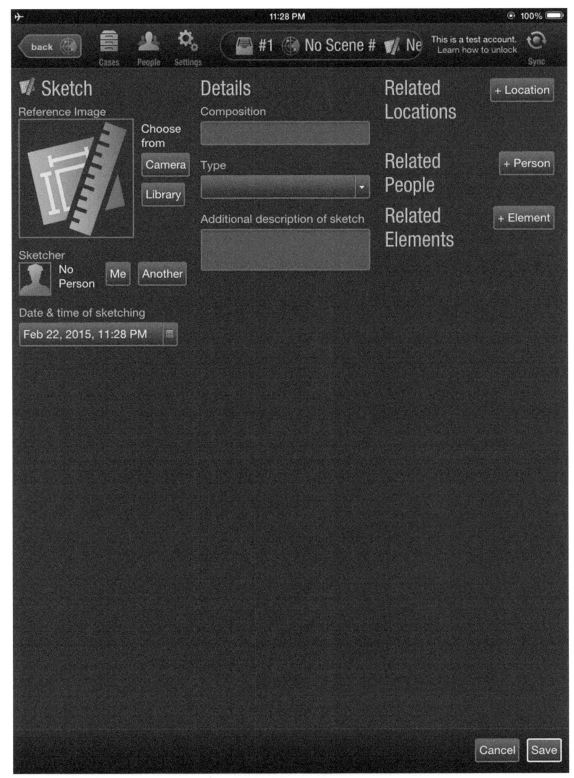

FIGURE 9.3   CrimePad app.

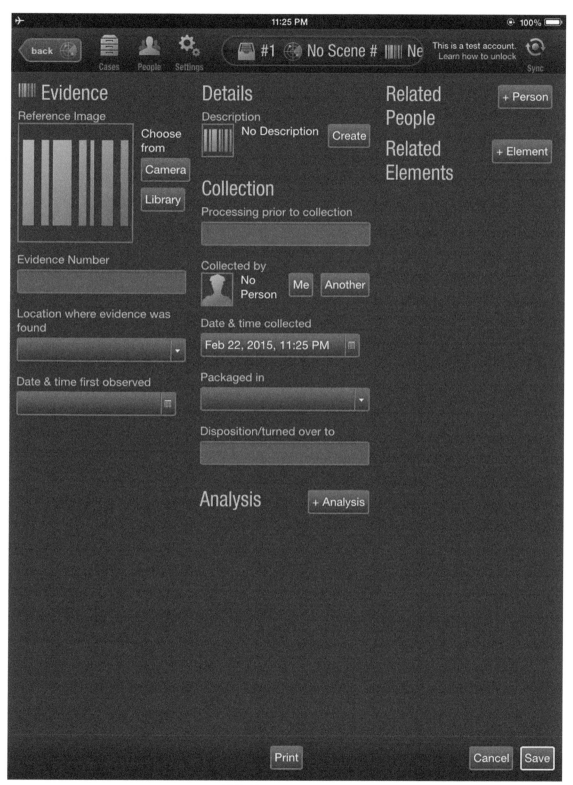

FIGURE 9.4   CrimePad app.

FIGURE 9.5   Leica ScanStation in use at a crime scene.

There are many types of units currently available to do this. They range from the handheld models such as the Faro Freestyle 3D, Leica ScanStation and LSI Laser, and a variety of brands of Total Stations (see Figs. 9.8−9.10).

These large format laser-measuring devices operate in two distinctly different ways. The LTI laser and Total Stations operate using a single laser beam that is reflected off a mirror that is held next to the object to be measured. These chosen data points can be collected in a handheld collector and transferred into a computer program to generate an accident or forensic scene. The benefit of the Faro or Leica laser measurers is that they send out a laser that scans an entire scene that is then downloaded into the respected proprietary computer program for documentation. This means that it generates millions of data points that can be checked at a later date for distance measurements. As can be imagined, the computers needed for this type of display need sufficient computing power to create the 3-D scene.

The 3-D laser scanners do an excellent job of documenting a crime scene and presenting a "real scene". They can be difficult to use with smaller indoor crime.

Therefore, a different option would be a smaller handheld laser measurer. It will allow the investigator to take as many measurements as needed and connect via Bluetooth to an app and create a sketch (see Figs. 9.11 and 9.12 below).

There are some interesting new technologies that have just arrived on the iOS platform that will use apps that can be used to measure forensic scenes.

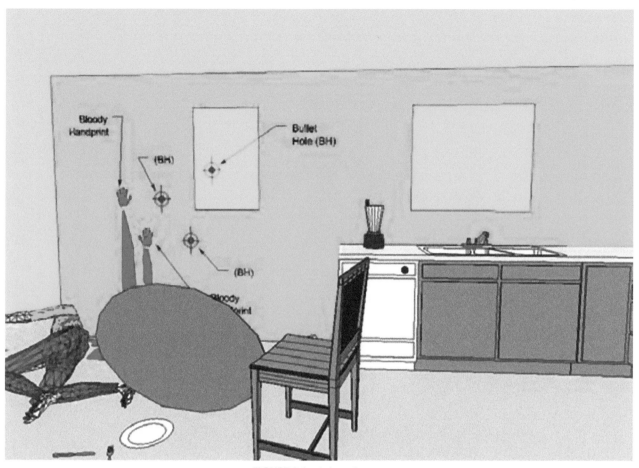

FIGURE 9.6   Animated scene.

FIGURE 9.7   Laser scanner distance-based image of scene.

FIGURE 9.8   LTI laser.

FORENSIC SCIENCE FROM THE LABORATORY TO THE SCENE

Raman Spectroscopy

The ability to take large pieces of equipment from a laboratory setting into the field, portability, allows the crime scene investigator to gather more details and information faster. The use of a portable Raman spectrophotometer to identify white powders, for example, can allow for an instantaneous identification of a suspected drug. This utilization of taking the forensic laboratory out to the crime scene accomplishes much more than just portability. More commonly used in the field are small presumptive test kits that can establish the probable cause to make an arrest (see Fig. 9.13 below with an example of a field test for suspected controlled substances).

The suspected drug must then be sent off to a forensic laboratory for confirmation that can take weeks for a result to be available. In order to utilize the field drug kit, the investigator needs to make a guess which of the many tests to perform. The handheld Raman spectrophotometer will make that identification. Oftentimes nefarious individuals try to sell imposter drugs for the real substance. Unlike the field test kit, which would show a negative reaction, the portable spectrophotometer will alert the investigator as to the identity of the fraudulent material. All that is needed is to utilize the supplied library or to add material into the library on your own. Raman has also shown some promise for the identification of physiological fluids, too.

Fourier Transform Infrared Spectroscopy

The next portable instrument is the FTIR, Fourier transform infrared spectroscopy. The portable FTIR can analyze and identify a material (solid or liquid) in less than 1 min. See Fig. 9.14 below for one example of an FTIR spectrometer. It has wireless transmission and built-in spectral libraries, is capable of mixture analysis, and is adept in identifying chemical warfare agents, explosives, toxic industrial chemicals, narcotics, and suspicious powders, among other dangerous chemical classes. This instrument is unique in that it is certified for use in harsh conditions and high-temperature operation.

FIGURE 9.9 Faro Freestyle 3-D.

FIGURE 9.10 Total Station.

FIGURE 9.11   Laser measurer.

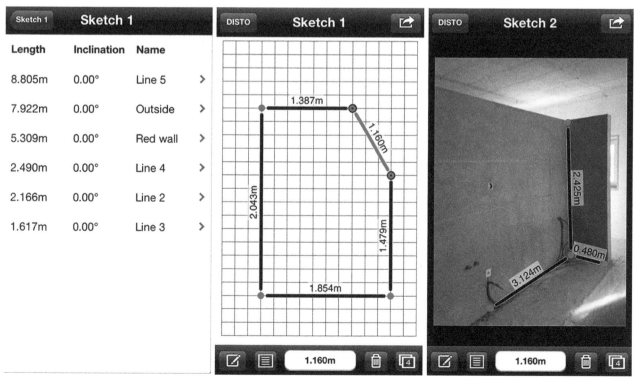

Length	Inclination	Name	
8.805m	0.00°	Line 5	>
7.922m	0.00°	Outside	>
5.309m	0.00°	Red wall	>
2.490m	0.00°	Line 4	>
2.166m	0.00°	Line 2	>
1.617m	0.00°	Line 3	>

FIGURE 9.12   Sketch from handheld laser measurer.

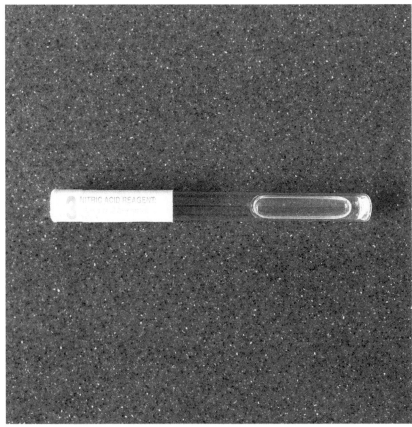

FIGURE 9.13   Presumptive field test kit.

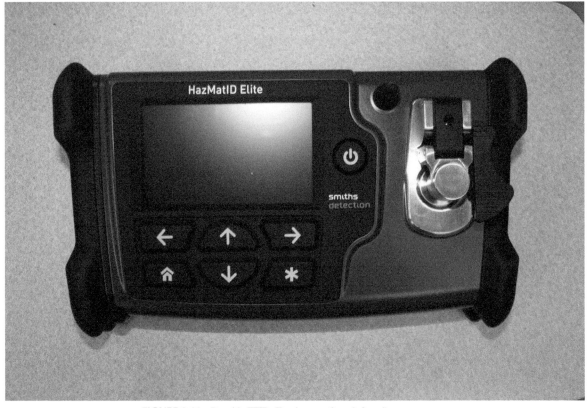

FIGURE 9.14   Portable FTIR (Fourier transform infrared) spectrometer.

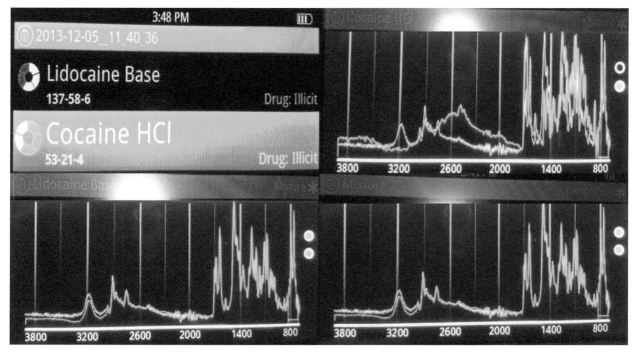

FIGURE 9.15   On-scene result for white powder: lidocaine and cocaine.

At the scene of a hit and run motor vehicle accident, paint chip evidence can be tested, and a result, available immediately as to manufacturer, model, and year of the offending vehicle. In an investigation, the precious moments shortly after an incident are always the most critical.

At the scene of a chemical spill, an investigator can rapidly identify the constituents of that spill immediately, allowing for proper evacuation and safety protocols to be enacted expeditiously.

If an agency has a response vehicle, there are slightly larger and more powerful portable FTIRs available. These instruments are only as good, however, as their library databases. The more powerful the library, the more likely the identification of the unknown. See Fig. 9.15 below that showing an FTIR spectrum result.

Portability has another use as well, the ability to search a scene quicker and in more detail. In the past, if an agency were to be looking for any type of evidence that might be buried, they would rely on an informant or request that an entire area be excavated costing sums of money and destroying property. More seized items than necessary might be sent to the crime laboratory just in case probative evidence might be found on it. The ability to narrow your search and gather appropriate amounts of relevant evidence is turning out to be key.

Ground-Penetrating Radar

Ground-penetrating radar (GPR) is an instrument that has been around for many years. It has been only recently that its use has been applied in a crime scene setting. A very experienced operator will be able to identify the object by the signature of the response of the waves. Others are able to determine if an anomaly exists.

These anomalies are marked on the instrument itself for location, as well as approximate depth. The use of surveyor flags aids in determining an above ground visual pattern. Once these anomalies are identified, the smaller areas can be excavated in an attempt to locate any potential physical evidence. See Figs. 9.16—9.18 below.

ADVANCEMENTS IN ALTERNATE LIGHT SOURCES

As discussed in an earlier chapter with regard to searching for evidence, the use of alternate light source (ALS) can greatly assist that search. The ability to see evidence is not always easy. Our eyes see only a small portion of the electromagnetic radiation spectrum, about 300 nm of an approximate 10,000 nm total. Research has shown that different body fluids behave differently at different wavelengths especially in the areas of the spectrum that are not visible to us. The use of an ALS makes it easier to locate those body fluids. While this is not a presumptive or a confirmatory test, this is a search method for locating forensic evidence that can be collected for further analysis in the forensic laboratory.

FIGURE 9.16   Ground-penetrating radar.

The concern over the years with ALS is the size of the unit and the strength of the light emitted. The ALS units used to be quite large and not very portable. They needed to be connected to a power outlet. The portable handheld ALS has been enhanced using LEDs as light sources and longer lasting, lighter batteries. The ability to handle a lighter and more efficient ALS has revolutionized the search for potential body fluids at the crime scene. See Fig. 9.19 below.

Another type of electromagnetic radiation, reflective ultraviolet imaging system (RUVIS), allows the user to search for latent fingerprints on surfaces that are nonporous and relatively smooth. It is best on surfaces that do not absorb the moisture left during the deposit of the fingerprint and that reflect light. The unenhanced latent fingerprints appear as white ridges on a dark backing. The advantage to this technique is that it allows preliminary scanning of objects or rooms so as to locate specific areas that can then be enhanced using chemical and physical methods as opposed to powder dusting or processing an entire room in the hopes of finding an identifiable latent fingerprint. The instrument is based on the use of shortwave ultraviolet light.

Infrared (IR) light energy is on the opposite side of the electromagnetic radiation spectrum from ultraviolet energy as discussed above. The IR spectrum alone goes from 700 to 100,000 nm. It is 300 times the range of the visible light spectrum. Since IR light can be diffracted like visible light, it also is reflected, absorbed, or transmitted in a very similar way. Objects imaged in IR light look different because of the different properties of the object; an object that is opaque to a wavelength of 500 nm (visible) may be transparent to a wavelength of 900 nm (IR). Digital cameras take advantage of this range of near-IR wavelengths for low-end night vision, as CCD and CMOS arrays are quite sensitive to the near-IR light.

However, owing to inappropriate use by some individuals, camera makers installed filters on their digital cameras. Now only certain IR cameras come with requisite filters necessary to allow the IR light to be captured by the camera. Specific types of evidence that it can assist with would include inks and handwriting, drugs, gunshot residue, and blood. IR photography can also verify a subject's statement.

Between 6,000 nm and 15,000 nm is the wavelength range used in thermography or visualizing heat signatures. It is this range that has forensic scene application. These functions range from locating missing individuals, to finding evidence,

FIGURE 9.17   Forensic scene investigator operating GPR (ground-penetrating radar).

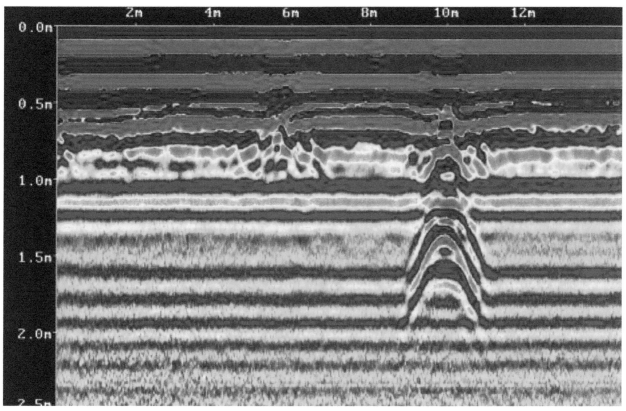

FIGURE 9.18   GPR (ground-penetrating radar) scan showing anomalies.

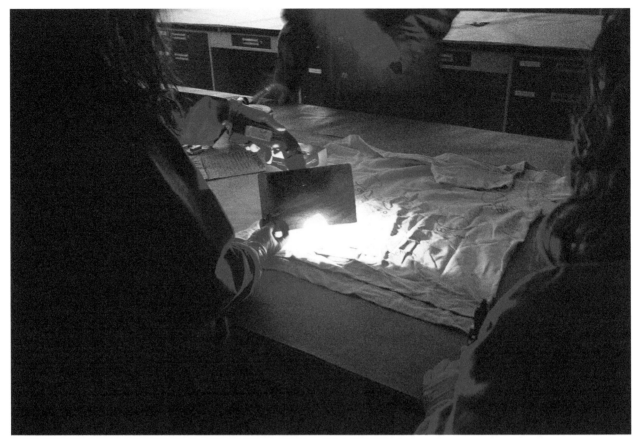

FIGURE 9.19 Using an alternate light source (ALS) to search for physiological fluids.

to locating hidden compartments in residences, and to detecting paths of foot or vehicular traffic. IR light can also be used to reveal patterns not visible, identify materials, and improve documentation. See Figs. 9.20−9.22 below.

RAPID DNA PROFILES

According to the National Academy of Sciences report on forensic science in 2009, nuclear DNA testing is the gold standard against which all other forensic disciplines are measured. The latest and even future technology, as it relates to nuclear DNA, is the improvement in the time it takes to produce a profile that would be compatible with the standard database protocols that are currently in use. Typically, it would take anywhere from 30 to 90 days from submission for profile results from a laboratory. Now using Rapid DNA technology, it takes approximately 90−120 min. The implication for using this new Rapid DNA technology is in situations of trying to identify an unknown individual. The longer it takes to identify an unknown victim, the more difficult the task is for the investigators to solve the case. This shortened time span is immeasurable for law enforcement (Figs. 9.23−9.25).

BIOMETRICS AT THE CRIME SCENE

One of the fastest growing areas of forensic science at the crime scene is the area of biometrics. Very simply defined, biometrics is metrics related to the human body. Examples of biometrics are facial recognition, voice analysis, ears, retinal and iris identification, venous patterns, and fingerprints. Some of this technology is used for non−law enforcement identifications, such as admission to amusement parks, smart phones, or time clocks (see Fig. 9.26 below).

Among law enforcement applications is the ability to photograph a developed latent fingerprint impression, or a patent fingerprint impression, and send it wirelessly to Integrated Automated Fingerprint Identification System (IAFIS) to search for an identity. These same instruments can also send a known impression of an unknown subject to IAFIS in an attempt to determine their identity. The device pictured in Fig. 9.27, a standalone AFIS, has an even greater advantage. It can capture

FIGURE 9.20   Infrared image of an animal.

FIGURE 9.21   Infrared image of the heat signature of a vehicle.

FIGURE 9.22   Infrared image of the heat signature of an individual inside a home.

FIGURE 9.23 Rapid DNA analyzer.

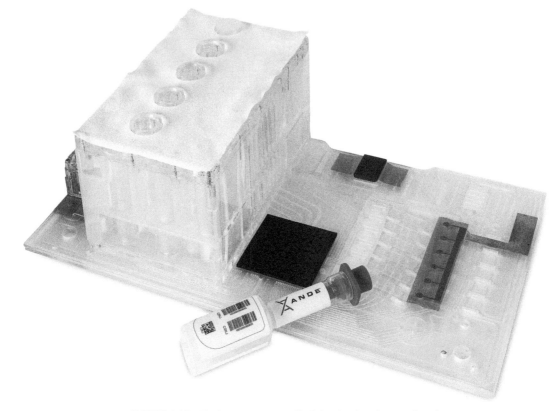

FIGURE 9.24 The key component—all of the chemistry is prepackaged.

FIGURE 9.25   The unit is very portable and can be handled by one individual.

not only a developed latent impression, a patent impression, but also an undeveloped latent impression. Using the onboard database which can be both populated on scene with a suspect or for elimination prints, it can be preloaded with a number of local known perpetrators to aid in an investigatory identification. This might allow for quicker apprehension (Fig. 9.28).

UNMANNED AERIAL VEHICLES OR DRONES

Over the past couple of years, the move of unmanned aerial vehicles (UAVs) going from a hobby or military use has transcended into the realm of forensic scene investigations. While very early, their potential is limitless. They are already outfitted with still cameras, video cameras, IR cameras, LiDAR, and 3-D laser scanner technology. The benefits of this are being able to gather information from above the forensic scene, when generally it has been difficult to do so prior to the development of UAVs. Oftentimes, it takes an aerial view to allow for a better understanding of what occurred and provides additional information to the court system. It will also reduce the number of individuals in forensic scenes minimizing contamination and possible destruction of evidence. See Fig. 9.29 below.

TELEFORENSICS

With over 18,000 police departments in the United States, not every agency has the capability to properly investigate forensic scenes. The cost to operate a unit is very expensive. One of the most important aspects of operating a unit is to have adequately trained personnel. Having trained and continuously investing in training of crime scene investigators, unfortunately, is not high on many agencies' budget requests. Teleforensics can be the answer to proper scene investigation. Teleforensics is the process to enable a trained, off-scene forensic specialist assist with most any on-scene case in real time from just about anywhere. The off-scene expert allows the on-scene investigator to identify, document, search for,

FIGURE 9.26   Biometric time clock.

and collect evidence that might be overlooked by on-scene untrained or undertrained investigators. Teleforensics may have an impact on increased case closures. An example of this technology is the raid in Pakistan for Osama bin Laden which was viewed in real time by government officials in Washington DC. Another use of teleforensics ties in with some of the aforementioned technologies. The portability of bringing typical forensic laboratory equipment to a forensic scene allows for near instant analysis. One of the pitfalls would be the training necessary to allow that investigator to corroborate and identify or analyze by off-scene scientists.

FIGURE 9.27   Portable biometric instrument.

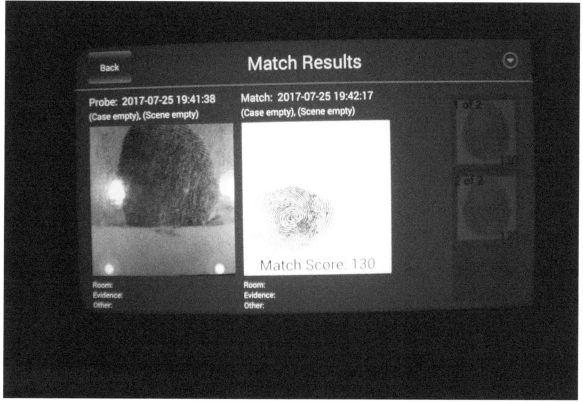

FIGURE 9.28   Portable biometric device results.

FIGURE 9.29   Unmanned aerial vehicle (UAV).

DATABASES

The final area of technology for forensic scene investigation is the use of databases. The compilation and storage of information has dramatically changed over the years. Historically law enforcement agencies do not communicate very well with other agencies or even within their own agency. Databases such as "I2 Coplink" allow for law enforcement agencies to organize all of the information from a forensic scene, as it relates to a particular investigation, but more importantly, compare information across other investigations in other agencies or places. It can create time-lines, develop leads for the investigation, and organize case information.

One of the many types of forensic evidence is firearms evidence. This includes firearms, projectiles, and cartridge casings. Creation of an automated ballistics identification system was completed years ago. There have been many different fractions of the system. Some looked at projectiles, and some looked at fired casings. Forensic scientists image the casings or projectiles and input data on both pieces of recovered evidence into the system. The database, now called the Integrated Ballistics Identification System (IBIS), allows users to share information worldwide. See Fig. 9.30 below.

One of the oldest databases is the Integrated Automated Fingerprint Identification System (IAFIS). This database searches and uses algorithms to compare minutiae in fingerprints in the attempt to identify individuals. The new technology integrates IAFIS with input directly from the forensic scene.

The Combined DNA Index System (CODIS) is the laboratory-based database for DNA, has been available for a few years, and allows for searches of individuals' profiles. The index contains nearly 11 million profiles. Like IAFIS, it will not be long before there will be connectivity to the forensic scene as Rapid DNA advances. What may hold even more promise is the advent of LODIS, a local DNA Index System. The premise behind it is very simple. Studies have shown that approximately 20% of individuals commit approximately 80% of crimes. LODIS is based on the fact that the profiles that are inputted into the database are from those known subjects from a specific region, city, or town. LODIS is generally operated by private enterprises, which usually shortens examination times and, therefore, quicker inclusion into the database and inclusion of profiles from all types of crimes, which may be limited by a governmental laboratory. These LODIS databases are also not governed by federal regulations that allow the local agencies to set up their own protocols for submissions. Currently because of the regulatory differences, LODIS does not connect with CODIS.

The final database is the Shoe Print Identification and Casework Management System or SICAR. This database allows the user to scan tire tread patterns and footwear sole patterns from a crime scene and determine the manufacturer of that item. See Fig. 9.31 below.

FIGURE 9.30 Integrated Ballistics Identification System (IBIS).

CONCLUDING THOUGHTS

New advances in technology are not just put into use when made available. The methods, instruments, and technology must meet certain criteria. *Frye v. United States* and *Daubert v. Merrell Dow Pharmaceuticals* establish the reliability of expert testimony and expert testimony based on technology and science. Daubert allows that evidence based on innovative or unusual scientific knowledge may be admitted only after it has been established that the evidence is reliable and scientifically valid. These cases strengthened the process so that junk science would not be allowed into court. It is up to

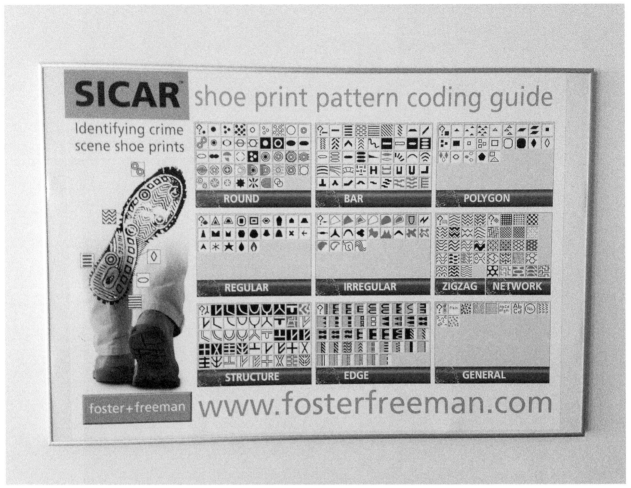

FIGURE 9.31   Shoe Print Identification and Casework Management System (SICAR).

the judge to make that decision based on four tests: testing, peer review, error rates, and acceptability in the relevant scientific community. The use of the new technologies discussed in this chapter must undergo extensive testing and validity analysis in order to be placed into use by any crime scene investigator.

DISCUSSION QUESTIONS

1. True or False—FTIR instruments allow for the testing of DNA?
2. What human characteristics can be identified by biometric means?
3. How long might it take to develop a DNA profile from a crime scene using Rapid DNA?
4. What are some of the advantages of using a laser-measuring device compared with a tape measure?
5. What is Daubert v. Merrell Dow Pharmaceuticals?

Chapter 10

Concluding Thoughts

Chapter Outline

Learning Objectives

Upon completion of this chapter the reader should be able to

- Explain the usefulness and probative value of physical evidence from the crime scene.
- Identify areas where a crime scene investigator encounters barriers or challenges.

PROBATIVE VALUE OF CRIME SCENE EVIDENCE

This textbook has spent a great amount of time instructing the reader how to recognize, document, search for, and correctly package physical evidence from a crime scene. It has shown what-to-do and what-not-to-do to accomplish those tasks. Ultimately, it is the determination of the probative value of the evidence found at the crime scene that is important. In other words, did the scene investigation produce reliable, valid, and relevant results?

Evidence can simply be defined as anything that helps to ascertain the truth of a matter or gives proof of a fact. Just because an investigator recognizes, records, searches for, and collects evidence from a crime scene along with having that evidence analyzed, does not necessarily mean that it is helpful in the investigation or subsequent prosecution. Probative evidence, evidence that is useful or significant to an investigation, is categorized in two ways: standing on its own or as part of lots of other evidence, i.e., a cumulative effect.

Usefulness or Probative Value of Physical Evidence

It is important for the scientific crime scene investigator to understand the value of physical evidence in a criminal investigation, as well as the limitations of physical evidence; the theory of evidence transfer; and the proper science-based methodologies for locating less-than-obvious evidence and the obvious evidence at the crime scene. Most of the clues that lead to the solution of the crime are at the crime scene in the form of physical evidence. It has been the purpose of this textbook to provide a means for the reader to do just that—use the physical evidence to reach the proper conclusion. Therefore, scientific crime scene investigators must use their knowledge of physical evidence as part of the total investigation. The experienced crime scene investigator also knows to expect the unexpected and not investigate a crime scene to produce evidence supporting a preconceived idea or theory.

The objectives of scientific crime scene investigation are to recognize, collect, interpret, and reconstruct all the relevant physical evidence at the crime scene. The major objective of the examination of physical evidence is to provide useful information for the criminal investigator in solving cases. It is the interaction of these objectives of crime scene investigation and physical evidence examination that is the basis of reliable, valid, and relevant scientific crime scene investigation.

The following are examples of science-based crime scene analysis and physical evidence examination interaction and the value of the interaction in criminal investigations.

Information on the Corpus Delicti

Corpus delicti, from the Latin term meaning "body of crime," is the determination of the essential facts that will show that a crime has occurred. The body of the crime is the physical evidence at the crime scene and the laboratory results from the testing of that evidence. Impacted bloodstain patterns, passive drops of blood, broken light switches, clean-up attempts, and a missing person (see Fig. 10.1) are examples of physical evidence that would be important in establishing a possible homicide.

Similarly, the location of a victim's blood found on baseboards as opposed to being found at shoulder height provides for information with regard to bloodshed locations that may be significant in the reconstruction of the homicide case.

Information on the Modus Operandi

Most experienced criminal investigators know that many criminals have a particular method of operation or modus operandi (MO), which is their "signature" or characteristic way of committing a crime. The physical evidence found at the crime scene can also be very instrumental in establishing a pattern of repeated behavior (see Fig. 10.2).

Cases that may seem to be unrelated can be associated by careful crime scene investigation of similar MOs. Association of cases by use of the physical evidence or MO is especially important in serial case investigations.

Linkage of Persons to Other Persons, Objects, or Scenes

Edmund Locard established the scientific basis used for all investigations in the 1930s. By using scientific research methodology, Locard showed that every contact leaves behind a trace—for his research, traces of dust on the feet of flies. For criminal investigations, the Locard Exchange Principle is the basis for linking persons, objects of evidence, and scenes. The linkage is multidirectional—linking suspects to victims to crime scenes. Sometimes the exchanged physical evidence is of such a small size, referred to as "trace," it can often be overlooked or contaminated. For the crime scene investigator, that means that the evidence must be subject to careful searching and kept or packaged separately to avoid loss and cross-contamination.

Direct linkage or association of a person (a suspect, a victim, or even a witness) to a particular crime scene location is accomplished by having the scene evidence analyzed in the forensic laboratory (and sometimes done right at the scene—teleforensics). An obvious example is the identification of an individual's fingerprints found at the crime scene, which is a direct link between the individual and a particular scene. This text has shown that on-scene identifications or analysis will greatly enhance the speed of the analysis and, therefore, the swift identification of associated evidence.

Some physical evidence such as footwear impressions, tire tread marks, toolmarks, or items belonging to persons found at the scene can be an indirect link or association. The directional, indirect linkage of the physical evidence is demonstrated by the fact that objects can be taken from the scene too. For example, fibers or debris from a suspect's home might be deposited on the victim's body or on a crime scene even though the victim has never been to the suspect's home.

Disproving or Supporting Suspect, Victim, or Witness Statements or Testimony

Proper crime scene investigation and analysis of physical evidence can often assist with the determination of the creditability of victims', eyewitnesses', or even suspects' statements or testimony. Blood found on a suspect's shoes can be tested and shown to belong to the victim or even shown to be not human blood (see Fig. 10.3).

Patterned physical evidence can be useful for the determination of credibility of statements, too. For instance, the size, shape, and distribution of gunshot residue on the shirt of a shooting victim can be used to determine the muzzle to target distance for the firearm used in a shooting. If eyewitnesses differ in their statements regarding how far away a shooting victim is from the shooter, a series of test firings of the firearm and ammunition in question will facilitate the determination of eyewitness credibility (See Fig. 10.4).

FIGURE 10.1 Physical evidence at the scene of a possible homicide.

FIGURE 10.2   Associated physical evidence indicating a particular suspect.

FIGURE 10.3   Blood on a suspect's shoes shown to belong to the victim.

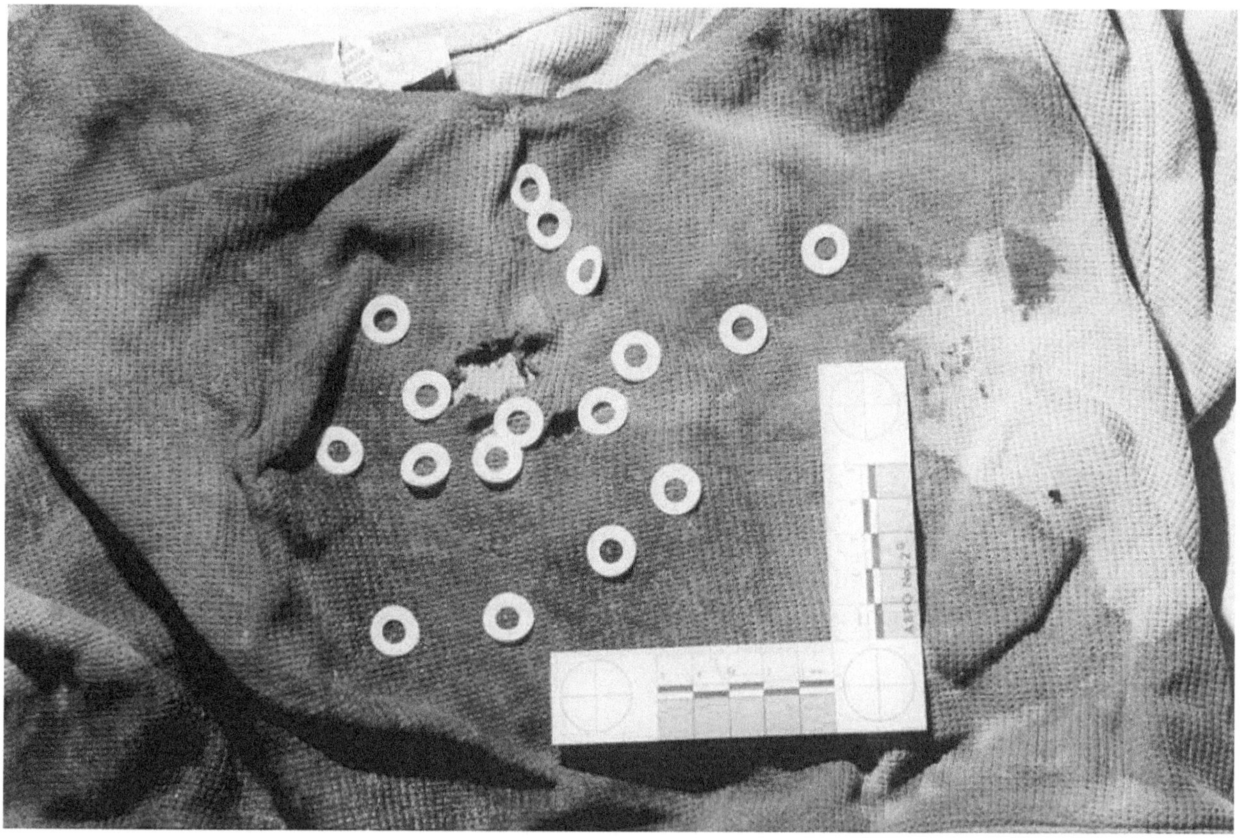

FIGURE 10.4   Range of fire determination.

Providing Investigative Leads

Probably one of the most significant uses of physical evidence from a crime scene is its ability to provide information that may direct an investigation along a productive path. Not all physical evidence will be directly linked or associated to or can identify a suspect. However, the physical evidence could provide indirect investigative information or lead to the solution of the crime. Not every crime scene will have a smoking gun or an eyewitness, but the scene will hold physical evidence that can provide help to the investigating officers. For example, the projectile removed from a drive-by-shooting victim can be located and possibly the manufacturer, model, and caliber of the firearm can be determined (see Fig. 10.5).

Blood found at the scenes of a series of burglaries can be analyzed and determine that the same individual is breaking into a number of residences in the same area. The number of different types of footwear impressions at the scene of a homicide (see Fig. 10.6) could indicate the number of persons at the crime scene, the locations of the impressions could yield information about a possible sequence of events at the scene, and the condition of the impressions could also help identify the activity of the scene.

Reconstruction of a Crime

As has been shown in previous chapters, the use of the physical evidence from crime scenes and their subsequent laboratory testing is a basic step in the crime scene reconstruction process. It is placed in this usefulness list because crime scene reconstruction is now readily accepted as part of most investigations.

The Cumulative Effect of Physical Evidence

Several pieces of class evidence link a suspect to a scene with greater probability than a single piece. In other words, the more the pieces of evidence to link a person to a crime, the greater the probative value of the evidence. Probative value is the ability of evidence to prove that something is related to a crime. This is the cumulative effect.

FIGURE 10.5 Projectile from victim used to determine make, model, and caliber.

As an example of the cumulative effect of evidence from crime scenes is the Way Williams case. Beginning in July 1979, 30 African-American children and young men in Atlanta, Georgia, were either reported missing or found to be victims of homicide. A task force was setup, and ultimately an individual was arrested and subsequently convicted. There was a large amount of evidence in the cases, but most importantly, the fibers found on the victims in the case illustrate the cumulative effect of physical evidence. Twenty-eight yellow-green nylon fibers and violet colored acetate fibers and dog hairs were recovered from the scenes or victims. The FBI Forensic Laboratory analyzed the fibers. A search of the suspect's home and car provided numerous fibers similar to those found at the scenes or on the victims' bodies.

During the trial, the defense sought to question the fiber evidence, arguing that a particular fiber might be discovered in the vehicle or home of any number of people not just the suspect's home. The prosecution however told a different story. It suggested to the jurors that they needed to consider the limited number of people who would have that particular carpet that was the source of one distinctive type of fiber; out of those, they asked how many could also be expected to have a particular bedspread that was the source of light green cotton fibers blended with violet acetate fibers. Of that limited number of individuals around Atlanta, how many would also drive a 1970 Chevrolet station wagon and own a German shepherd? On their own, these facts might have little bearing on the conviction, whereas cumulative, the probability of all of these occurring at random was very low. The probative value of all of these items of evidence was extremely high.

A second example of the cumulative effect of physical evidence is to consider how a particular piece of evidence ends up in a particular location. Sex offenses are good examples. If two people engage in consensual sex, then there will be transfer of a variety of evidentiary items. Even if two people engage in nonconsensual sex, there will be that same transfer of evidence. Oftentimes, the determination of consensual versus nonconsensual sex is based on who is more truthful in their testimony or statements. Sometimes it does not. In 1987, a young female was sexually assaulted and murdered. Two pubic hairs were located on the victim's buttocks. These hairs were determined to be microscopically similar and possessed similar mitochondrial DNA as consistent with the suspect. As stand-alone evidence, they may mean little. However, in the investigation the defendant used an alibi defense that he was never in contact with the victim. The probative value of

FIGURE 10.6 Multiple bloody footwear patterns at a homicide scene.

finding evidence with several confirmations of identification or linking to the suspect was very high considering his statement.

CHALLENGES AND BARRIERS

The Harassed and Hurried Crime Scene Investigator

What does the usefulness or probative value of physical evidence mean to the crime scene investigator? Seemingly one never knows what value a particular item of evidence found at a crime scene will have. Therefore, it becomes singularly incumbent to the scene investigator to conduct a thorough search, with a wide breadth of knowledge of what might be evidence and what a forensic laboratory can do to analyze it. Knowledge, proper training, correct and essential equipment for locating, preliminary and on-scene testing, and proper preserving or packaging evidence is critical. Taking all of the time necessary to do a complete job is of utmost importance. In an era of being hurried and pushed for answers, the crime scene investigator cannot ever rush, skimp, or "gloss over" the proper job at the crime scene. Only careful, systematic, methodical, science-based processes at the scene will ensure the reliability, validity, and relevancy of the scene and its physical evidence. As with Mincey, an investigator often goes in without specific knowledge of what those items of evidence might turn out to be that would allow for a successful prosecution or to evoke a plea agreement.

Sworn versus Nonsworn Crime Scene Investigator

Another challenge faced in crime scene investigation is the use of sworn versus nonsworn personnel. There are clearly advantages for both uses. One clear advantage of nonsworn over sworn is that nonsworn investigators tend not to get promoted or transferred out of a crime scene unit, whereas the same cannot be said for sworn personnel. Promotions and transfers often lead to instability in effective staffing of a crime scene unit.

Budgets and Funding

In the era of shrinking budgets, proper funding for training and equipment including new technology and proper safety equipment is a significant challenge for crime scene investigation units. Oftentimes, evidence storage is an afterthought leading to improper storage. This improper storage can contaminate evidence. Inadequate facilities can lead to loss of evidence. Evidence storage staff should never be used as a means for punishment or for using an officer near retirement. This type of personnel placement can often cause a critical stop in the effort to preserve the chain of custody.

CONCLUDING THOUGHT

In the modern world, it is less and less of the science that is being challenged in courts of law; it is more about the lack of productivity or the improper efforts by the crime scene investigator. This was lack of responsibility or caring by the scene investigator that was and still remains the impetus behind this book. In the end, just do and care about your job and its consequences!

DISCUSSION QUESTIONS

1. What is probative evidence?
2. What are some of the challenges of a crime scene investigator?
3. What does the cumulative effect of evidence mean?
4. What are the ways in which physical evidence can be probative?
5. How would you as a crime scene investigator assure reliability, validity, and relevancy to your work at the crime scene?

Appendix 1

Crime Scene Investigation Necessities

TELECOMMUNICATIONS

- Cellular telephones
- Laptop computer
- Wi-Fi access
- Portable printer/copier/scanner

ASSORTED TOOLS

- Scissors, knives, scalpel, and single-edge razor blades
- Forceps—plastic and steel, fine-tip and wide
- Power tools as needed, saws, screwdrivers, etc.
- Portable generators
- Dissecting tools
- Spatulas—small to large, plastic to metal
- Toothpicks
- Mirrors with extension rods
- Metal scribes
- Portable vacuum with filters or evidence trap
- Ladders—step stool to extension
- Table and chairs (and cover tent)
- Metal detector, spade, shovel, trowels, sieves, etc.

CRIME SCENE VEHICLE

- Sufficient to carry equipment and evidence-locking storage, drying racks
- Refrigeration
- Hard line and generator power sources
- Four-wheel drive, off-road capabilities

PERSONNEL PROTECTION

- Surgical and latex gloves, heavy rubber gloves
- Disposable gowns, hair nets, and booties
- Dust-filter masks
- Gas masks, HEPA filters
- Self-contained breathing apparatus
- Boots
- Eyewash

- Cleaning solutions with sprayers
- Tissues and paper towels
- Insect repellent

SUPPLIES FOR SCENE SECURITY

- Barrier tape
- Rope and cord
- Sawhorses
- Signs and poles
- Color spray paints
- Duct tape or adhesive materials (Velcro, etc.)
- Security and safety lighting devices
- Police or marked vehicles
- Emergency response equipment
- Tents and tarps

EQUIPMENT OR SUPPLIES FOR CRIME SCENE DOCUMENTATION

Visual Records

- Digital Single-Lens Reflex (SLR) camera with wide angle, normal, and telephoto lenses
- Image cards (minimum 16 GB) and readers
- Alternate Light Source (ALS) barrier filters for lenses (orange, yellow, and red)
- Numbered markers
- Scales and rulers
- Remote or auxiliary flash units with synch cords or wireless synch
- Tripods
- Digital video cameras and equipment
- Charged extra batteries
- Permanent markers (fine tip to wide)
- Placards

Sketching Equipment

- Assorted papers, pens, and clipboards
- Tape measures, various length- or laser-measuring devices
- Rainproof write on papers
- Protractors, angle-measuring devices
- Grid overlays—volume determination, droplet count
- Handheld GPIs (ground positioning instruments)
- Drafting templates
- Stick-on scales, numbers, and letters
- Laptops or tablets with drawing apps

EVIDENCE PACKAGING MATERIAL

- Paper bags and envelopes (various sizes)
- Butcher paper
- Boxes (specialty and various sizes)
- Evidence sealing tape
- Scotch tape
- Metal paint cans
- Pillboxes (various sizes)

- Sharps containers (cardboard, plastic tubes, boxes, etc.)
- Sterile swabs and swab boxes
- Gunshot Residue (GSR) collection kits
- Sexual assault evidence collection kits—victim
- Sexual assault evidence collection kits—suspect
- Tape and gel lifters
- Evidence tags/labels
- Strings
- Labels and markers
- Glassine weighing paper for druggist's folds
- Evidence tags and labels
- Casting materials—microsil to dental stone, rubber bowls, water

VISUALIZATION AND ENHANCEMENT REAGENTS

- Presumptive blood tests—drops or sprays
- Presumptive protein tests—drops or sprays
- Bloody print enhancement reagents
- Latent print processing chemicals
- Entomology sample preservatives
- Clorox/cleansing reagents
- Saline/distilled water
- Drug field tests reagents

LIGHTING EQUIPMENT

- Auxiliary lights-flood to penlight lasers
- Generators
- Flashlights
- Forensic light units—fixed wavelengths to variable, portable
- Ultraviolet lights

SPECIAL EVIDENCE SUPPLIES OR KITS

Latent Fingerprint Kit

- Assorted color fingerprint powders
- Fingerprint brushes
- Magna brush and magna powder
- Lifting tape—variety of sizes
- Lift cards—variety of sizes
- Gel lifters—large to small
- Fingerprint cards
- Backing latent lift cards—white and black
- Inked pad
- Flashlight
- Magnifier

Imprint and Impression Collection Kit

- Electrostatic dust lifter
- Dental stone
- Mixing bowls and spatulas
- Retaining borders

- Reinforcing material
- Release agent
- Silicone rubber
- Snow wax
- Cardboard box
- Large tape lifters

Appendix 2

DEATH SCENE INVESTIGATION CHECKLIST

Case No. _____   Date _____

Incident Type _____
Location _____
Time Notified _____   Notified by _____
Time of Arrival _____
Officer in Charge _____
Lead Investigator _____
Lead Scene Investigator _____

SCENE SECURITY

Was Scene Secured? Yes ❑ No ❑
Method: officer _____   barrier tape _____   other _____
Entry Log Started? Yes ❑ No ❑ Started by _____

STATE'S ATTORNEY

State's Attorney Notified?   Yes ❑ No ❑ Name: _____
Notified by: _____   Time: _____
Name of SA: _____
At scene? Yes ❑ No ❑ Time: _____
Search Warrant needed? Yes ❑ No ❑
Affiants:_____ Judge:_____
Date: _____   Time: _____
Consent to Search? Yes ❑ No ❑ Date: _____ Time: _____
Obtained from: _____ By: _____

+--+
| **REMARKS** |
| |
| |
| |
| |
| |
| |
+--+

Person(s) entering scene prior to CSU arrival

First Responders

Name	Agency	Phone

EMS/Fire Personnel

Name	Agency	Phone

Civilians

Name	Status	Address	Phone

Medical Examiner

DATE/TIME NOTIFIED:_____ BY: _____
OCME CASE #:_____
ASSISTANT ME / INVESTIGATOR AT SCENE: _____
DATE / TIME ARRIVED: _____ DEPARTED: _____

BODY REMOVAL

FUNERAL HOME: ❏
COMPANY NOTIFIED FOR REMOVAL: _____
DATE/TIME OF NOTIFICATION:_____ BY: _____
TIME ARRIVED: _____ DEPARTED:_____
PERSONNEL: _____
_____

OCME: ❏
DATE/TIME OF NOTIFICATION: _____ BY: _____
TIME ARRIVED: _____ DEPARTED:_____
PERSONNEL: _____

BODY BAG SEALED: Yes ❏ No ❏   METHOD:_____
BODY TRANSPORTED TO:

REMARKS

DECEASED INFORMATION IDENTIFICATION

Last: _____ First:_____ Middle _____
Address: _____
Phone: _____ Cell:_____ Carrier: _____
D.O.B. _____ SSN: _____ Age:_____
Race: _____ Gender: _____ Height: _____ Weight: _____
Hair Color: _____ Eye Color: _____ Facial Hair: Yes ____ No ____
Describe: _____ Tattoos: Yes ____ No ____
Describe:
_____
_____

REMARKS

DECEASED FOUND BY

LAST:_____ FIRST:_____ MIDDLE:_____
ADDRESS: _____
DOB:_____ TELEPHONE: _____

LAST:_____ FIRST:_____ MIDDLE:_____
ADDRESS: _____
DOB:_____ TELEPHONE: _____

DATE /TIME FOUND:_ _ _ _ _ _ _ _ _ _ DEATH WITNESSED: Yes ❑ No ❑

DECEASED IDENTIFIED: Yes ❑ No ❑ METHOD:_ _

REMARKS

LOCATION WHERE DECEASED WAS FOUND

CHECK THE PROPER SECTION PAGE NUMBER BELOW FOR THE BODY LOCATION AND REFER TO THAT SECTION TO CONTINUE DOCUMENTATION

❑ **BODY IN STRUCTURE—Page 227**

❑ **BODY IN WATER—Page 231**

❑ **BODY IN VEHICLE—Page 235**

❑ **BODY IN OPEN AREA—Page 239**

❑ **VICTIM REMOVED FROM SCENE PRIOR TO DEATH—Page 241**

UPON COMPLETION OF THE APPROPRIATE SECTION, PROCEED TO PAGE 21 TO CONTINUE THE DEATH SCENE CHECKLIST.

BODY FOUND IN STRUCTURE

LOCATION AND TYPE OF STRUCTURE

Apartment ☒ Duplex ☒ House ☒ Garage ☒ Outbuilding Other

DESCRIBE:

ADDRESS: _____

TELEPHONE: _____ NUMBER OF ROOMS: _____ ____ _____

BASEMENT: Full ❑   Partial ❑   None ❑   Other ❑ _____

POINT OF ENTRY: Door Forced ❑ Key ❑ Cutting Chain ❑ Window ❑ Undetermined ❑ Other ❑

DESCRIBE:

EVIDENCE OF ROBBERY / LARCENY: Yes ❑ No ❑ Undetermined ❑

DESCRIBE:

CONDITION OF DOOR: Open ❑   Closed ❑   Locked ❑   Unlocked ❑

CONDITION OF DOOR: Open ❑   Closed ❑   Locked ❑   Unlocked ❑

CONDITION OF DOOR: Open ❑   Closed ❑   Locked ❑   Unlocked ❑

CONDITION OF DOOR: Open ❑   Closed ❑   Locked ❑   Unlocked ❑

GARAGE DOOR(s): Yes ❑ No ❑ Unlocked ❑   IF YES: Open ❑   Closed ❑   Locked ❑

CONDITION OF WINDOW: Open ❑   Closed ❑   Locked ❑   Unlocked ❑   Broken ❑

CONDITION OF WINDOW: Open ❑   Closed ❑   Locked ❑   Unlocked ❑   Broken ❑

CONDITION OF WINDOW: Open ❑   Closed ❑   Locked ❑   Unlocked ❑   Broken ❑

CONDITION OF WINDOW: Open ❑   Closed ❑   Locked ❑   Unlocked ❑   Broken ❑

CONDITION OF INTERIOR: Neat and Orderly ❑ Disarray ❑ Ransacked ❑

DESCRIBE:

LIGHTS ON?: Yes ❑ No ❑

> IF YES, LIST LIGHTS AND LOCATIONS:

APPLIANCES ON: TV ❑ Radio ❑ Stereo ❑ Range ❑ Microwave ❑ Dishwasher ❑ Washer/Dryer ❑ Other ❑

> DESCRIBE:

COMPUTER: Yes ❑ No ❑   IF YES: On ❑ Off ❑

TELEPHONE: Yes ❑ No ❑   WORKING?: Yes ❑ No ❑

TELEPHONE NUMBER:_____

ANSWERING MACHINE: Yes ❑ No ❑   IF YES: On ❑ Off ❑

> CHECK FOR MESSAGES AND DESCRIBE:

HEATER: On ❑ Off ❑   AIR CONDITIONER: On ❑ Off ❑

THERMOSTAT SETTING:_____

ANIMALS PRESENT: Yes ❑ No ❑

> IF YES, DESCRIBE TYPE CONDITION AND DISPOSITION:

DATED MATERIAL: Yes ❑ No ❑

MAIL: _____

NEWSPAPERS: _____

RECEIPTS: _____

OTHER: _____

EVIDENCE OF LAST FOOD PREPARATION: Yes ❏ No ❏

DESCRIBE:

ALCOHOL PRESENT: Yes ❏ No ❏

DESCRIBE:

LOCATION OF BODY IN STRUCTURE

Living Room ❏ Dining Room ❏ Bedroom ❏ Kitchen ❏ Bathroom ❏ Family Room ❏ Hallway/Foyer ❏ Basement ❏ Attic ❏ Garage ❏ Other ❏

DESCRIBE:

POSITION OF BODY

Supine ❏ Prone ❏ Left Side ❏ Right Side ❏ Seated ❏ Hanging ❏ Other ❏

DESCRIBE:

CLOTHING AND JEWELRY

Fully Clothed ❏ Partially ❏ Clothed ❏ Nude ❏

DESCRIBE:

JEWELRY ON BODY: Yes ❏ No ❏

DESCRIBE:

CONDITION OF BODY

Well Preserved ❏ Partial Decomposition ❏ Decomposed ❏ Skin Slippage ❏ Skeletal Remains ❏

DESCRIBE:

ESTIMATE OF RIGOR: Complete ❏ Neck ❏ Arms ❏ Legs ❏ TIME:

DESCRIBE:

LIVIDITY: Front ❏ Back ❏ Localized ❏

BODY FOUND IN WATER

LOCATION

WATER TYPE: Pond ❑ Lake ❑ River ❑ Stream ❑ Other ❑
NAME OF BODY OF WATER:_____
LOCATION:_____
NEAREST STRUCTURE OVER WATER:_____
DISTANCE AND DIRECTION TO SCENE:_____
NEAREST ROAD TO SCENE:_____
DISTANCE AND DIRECTION TO SCENE:_____

DESCRIBE:

BLOOD: Absent ❑ Present ❑

IF PRESENT, GIVE LOCATION:

ANYTHING TIED TO BODY?: Yes ❑ No ❑

IF YES, DESCRIBE:

LIGATURE MARKS: Yes ❑ No ❑

IF YES, DESCRIBE:

AIR TEMP: _____ WATER TEMP: _____ WATER DEPTH: _____

WIDTH: _____ CURRENT: Yes ❏ No ❏ DIRECTION: _____

```
DESCRIBE:




```

WATER CLAIRITY: Clear ❏   Muddy ❏   Cloudy ❏

LAST PRECIPITATION IN AREA: _____ AMOUNT: _____ Type: _____

LOCATION OF BODY IN WATER: In Water ❏   Partially In Water ❏   On Shore ❏

IF IN WATER, DISTANCE FROM SHORE: _____

SHORE / BANK TYPE: Sand ❏   Rock ❏   Gravel ❏   Dirt ❏   Grass ❏

SHORE / BANK HEIGHT: _____

NEAREST BOAT RAMP: _____

NEAREST DAM: _____

BODY POSITION

Floating ❏ Partially Submerged ❏ Submerged ❏ On Back ❏ Face Down ❏ Right Side ❏ Left Side❏
Other ❏

```
DESCRIBE:




```

CONDITION OF BODY

Well Preserved ❏ Partial Decomposition ❏ Decomposed ❏ Skin Slippage ❏ Skeletal Remains ❏

ESTIMATE OF RIGOR: Complete ❏ Neck ❏ Arms ❏ Legs ❏ TIME:

```
DESCRIBE:




```

LIVIDITY: Front ❑ Back ❑ Localized ❑

DESCRIBE:

BLOOD: Absent ❑ Present ❑

IF PRESENT, GIVE LOCATION:

ANYTHING TIED TO BODY?: Yes ❑ No ❑

IF YES, DESCRIBE:

LIGATURE MARKS: Yes ❑ No ❑

IF YES, DESCRIBE:

JEWELRY ON BODY: Yes ❑ No ❑

DESCRIBE:

SEARCH BY DIVERS

AREA SEARCHED BY DIVERS: Yes ❑ No ❑

DATE: _____TIME STARTED: _____ ENDED: _____

AREA SEARCHED:_____

ITEMS RECOERED: Yes ❑ No ❑

DESCRIPTION AND LOCATION:

DIVER'S NAME	AGENCY/DEPARTMENT

REMARKS

BODY FOUND IN VEHICLE

VEHICLE LOCATION

SPECIFIC LOCATION: _____

Roadway ❑ Driveway ❑ Parking Lot ❑ Field/Woods ❑ Other ❑

DESCRIBE:

SURFACE CONDITION: Asphalts ❑ Concrete ❑ Gravel ❑ Dirt ❑ Grass ❑ Other ❑

DESCRIBE:

NEAREST RESIDENCE TO BUSINESS:

NEAREST ROAD TO SCENE:

DIRECTION/DISTANCE:

VEHICLE INFORMATION

VEHICLE TYPE: Car ❑ Van ❑ Pickup Truck ❑ Large Truck ❑ Motor Home ❑ Bus ❑ Trailer ❑ Other ❑

NUMBER OF DOORS: 2dr ❑ 3dr ❑ 4dr ❑ Hatchback ❑ Other ❑_____

PICKUP TRUCK: Short Bed ❑ Long Bed ❑ Flat Bed ❑ No Bed ❑ Camper ❑ Cap ❑

Other ❑ _____

VEHICLE MAKE:_____MODEL: _____YEAR:_____

REGISTRATION #: _____ VIN: _____

COLOR:_____

ODOMETER READING:_____TRIP ODOMETER:_____

DOORS: Open ❑ Closed ❑ Locked ❑ Unlocked ❑

DESCRIBE:

WINDOWS: Open ❑ Closed ❑ Broken ❑ Other ❑

DESCRIBE:

DAMAGE TO VEHICLE: Yes ❑ No ❑

DESCRIBE:

KEYS PRESENT: Yes ❑ No ❑

DESCRIPTION AND LOCATION:

IGNITION: On ❑ Off ❑
ENGINE: On ❑ Off ❑ GASGAUGE:_____
TRANSMISSION: Standard ❑ Automatic ❑ Floor ❑ Column ❑ GEAR:_____
EMERGENCY BRAKE: On ❑ Off ❑
RADIO: On ❑ Off ❑ STATION: _____ VOLUME: _____
TAPE/CD PLAYER: On ❑ Off ❑ None ❑_____

LIGHTS ON: Headlights ❑ Parking Lights ❑ Turn Signal ❑ Interior Lights ❑

DESCRIBE:

BATTERY CONDITION: Good ❑ Dead ❑
TIRES: No Flats ❑ Tire(s) Flat ❑

CONTENTS OF ASH TRAY:

VEHICLE INVENTORIED: Yes ❑ No ❑

LOCATION OF BODY

Front Seat ❑ Back Seat ❑ Trunk ❑ Driver's Side ❑ Passenger's Side ❑ Front Floor ❑ Rear Floor ❑ Pickup Bed ❑ Outside of Vehicle ❑ Other ❑

DESCRIBE:

BODY POSITION: Sitting ❑ Supine ❑ Prone ❑ Right Side ❑ Left Side ❑

DESCRIBE:

CONDITION OF BODY

Well Preserved ❏ Partial Decomposition ❏ Decomposed ❏ Skin Slippage ❏ Skeletal Remains ❏

DESCRIBE:

ESTIMATE OF RIGOR: Complete ❏ Neck ❏ Arms ❏ Legs ❏ TIME:

DESCRIBE:

LIVIDITY: Front ❏ Back ❏ Localized ❏

DESCRIBE:

BLOOD: Absent ❏ Present ❏

IF PRESENT, GIVE LOCATION:

ANYTHING TIED TO BODY?: Yes ❏ No ❏

IF YES, DESCRIBE:

LIGATURE MARKS: Yes ❑ No ❑

IF YES, DESCRIBE:

CLOTHING AND JEWELRY

Fully Clothed ❑ Partially Clothed ❑ Nude ❑

DESCRIBE:

JEWELRY ON BODY: Yes ❑ No ❑

DESCRIBE:

REMARKS

BODY FOUND IN OPEN AREA

LOCATION

Roadway ❑ Parking ❑ Lot ❑ Driveway ❑ Field ❑ Woods ❑ Other ❑

DESCRIBE:

GROUND CONDITION: Paved ❑ Gravel ❑ Dirt ❑ Grass ❑ Woods ❑ Rocky ❑
WATER IN AREA: Yes ❑ No ❑

IF YES, DESCRIBE::

NEAREST RESIDENCE / BUSINESS: _____
DISTANCE AND DIRECTION: _____
NEAREST ROAD TO SCENE: _____
DISTANCE AND DIRECTION: _____

POSITION OF BODY

Supine ❑ Prone ❑ Left Side ❑ Right Side ❑ Seated ❑ Hanging ❑ Other ❑

DESCRIBE:

CLOTHING AND JEWELRY

Fully Clothed ❑ Partially Clothed ❑ Nude ❑

DESCRIBE:

JEWELRY ON BODY: Yes ❑ No ❑

DESCRIBE:

CONDITION OF BODY

Well Preserved ❑ Partial Decomposition ❑ Decomposed ❑ Skin Slippage ❑ Skeletal Remains ❑

DESCRIBE:

ESTIMATE OF RIGOR: Complete ❑ Neck ❑ Arms ❑ Legs ❑ TIME:

DESCRIBE:

LIVIDITY: Front ❑ Back ❑ Localized ❑

DESCRIBE:

BLOOD: Absent ❑ Present ❑

IF PRESENT, GIVE LOCATION:

ANYTHING TIED TO BODY?: Yes ❑ No ❑

IF YES, DESCRIBE:

LIGATURE MARKS: Yes ❑ No ❑

IF YES, DESCRIBE:

VICTIM REMOVED FROM SCENE PRIOR TO DEATH

DECEASED TRANSPORTED TO: _____

DATE AND TIME: _____

TRANSPORTED BY: EMS ❑ Police ❑ Civilian ❑

NAME	AGENCY	PHONE	VEHICLE USED

IF CIVILIAN:

LAST: _____ First: _____ Middle: _____

ADDRESS: _____

D.O.B.: _____

VEHICLE USED: _____

REMARKS

DATE AND TIME DEATH PRONOUNCED: _____

LOCATION: _____ By: _____

INVESTIGATOR PRESENT: Yes ❑ No ❑ IF YES, WHO: _____

REMARKS

WOUNDS / WEAPONS / DRUGS / MEDICATIONS

APPARENT WOUNDS

PRESENT: Yes ❏ No ❏

LOCATION: _____

TYPE OF WOUND: Gunshot ❏ Penetrating ❏ Laceration ❏ Incision ❏ Bruise ❏ Defensive ❏ Other ❏

DESCRIBE:

LOCATION: _____

TYPE OF WOUND: Gunshot ❏ Penetrating ❏ Laceration ❏ Incision ❏ Bruise ❏ Defensive ❏ Other ❏

DESCRIBE:

LOCATION: _____

TYPE OF WOUND: Gunshot ❏ Penetrating ❏ Laceration ❏ Incision ❏ Bruise ❏ Defensive ❏ Other ❏

DESCRIBE:

LOCATION: _____

TYPE OF WOUND: Gunshot ❏ Penetrating ❏ Laceration ❏ Incision ❏ Bruise ❏ Defensive ❏ Other ❏

DESCRIBE:

LOCATION: _____

TYPE OF WOUND: Gunshot ❏ Penetrating ❏ Laceration ❏ Incision ❏ Bruise ❏ Defensive ❏ Other ❏

DESCRIBE:

MARKS ON BODY: Yes ❏ No ❏
LOCATION:

DESCRIBE:

LOCATION:

DESCRIBE:

LOCATION:

DESCRIBE:

TATTOOS OR SCARS: Yes ❏ No ❏
LOCATION:

DESCRIBE:

WEAPONS PRESENT

Yes ❏ No ❏

FIREARM TYPE: Handgun ❏ Rifle ❏ Shotgun ❏ Other ❏ _____

TYPE OF ACTION: Single Shot ❏ Bolt Action ❏ Semi-automatic ❏ Pump Action ❏

Revolver ❏ Lever Action ❏ Automatic/Selective Fire ❏

MAKE:_____ MODEL:_____ CALIBER:_____

SERIAL NUMBER:_____ LENGTH: _____ BARREL LENGTH: _____

FINISH:_____ MAGAZINE / CYLINDER CAPACITY: _____

EJECTION PORT: Left ❏ Right ❏ CYLINDER ROTATION: Left ❏ Right ❏

NUMBER OF CARTRIDGES IN WEAPON: _____

NUMBER OF EXPENDED CARTRIDGES IN WEAPON:_____

AMMUNITION TYPE:_____

HEADSTAMP:_____

LOCATION AND FURTHER DESCRIPTION:

EXPENDED CARTRIDGES AT SCENE: Yes ❑ No ❑ # CASINGS:

LOCATION AND DESCRIPTION:

KNIFE: Yes ❑ No ❑

BRAND: MODEL: BLADE LENGTH:

LOCATION AND DESCRIPTION:

OTHER WEAPON: Yes ❑ No ❑

LOCATION AND DESCRIPTION:

BLOOD ON WEAPON: Yes ❑ No ❑ Presumptive test(s) Yes:_____ No:_____

Results:_____ Type:_____

Standard Tested? Yes: _____ No: _____ Result:_____

DESCRIBE:

MEDICATIONS/DRUGS

EVIDENCE OF DRUG USE: Yes ❑ No ❑   PRESCRIPTION MEDS: Yes ❑ No ❑

MEDICATION	DOCTOR	RX #	PHARMACY	DATE

LOCATION OF MEDICATION:

ILLEGAL DRUGS PRESENT: Yes ❑ No ❑

Describe:

DRUG PARAPHERNALIA PRESENT: Yes ❑ No ❑

DESCRIPTION AND LOCATION:

EVIDENCE OF SEXUAL DEVIATE PRACTICE: Yes ❑ No ❑

DESCRIBE:

EVIDENCE OF SEXUAL ASSAULT: Yes ❑ No ❑

Describe:

SCENE PROCESSING

START TIME:_____END TIME:_____

TRACE EVIDENCE

Blood ❑ Hair ❑ Fibers ❑ Stains ❑ Glass Fragments ❑ Soil ❑ Tool Marks ❑ Liquid ❑
Other ❑ _____
ALTERNATE LIGHT USED: Yes ❑ No ❑ TYPE:_ _ _ _ _ _

LOCATION/DESCRIPTION:
EXHIBIT #   KM: (+) ❑ (-) ❑

Blood ❑ Hair ❑ Fibers ❑ Stains ❑ Glass Fragments ❑ Soil ❑ Tool Marks ❑ Liquid ❑
Other ❑ _____
ALTERNATE LIGHT USED: Yes ❑ No ❑ TYPE:_ _ _ _ _ _

LOCATION/DESCRIPTION:
EXHIBIT #   KM: (+) ❑ (-) ❑

Blood ❑ Hair ❑ Fibers ❑ Stains ❑ Glass Fragments ❑ Soil ❑ Tool Marks ❑ Liquid ❑
Other ❑ _____
ALTERNATE LIGHT USED: Yes ❑ No ❑ TYPE:_ _ _ _ _ _

LOCATION/DESCRIPTION:
EXHIBIT #   KM: (+) ❑ (-) ❑

Blood ❑ Hair ❑ Fibers ❑ Stains ❑ Glass Fragments ❑ Soil ❑ Tool Marks ❑ Liquid ❑
Other ❑ _____
ALTERNATE LIGHT USED: Yes ❑ No ❑ TYPE:_ _ _ _ _ _

LOCATION/DESCRIPTION:
EXHIBIT #   KM: (+) ❑ (-) ❑

Blood ❏ Hair ❏ Fibers ❏ Stains ❏ Glass Fragments ❏ Soil ❏ Tool Marks ❏ Liquid ❏
Other ❏ _____
ALTERNATE LIGHT USED: Yes ❏ No ❏ TYPE:_ _ _ _ _ _

LOCATION/DESCRIPTION:

EXHIBIT #   KM: (+) ❏ (-) ❏

Blood ❏ Hair ❏ Fibers ❏ Stains ❏ Glass Fragments ❏ Soil ❏ Tool Marks ❏ Liquid ❏
Other ❏ _____
ALTERNATE LIGHT USED: Yes ❏ No ❏ TYPE:_ _ _ _ _ _

LOCATION/DESCRIPTION:

EXHIBIT #   KM: (+) ❏ (-) ❏

Blood ❏ Hair ❏ Fibers ❏ Stains ❏ Glass Fragments ❏ Soil ❏ Tool Marks ❏ Liquid ❏
Other ❏ _____
ALTERNATE LIGHT USED: Yes ❏ No ❏ TYPE:_ _ _ _ _ _

LOCATION/DESCRIPTION:

EXHIBIT #   KM: (+) ❏ (-) ❏

Blood ❏ Hair ❏ Fibers ❏ Stains ❏ Glass Fragments ❏ Soil ❏ Tool Marks ❏ Liquid ❏
Other ❏ _____
ALTERNATE LIGHT USED: Yes ❏ No ❏ TYPE:_ _ _ _ _ _

LOCATION/DESCRIPTION:

EXHIBIT #   KM: (+) ❏ (-) ❏

OTHER PHYSICAL EVIDENCE SEIZED

LOCATION/DESCRIPTION:

EXHIBIT #

LOCATION/DESCRIPTION:

EXHIBIT #

LOCATION/DESCRIPTION:

EXHIBIT #

LOCATION/DESCRIPTION:

EXHIBIT #

LOCATION/DESCRIPTION:

EXHIBIT #

LOCATION/DESCRIPTION:

EXHIBIT #

LOCATION/DESCRIPTION:

EXHIBIT #

LOCATION/DESCRIPTION:

EXHIBIT #

FOOTWARE/TIRE IMPRESSION INFORMATION

FOOTWARE IMPRESSIONS AT SCENE: Yes ❑ No ❑ MEDIUM: Dirt/Soil ❑ Blood ❑ Snow ❑
Other ❑ _____ PHOTOGRAPHED: Yes ❑ No ❑
CASTING: Yes ❑ No ❑ ELECTROSTATIC LIFT: Yes ❑ No ❑

DESCRIPTION/LOCATION:
EXHIBIT #:

FOOTWARE IMPRESSIONS AT SCENE: Yes ❑ No ❑ MEDIUM: Dirt/Soil ❑ Blood ❑ Snow ❑
Other ❑ _____ PHOTOGRAPHED: Yes ❑ No ❑
CASTING: Yes ❑ No ❑ ELECTROSTATIC LIFT: Yes ❑ No ❑

DESCRIPTION/LOCATION:
EXHIBIT #:

FOOTWARE IMPRESSIONS AT SCENE: Yes ❑ No ❑ MEDIUM: Dirt/Soil ❑ Blood ❑ Snow ❑
Other ❑ _____ PHOTOGRAPHED: Yes ❑ No ❑
CASTING: Yes ❑ No ❑ ELECTROSTATIC LIFT: Yes ❑ No ❑

DESCRIPTION/LOCATION:
EXHIBIT #:

REMARKS:

TIRE IMPRESSIONS PRESENT: Yes ❑ No ❑
MEDIUM: Dirt/Soil ❑ Blood ❑ Snow ❑ Other ❑_____
PHOTOGRAPHED: Yes ❑ No ❑ CASTING: Yes ❑ No ❑

DESCRIPTION/LOCATION:
EXHIBIT #:

TIRE IMPRESSIONS PRESENT: Yes ❑ No ❑
MEDIUM: Dirt/Soil ❑ Blood ❑ Snow ❑ Other ❑_____
PHOTOGRAPHED: Yes ❑ No ❑ CASTING: Yes ❑ No ❑

DESCRIPTION/LOCATION:
EXHIBIT #:

REMARKS:

FINGERPRINT/FOOTPRINT EVIDENCE

AREAS EXAMINED:

TYPE OF PRINT DISCOVERED: Latent ❑ Patent ❑ Plastic ❑

METHOD USED: None (visible) ❑ Standard Powders ❑ Magnetic Powders ❑

Fluorescent Powders ❑ Superglue ❑ Iodine Fuming ❑ SPR ❑

Alternate Light ❑ _____

PHOTOGRAPHED: Yes ❑ No ❑   LIFTED: Yes ❑ No ❑

DESCRIPTION/LOCATION:

LP#:   EXHIBIT#:

TYPE OF PRINT DISCOVERED: Latent ❑ Patent ❑ Plastic ❑

METHOD USED: None (visible) ❑ Standard Powders ❑ Magnetic Powders ❑

Fluorescent Powders ❑ Superglue ❑ Iodine Fuming ❑ SPR ❑

Alternate Light ❑ _____

PHOTOGRAPHED: Yes ❑ No ❑   LIFTED: Yes ❑ No ❑

DESCRIPTION/LOCATION:

LP#:   EXHIBIT#:

TYPE OF PRINT DISCOVERED: Latent ❑ Patent ❑ Plastic ❑

METHOD USED: None (visible) ❑ Standard Powders ❑ Magnetic Powders ❑

Fluorescent Powders ❑ Superglue ❑ Iodine Fuming ❑ SPR ❑

Alternate Light ❑ _____

PHOTOGRAPHED: Yes ❑ No ❑   LIFTED: Yes ❑ No ❑

DESCRIPTION/LOCATION:

LP#:   EXHIBIT#:

TYPE OF PRINT DISCOVERED: Latent ❏ Patent ❏ Plastic ❏

METHOD USED: None (visible) ❏ Standard Powders ❏ Magnetic Powders ❏

Fluorescent Powders ❏ Superglue ❏ Iodine Fuming ❏ SPR ❏

Alternate Light ❏ _____

PHOTOGRAPHED: Yes ❏ No ❏   LIFTED: Yes ❏ No ❏

DESCRIPTION/LOCATION:

LP#:   EXHIBIT#:

TYPE OF PRINT DISCOVERED: Latent ❏ Patent ❏ Plastic ❏

METHOD USED: None (visible) ❏ Standard Powders ❏ Magnetic Powders ❏

Fluorescent Powders ❏ Superglue ❏ Iodine Fuming ❏ SPR ❏

Alternate Light ❏ _____

PHOTOGRAPHED: Yes ❏ No ❏   LIFTED: Yes ❏ No ❏

DESCRIPTION/LOCATION:

LP#:   EXHIBIT#:

TYPE OF PRINT DISCOVERED: Latent ❏ Patent ❏ Plastic ❏

METHOD USED: None (visible) ❏ Standard Powders ❏ Magnetic Powders ❏

Fluorescent Powders ❏ Superglue ❏ Iodine Fuming ❏ SPR ❏

Alternate Light ❏ _____

PHOTOGRAPHED: Yes ❏ No ❏   LIFTED: Yes ❏ No ❏

DESCRIPTION/LOCATION:

LP#:   EXHIBIT#:

TYPE OF PRINT DISCOVERED: Latent ❏ Patent ❏ Plastic ❏

METHOD USED: None (visible) ❏ Standard Powders ❏ Magnetic Powders ❏

Fluorescent Powders ❏ Superglue ❏ Iodine Fuming ❏ SPR ❏

Alternate Light ❏ _____

PHOTOGRAPHED: Yes ❏ No ❏   LIFTED: Yes ❏ No ❏

DESCRIPTION/LOCATION:

LP#:   EXHIBIT#:

VEHICLES AT CRIME SCENE

VEHICLES PRESENT: Yes ❏ No ❏

VEHICLE INFORMATION

VEHICLE #1
MAKE:_____MODEL:_____YEAR:_____
VIN:_____REGISTRATION:_____
REGISTERED OWNER:_____
VEHICLE LOCATION:_____
VEHICLE PROCESSED: Yes ❏ No ❏ SEE VEHICLE INVENTORY REPORT ❏

VEHICLE #2
MAKE:_____MODEL:_____YEAR:_____
VIN:_____REGISTRATION:_____
REGISTERED OWNER:_____
VEHICLE LOCATION:_____
VEHICLE PROCESSED: Yes ❏ No ❏ SEE VEHICLE INVENTORY REPORT ❏

VEHICLE #3
MAKE:_____MODEL:_____YEAR:_____
VIN:_____REGISTRATION:_____
REGISTERED OWNER:_____
VEHICLE LOCATION:_____
VEHICLE PROCESSED: Yes ❏ No ❏ SEE VEHICLE INVENTORY REPORT ❏

REMARKS:

SCENE RELEASE INFORMATION

SCENE RELEASED BY AUTHORITY OF:_____

DATE:_____TIME:_____

CLEARED BY DETECTIVE(s):Yes ❑ No ❑

Name	Agency

SCENE SECURED AT TIME OF RELEASE: Yes ❑ No ❑

METHOD USED:_____

SCENE RELEASED BY:_____

DATE:_____TIME:_____

RELEASED TO:_____

ADDRESS:_____

PHONE:_____

COPY OF SEARCH WARRANT LEFT: Yes ❑ No ❑   PAGE 5 ONLY: Yes ❑

TIME OF DEPARTURE: _____

REMARKS:

Appendix 3

Recipes for Commonly Used Reagents at the Crime Scene

SCREENING TESTS FOR SUSPECTED DRUGS

Benedict

Copper sulfate	2 g
Sodium citrate	20 g
dH$_2$O	Fill to total volume of 100 mL
Reactions	
Aldehydes	Black

Cobalt Thiocyanate

Cobalt (II) thiocyanate	2 g
dH$_2$O	100 mL
Reactions	
Cocaine	Green/blue or blue
Darvon	Green/blue
Demerol	Green/blue
Heroin	Green/blue
Methadone	Violet to blue/green to blue
Opium	Green
Phencyclidine	Green/blue
Procaine	Green/blue to blue
Ritalin	Green/blue

Dille—Koppanyi, Modified

Solution A	Cobalt (II) acetate dihydrate	0.1 g
	Methanol	100 mL
	Glacial acetic acid	0.2 mL
Solution B	Isopropylamine	5 mL
	Methanol	95 mL
Procedure: Add two drops of solution A to sample. Wait for 10 s. Add one drop of solution B to sample and note any color change.		
Reactions		
Pentobarbital	Purple	
Phenobarbital	Purple	
Secobarbital	Purple	

Duquenois—Levine

Solution A	Acetaldehyde	2.5 mL
	Vanillin	2 g
	95% ethanol	100 mL
Solution B	HCl	
Solution C	Chloroform	
Procedure: Add one drop of solutions A and B to the drug in order in a spot plate. Note the color produced. Add three drops of solution C and note if the color produced is extracted from the mixture of A and B.		
Reactions		
Cannabinoids	Purple or violet	
**Shelf life only about 3 months		
**HCl must be concentrate		
**Store in the fridge		

Ferric Chloride

Anhydrous ferric chloride	2 g
dH$_2$O	100 mL
Reactions	
Morphine	Red/orange to orange to orange/yellow

Mayer Reagent

Mercuric chloride	1.3 g
Potassium iodide	5 g
dH$_2$O	Fill to total of 100 mL
Reactions	
Alkaloids	Cream-colored precipitate

Ammoniacal Chloroform

Ammonium hydroxide	5–10 mL
dH$_2$O	5–10 mL
Chloroform	300 mL
Mix in separatory funnel. Allow to separate. Place chloroform layer in bottle with sodium sulfate. Cap bottle tightly.	

Bismuth Iodide

Solution A	Bismuth subnitrate	50 g
	HNO$_3$	70 mL
	dH$_2$O	Dilute to 100 mL
Solution B	KI	5 g
	dH$_2$O	8 mL
Solution C	H$_2$SO$_4$	10 mL
	dH$_2$O	30 mL
Working solution: Mix one drop of solution A, five drops of solution B, and five drops of solution C.		
**Shelf life: 2 days.		
Reactions		
Mescaline	Color is pale brownish-red	

Ehrlich

p-DMAB	1 g
Ethanol	25 mL
Concentrated HCl	25 mL
Reactions	
LSD	Purple

Fehling's Test

Solution A	Cupric sulfate	35 g
	dH$_2$O	500 mL
Solution B	Rochelle salt	173 g
	KOH	125 g
	dH$_2$O	For a total of 500 mL
Reactions		
Sugars	Green solution and red precipitate	

Folin–Wu

Phosphomolybdic acid	1 g
Glacial acetic acid	100 mL
Reactions	
Sugars	Blue color

Froehde

Molybdic acid (or sodium molybdate)	0.5 g
Hot concentrated sulfuric acid	100 mL
Reactions	
Codeine	Olive/brown to yellow/green to olive/green to green
Darvon	Gray/red/orange to red/brown to gray/olive to blue/purple
Heroin	Purple/red
LSD	Yellow/green
MDA	Olive to red/brown to olive/black to green/black
Mescaline	Yellow
Morphine	Purple/red
Opium	Red to red/brown to olive/brown
Oxycodone	Yellow
Phencyclidine	Pink

Janovski

Solution A	2% *m*-dinitrobenzene in absolute ethanol
Solution B	5N KOH
Reactions	
Benzodiazepines	Violet

Liebermann

Potassium nitrate	1 g
Concentrated sulfuric acid	10 mL (slowly)
Reactions	
Cocaine	Yellow
Morphine	Black

Mandolin

Ammonium vanadate	1 g
Concentrated sulfuric acid	100 mL
Reactions	
Cocaine	Orange
Codeine	Olive/brown to olive
Amphetamine	Green to olive to olive/green to blue/green
Methamphetamine	Yellow/green
Darvon	Gray/red/brown to red/brown
Heroin	Red/brown
Mescaline	Yellow/green to olive/brown to black
Methadone	Yellow/pink
Morphine	Red/orange to red/brown to gray/red/brown
Opium	Olive/brown
Oxycodone	Orange/yellow
Procaine	Yellow/pink to olive
Ritalin	Orange/yellow
Psilocybin	Green
LSD	Orange to green to gray
MDA	Red to purple/black

Marquis

40% formaldehyde	10 mL (slowly add)
Concentrated sulfuric acid	100 mL
Reactions	
Codeine	Red to violet
Amphetamine	Orange to red/orange to red/brown
Methamphetamine	Orange to red/orange to red/brown
Darvon	Red/purple to black/purple
Demerol	Orange to brown
Heroin	Red to purple/red
LSD	Brown to gray/brown to brown/black to purple/gray to purple/black
Mescaline	Red/orange
Morphine	Red/purple
Opium	Red/brown
Oxycodone	Yellow to olive/brown to purple to purple/blue
Pentobarbital	Orange/yellow to yellow to yellow/brown
Phencyclidine	Pink
Phenobarbital	Orange/yellow to yellow to yellow/brown
Ritalin	Orange/yellow
Secobarbital	Orange/yellow to yellow to yellow/brown
Psilocybin	Orange
MDA	Black

Mecke

Selenious acid	1 g
Concentrated sulfuric acid	100 mL
Reactions	
Codeine	Green/blue to blue/green
Darvon	Yellow/brown to brown/orange to brown to red/brown
Heroin	Olive to olive/green to green to blue/green
LSD	Blue/green to black/green
Mescaline	Olive/yellow to yellow/brown to olive to olive/black
Morphine	Green/blue
Opium	Gray/olive/brown to gray/olive to olive/black
Oxycodone	Yellow to olive/brown to olive
Phencyclidine	Pink
MDA	Olive to blue/green to blue

Nitric Acid

Concentrated Nitric Acid	
Reactions	
Codeine	Red/orange to orange to green/yellow
Heroin	Yellow
LSD	Brown/orange
Mescaline	Red to red/brown
Morphine	Red/orange to orange to green/yellow
Opium	Red/orange to orange to green/yellow
Oxycodone	Yellow
MDA	Green/yellow

Sanchez

Furfural	6.9 mL
dH$_2$O	100 mL
Reactions	
Procaine	Red color

Sodium Nitroprusside

Solution A	Sodium nitroprusside	1 g
	Acetaldehyde	10 g
	dH$_2$O	100 mL
Solution B	2% sodium carbonate in dH$_2$O	
Procedure: Add one drop of solution A followed by two drops of solution B.		
Reactions		
Methamphetamine	Dark blue violet color	

VAN URK REAGENT (SEE EHRLICH'S REAGENT)

Wagner

Iodine	2 g
KI	4 g
dH$_2$O	100 mL
Reactions	
Starch	Black color

Weber

Solution A	Fast blue B	10 mg
	dH_2O	10 mL
Solution B	Concentrated HCl	
Reactions		
Psilocin/Psilocybin	Blue	

Zwikker

Solution A	Copper (II) sulfate pentahydrate	0.5 g
	dH_2O	100 mL
Solution B	Pyridine	5 mL
	Chloroform	95 mL
Procedure: Add one drop of solution A followed by one drop of solution B.		
Reactions		
Pentobarbital	Purple	
Phenobarbital	Purple	
Secobarbital	Purple	

SCREENING TESTS FOR SUSPECTED EXPLOSIVES AND GUNSHOT RESIDUE

Alcoholic KOH

10 g	Potassium hydroxide
100 mL	Butanol
Store in amber bottles. Shelf life: 1 year	
Procedure: Add one drop of solution to sample. A red to red-violet color indicates the presence of TNT and similar compounds.	

Barium Chloride

Solution A	Barium chloride	5 g
	dH_2O	100 mL
Solution B	Concentrated acetic acid	
Procedure: Using a clear spot plate, add one drop of solution A. A white precipitate may form. Add one drop of solution B. If white precipitate redissolves, indicates a presence of carbonates. If white precipitate remains, indicates presence of sulfates.		
**Store in amber bottles.		
**Shelf life: 1 year.		

DPA

Diphenylamine	1 g
Concentrated sulfuric acid	100 mL
Procedure: Add one drop of DPA. A blue to blue/black color indicates a positive for nitrates, chlorates, or ferric ions.	
(+) nitrates, (+) iodide, (+) chlorate	
**Store in amber bottles.	
**Shelf life: 1 year.	

Griess Reagent

Solution A	Sulfanilic acid	1 g
	30% acetic acid	100 mL
Solution B	α-napthylamine**	1 g
	dH$_2$O	230 mL
*These are two separate solutions, do not mix them together.		
**α-Naphthylamine is also known as 1-aminonaphthalene (needs about 15 drops of concentrated HCl to go into solution); it may be replaced with *N*-(1-naphthyl)ethylenediamine dihydrochloride.		
Procedure: Add one drop of solution A. Note any color change. Add one drop of solution B to the same well. A strong red color fading to yellow indicates an inorganic nitrite reaction. If no color develops, add a few grains of powdered zinc. The development of a red color indicates the presence of nitrates.		

J-Acid

6-amino-1-naphthol-3-sulfonic acid	1 g
Concentrated sulfuric acid	100 mL
Procedure: Add one drop of solution to sample. An orange/brown color indicates the presence of explosives.	
**Store in amber bottles.	

Methylene Blue

Solution A	Methylene blue	1 g
	Ethanol	100 mL
Solution B	KOH	0.03 g
	dH$_2$O	300 mL
Procedure: Add one drop of solution A. Note any color change. Add one drop of solution B to the same sample. A blue color and/or precipitate indicates a positive for explosives. Reaction can take 1−2 min.		
*These are two separate solutions, do not mix them together.		
**Store in amber bottles.		
**Shelf life: 1 year.		

Nitron

Nitron (diphenylenedianilohydrotriazole)	1 g
88% formic acid	20 mL
Procedure: Using a clear spot plate, add one drop of solution. Mix with a toothpick. The presence of a white precipitate indicates a positive for nitrates or perchlorates.	
**Shelf life: 1 month.	

Silver Nitrate

Solution A	Silver chloride	5 g
	dH$_2$O	100 mL
Solution B	Concentrated ammonium hydroxide	
Procedure: Add one drop of solution A. Note if white precipitate forms (sulfates present). Add one drop of solution B. If precipitate redissolves, it confirms the presence of chloride.		
**Store in amber bottles.		

Sodium Rhodizonate

Solution A	Place a small amount of sodium rhodizonate in a beaker and add enough to make a saturated solution. (It should appear the color of a very strong tea.) It is saturated if there is slight sediment on the bottom of the beaker after stirring with a glass rod.	
	**Shelf life: 1 day	
Solution B	Sodium bitartrate	1.9 g
	Tartaric acid	1.5 g
	dH$_2$O	100 mL
Dissolve using magnetic stirrer. Store in uncontaminated, sealed container.		
Solution C	Concentrated HCl	5 mL
	dH$_2$O	95 mL
Store in uncontaminated, sealed bottle.		
Test procedure		

1. Spray the appropriate area with solution A.
2. Spray the same area with solution B. Lead and a few other metals which may be present will be in pink color.
3. Spray the same area with solution C. The pink color will fade and leave a blue-violet color in its place if lead is present.

SCREENING TESTS OR ENHANCEMENT REAGENTS FOR BLOODSTAINS

Amido Black (Water Based)

Add in Order While on a Stir Plate	
dH_2O	500 mL
5-sulfosalicylic acid	20 g
Naphthol blue black	3 g
Sodium carbonate	3 g
Formic acid	50 mL
Glacial acetic acid	50 mL
Kodak Photo-Flo 600 solution	12.5 mL
Dilute this mixture to 1 L using dH_2O. Although this mixture will be ready to use following dilution, allow the mixture to stand for several days prior to use for best results.	
**Shelf life: indefinite	
Procedure: Apply the amido black to the specimen by dipping or using a squirt bottle. Leave the amido black on the specimen for 3–5 min, then rinse using tap water. Repeat until desired contrast is obtained.	

Coomassie Brilliant Blue

Staining solution	Coomassie	0.44 g
	Glacial acetic acid	40 mL
	Methanol	200 mL
	dH_2O	200 mL
Mix on stirrer for approximately 30 min.		
**Shelf life: Indefinite		
**Keep refrigerated		
Destaining solution	Glacial acetic acid	40 mL
	Methanol	200 mL
	dH_2O	200 mL
**Shelf life: Indefinite		
**Keep refrigerated		
Procedure: Apply staining solution by dipping or using squirt bottle/sprayer. Leave solution on for about 60 s, then apply destaining solution. These steps can be repeated until a maximum contrast is achieved. When this has occurred, apply a final bath of distilled water.		

Fluorescein

Stock solution	Fluorescein	2 g
	Potassium hydroxide	20 g
	dH$_2$O	100 mL
Reflux with 20 g powdered zinc for at least 6 h. Final product is pale orange. Store in dark with zinc in bottom of bottle.		
**Shelf life: 1 month.		
Working solution	Stock solution	20 mL
	dH$_2$O	80 mL
Procedure: In hood, spray test area with working solution. Allow to dry.		

Leuco Crystal Violet

| Dissolve 10 g of 5-sulfosalicylic acid in 500 mL of 3% hydrogen peroxide. Add and dissolve 4.4 g of sodium acetate. Add and dissolve 1.1 g of leuco crystal violet (LCV). (If LCV crystals have become yellow instead of white, obtain fresh LCV.) Store in amber bottle and refrigerate. |
| **Shelf life: 1 month |
| Procedure: Spray test area with finest mist possible. The development should occur within 30 s. Blot the area with a tissue or paper towel. The preceding steps may be repeated when the area is dry for more contrast. |

Leucomalachite Green

Leucomalachite green	0.1 g
Sodium perborate	3.2 g
Acetic acid	66 mL
dH$_2$O	33 mL
Stir with magnetic stirrer with zinc powder. Filter out zinc with filter paper when the solution has turned gray.	
**Store in amber bottles in refrigerator.	
**Shelf life: 3 months.	
Procedure: Immerse the object in methyl alcohol for about 5 min. Apply several drops of leucomalachite green to cover the blood stain. Allow to air dry before examining.	

Luminol

Recipe 1	
Mix	0.5 g luminol
	25 g sodium carbonate (anhydrous)
	500 mL dH$_2$O
Right before use, add 3.5 g of sodium perborate, and mix well.	

Recipe 2	
For a demo batch	
Mix	0.17 g luminol
	8.33 g sodium carbonate
	167 mL dH$_2$O
Then add 1.17 g of sodium perborate	
Recipe 3	
Solution A	0.1 g luminol
	50 mL dH$_2$O
	20 mL ethanol
Solution B	0.5 g sodium carbonate
	0.7 g sodium perborate
	30 mL dH$_2$O
Mix solutions A and B immediately before use.	
**Cover all luminol bottles with aluminum foil to avoid UV exposure.	

O-Tolidine

O-tolidine	1.6 g
Ethanol	40 mL
Acetic acid	30 mL
dH$_2$O	30 mL
Procedure: Add one drop of *o*-tol solution to stain cutting. Wait 10 s and note any color change. Then add one drop of H$_2$O$_2$ and note any color change. A dark blue after adding the H$_2$O$_2$ indicates a positive for blood.	
**Store in amber bottle in the refrigerator.	
**Shelf life: 6 months.	

Phenolphthalein (Kastle—Meyer Reagent)

Stock solution	Phenolphthalein	2 g
	Potassium hydroxide	20 g
	dH$_2$O	100 mL
	Granular zinc	20 g
Reflux stock solution until solution becomes colorless ($\sim$2 h). Store stock solution in dark bottle in fridge with some zinc in the bottle to keep it colorless.		
**Shelf life: 3 months		
Working solution	Phenolphthalein stock	20 mL
	Ethanol	80 mL
Store working solution in dark bottles in the fridge with some zinc in the bottom to keep it colorless.		
**Shelf life: 3 months		
Procedure: Apply one drop of working solution to stain cutting. Wait 10 s and note any color change. Add one drop of H$_2$O$_2$ and note any color change. A pink color indicates a positive screen for blood.		

TMB

Acetate buffer	Dissolve 5 g of sodium acetate in 43 mL of glacial acetic acid, then add 50 mL of dH_2O	
**Store in refrigerator up to 6 months		
Tetramethylbenzidine	TMB	0.2 g
	Acetate buffer	10 mL
**Store in refrigerator up to 6 months		
TMB spray reagent	Add 0.5 g of sodium perborate to 6 mL of solution B and mix well. Then, add 120 mL of solution C and mix well.	
Should be freshly made!		
Procedure: Carcinogenic! Use in Hood! Pour working solution into fine mist bottle. In hood, spray on area where blood may be present. Let dry in hood.		

REAGENTS FOR ENHANCING DUST FINGERPRINTS

Ammonium Thiocyanate

Ammonium thiocyanate	3 g
dH_2O	15 mL
Acetone	120 mL
Concentrated nitric acid	8 mL
In a large reaction vessel, ammonium thiocyanate is dissolved in distilled water, and then the acetone is added and thoroughly mixed. Nitric acid is added slowly.	
Procedure: Spray a test print to ensure the reagent is active. Latent impressions in dust will turn lavender or brown if the reagent is good. Spraying must be done in a well-ventilated area or under a fume hood. Use a fine mist. Spray until maximum contrast is achieved.	

Potassium Thiocyanate

Acetone	120 mL
dH_2O	15 mL
Potassium thiocyanate	15 g
10% sulfuric acid	8.5 mL
Procedure: First the acetone and water are mixed together, then potassium thiocyanate is added and the solution is vigorously stirred or shaken. The dilute sulfuric acid is now added to the reagent. A milky mixture will result and after a few moments, it will separate into two layers, a cloudy layer on the bottom and the clear one on top. The top clear layer is the solution to be sprayed on the impressions, whereas the cloudy layer is discarded. A separatory funnel will facilitate this process.	

CHEMICAL ENHANCEMENT REAGENTS FOR LATENT PRINTS ON NONPOROUS SURFACES

Ardrox

Ardrox	1 mL
Isopropanol	9 mL
Methyl ethyl ketone	15 mL
dH$_2$O	75 mL
Shake vigorously before applying to surface using a spray bottle.	
**Shelf life: 1 year.	
*Ardrox is a fluorescent dye used to make cyanoacrylate-developed latent prints more visible on various colored surfaces. Use in conjunction with a UV or alternate light source (ALS).	

Cyanoacrylate (Superglue) Fuming

Procedure using wand: Place items to be fumed in appropriate fuming chamber (inside hood). Set up wand by filing with butane, and placing new superglue cartridge on end. Place wand into hole on side of chamber, and support with sing stand. Allow to fume for approximately 10 min. When finished, open chamber slightly to allow fumes to escape into hood. Prints will be permanently developed on items.
*There are a number of dyes that may be used in conjunction with fuming to make prints more visible, typically under UV light or ALS.

Cyanoacrylate Fluorescent Dye (RAM)

Stock solution 1	Rhodamine 6G	1 g
	Methanol	1 L
Combine and place on stirring device until rhodamine is completely dissolved. Store in dark bottle.		
**Shelf life: Indefinite.		
Stock solution 2	MBD	1 g
	Acetone	1 L
Combine and place on stirring device until MBD is completely dissolved. Store in dark bottle.		
**Shelf life: Indefinite.		
RAM working solution	Stock solution 1	3 mL
	Ardrox P133D	2 mL
	Stock solution 2	7 mL
	Methanol	20 mL
	Isopropanol	10 mL
	Acetonitrile	8 mL
	Petroleum ether	950 mL
Combine in the order listed. Do not place on magnetic stirrer.		
**Shelf life: 1 month.		
Procedure: Apply using squirt bottle to prints developed with cyanoacrylate. Observe under UV light.		

R.A.Y.

Basic yellow 40 dye	0.5 g
Glacial acetic acid	10 mL
Rhodamine 6 dye	0.05 g
Ardrox P133D	4 mL
Isopropanol	450 mL
Acetonitrile	40 mL
Combine above ingredients in the order listed.	
Procedure	
1. Spray, dip, or use a squirt bottle to apply R.A.Y. 2. Examination under a laser of forensic light source of 450–550 nm. Use orange–or red-colored goggles.	

CHEMICAL ENHANCEMENT OF LATENT PRINTS ON POROUS SURFACES

1,2-Indanedione

1,2-Indanedione	2 g
Ethyl acetate	70 mL
HFE 7100	930 mL
Mix in the above order.	
Procedure	
1. Dip, spray, or wash the item in the reagent. 2. Air-dry the item. 3. Oven bake at 100 °C for 10–20 min at 60% relative humidity or with no added humidity. 4. View under a forensic light source. For most papers, view at 515 nm with an orange barrier filter. For manila, brown paper bags, cardboard items, and kraft paper, view at 515–570 nm with orange or red barrier filters. Option: 1. Spray lightly with zinc chloride and/or cool the treated item with liquid nitrogen. View with forensic light source.	

Iodine Fuming

Procedure: Place iodine crystals in a glass dish and place the specimen and dish in a fuming chamber. Apply heat to the crystals and observe development. Must be photographed immediately.
*Iodine fumes adhere to grease or oils and appear as a yellow stain.

Iodine Spray Reagent

Solution A	Iodine crystals	1 g
	Cyclohexane	1000 mL
Stir for about 30 min. Store at room temperature.		
**Shelf life: Indefinite.		
Solution B	α-Naphthoflavone	5 g
	Methylene chloride	40 mL
Mix manually until dissolved. Store in refrigerator.		
**Shelf life: 1 month.		
Working solution	Solution A	2 mL
	Solution B	100 mL
Mix thoroughly on stirrer for 5 min. Filter directly into a fine mist sprayer.		
**Shelf life: 24 h.		
Procedure: Spray onto test area using a fine mist sprayer in a hood. Allow to dry.		

MRM 10 (Fluorescent Dye)

Stock solution A	Rhodamine 6G	1 g
	Methanol	1 L
Combine on stirring device until rhodamine is dissolved. Store in dark bottle.		
**Shelf life: Indefinite		
Stock solution B	Maxillon flavine 10GFF	2 g
	Methanol	1 L
Combine on stirring device until maxillon flavine 10GFF is dissolved. Not all of it will dissolve, leaving a settlement in the bottom of the storage bottle. Store in dark bottle.		
**Shelf life: Indefinite		
Stock solution C	MBD	1 g
	Acetone	1 L
Combine on stirring device to dissolve MBD. Store in dark bottle.		
**Shelf life: Indefinite		
MRM 10 working solution	Stock solution A	3 mL
	Stock solution B	3 mL
	Stock solution C	7 mL
	Methanol	20 mL
	Isopropanol	10 mL
	Acetonitrile	8 mL
	Petroleum ether	950 mL
Combine ingredients in the order listed. Do not place on stirring device. Store in dark bottle.		
**Shelf life: 6 months		
Procedure: Same as above dyes.		
*Used in conjunction with cyanoacrylate fuming on various colored surfaces.		

Ninhydrin

2,2-dihydroxy-1,3-indanedione monohydrate	1.25 g
Acetone	100 mL
Solution must be stored in the dark.	
**Shelf life: 1 year	
Procedure: Place the solution in a fine mist spray bottle and spray the test area in a hood. Once applied, it must be dried before any attempt is made to accelerate the development process. Once dry, run a warm iron over the top (can also be placed into oven to shorten developing time).	
*Ninhydrin reacts with the amino acids in perspiration. Positive result: Print turns purple.	

Ninhydrin With HFE 7100

Ninhydrin crystals	0.5 g
Ethyl alcohol	4.5 mL
Ethyl acetate	0.2 mL
Acetic acid	0.5 mL
HFE 7100	100 mL
Solution must be stored in the dark.	
**Shelf life: 1 month	
**Only make when specifically requested!	
Procedure: Same as above.	

Rhodamine 6G (Fluorescent Dye)

Stock solution	Rhodamine 6G	1 g
	Methanol	1 L
Dissolve rhodamine using magnetic stirrer. Store in dark bottle.		
**Shelf life: Indefinite		
Working solution	Stock solution	3 mL
	Acetone	15 mL
	Acetonitrile	10 mL
	Methanol	15 mL
	Isopropanol	32 mL
	Petroleum ether	925 mL
Combine above ingredients in the order listed. Do not place on magnetic stirrer. Store in dark bottle.		
**Shelf life: 6 months		
*Used in conjunction with cyanoacrylate fuming on various colored surfaces.		

Zinc Chloride Solution

Zinc chloride crystals	5 g
Dissolve crystals in 2 mL glacial acetic acid and 100 mL methanol. Add 400 mL 1,1,2-trichlorotrifluoroethane and stir. Add 2 mL 5% sodium hypochlorite solution (bleach).	
**Shelf life: 3 months	
*Zinc chloride is applied after the use of ninhydrin to enhance the prints. This can be done using a fine mist spray bottle or by dipping.	

ENHANCEMENT REAGENTS FOR PRINTS ON STICKY SURFACES

5-MTN

5-Methylthioninhydrin crystals	3 g
Petroleum ether	1 L
Procedure	

1. **a.** Submerge item in reagent for 5 s
   b. Brush solution onto item—until coated.
   c. Spray solution onto item—until coated.
2. Heat up to 80°C and humidity exposure at 60%—70% relative humidity. Monitor development or use a steam iron.
3. Photograph the developed detail using a green-colored (Wratten#58) filter.
4. View non-zinc chloride latent prints under a forensic light source at 530 nm using no barrier filter.
5. Item may be treated with zinc chloride. View under a forensic light source at 530 nm using orange barrier filter.

5-MTN/5-MTN Hemiketal

Working solution	5-MTN/5-MTN Hemiketal	3.4 g/3.0 g
	99%—100% acetic acid	10 mL
	Isopropanol	25 mL
	Ethyl acetate	145 mL
	MTBE (methyl-tert-butyl ether)	100 mL
	Petroleum ether (40—60° or 60—80°)	700 mL
Procedure: Dissolve the crystals in the acetic acid and ethyl acetate and isopropanol (which will take 10—15 min with stirring) to form a concentrated solution. After it is fully dissolved, add the MTBE and the petroleum ether.		
**Shelf life: Can last for extensive periods of time as long as it is at room temperature.		
Used in conjunction with a zinc chloride solution	Zinc chloride	30 g
	MTBE	500 mL
	Ethanol (anhydrous)	20 mL
	Glacial acetic acid	15 mL
	Petroleum ether, heptanes, or pentane	
Procedure: Dissolve 30 g of ZnCl in 500 mL MTBE and ethanol and stir for 60 min. After it dissolves, add 15 mL of glacial acetic acid. Dilute to 1000 mL with petroleum ether, pentane, or heptanes. Store in a brown bottle and stable at low temperatures.		

Alternate Black Powder

Lightning black powder	1 tsp
Liqui-Nox solution (diluted 1:1 with water)	40 drops
Combine in petri dish and stir until solution has consistency of shaving cream.	
**Shelf life: Prepare as needed	
Procedure: Apply the solution with a small brush to the adhesive side of the tape. Allow to set for 30–60 s, then rinse off with cold tap water. Allow to dry.	
*Use the Liqui-Nox recipe in this cookbook instead of this recipe.	

Ash Gray Powder

Ash gray powder	1 tsp
Photo-Flo 200 or 600 solution	
Place powder in a dish and add Photo-Flo solution. Stir the mixture until it reaches the consistency of paint.	
Procedure: Same as alternate black powder.	
*This method is useful on dark-colored and black tape.	

Crowle's Double Stain

Developer solution	Crocein Scarlet 7B	2.5 g
	Coomassie Brilliant Blue R	150 mg
	Glacial acetic acid	50 mL
	Trichloroacetic acid	30 mL
	dH_2O	1 L
Stir for about 20 min until all is dissolved.		
Rinse solution	Glacial acetic acid	30 mL
	dH_2O	970 mL
Store in clear or dark bottles.		
**Shelf life: Indefinite		
Procedure: Apply developer by dipping or using a squirt bottle/sprayer. Leave the developer on for about 60 s, then apply the rinse. Repeat these steps for higher contrast. Apply a final bath of distilled water when contrast is achieved.		

Crystal (Gentian) Violet

Gentian violet	1 g
dH_2O	1 L
**Shelf life: Indefinite	
Procedure: Dip specimen into solution for about 1–2 min, then rinse with cold tap water. The gentian violet solution may be reused.	
*Additional info available in reference manual.	

DFO (1,8-Diazafluoren-9-One)

Stock solution	DFO	1 g
	Methanol	200 mL
	Ethyl acetate	200 mL
	Acetic acid	40 mL
Working solution	Start with stock solution and dilute to 2 L with petroleum ether (Pentane may be used in substitute for petroleum ether). Store in dark bottle.	
**Shelf life: 6 months		
Procedure: DFO can be dipped or sprayed. The specimen must then be dried and placed in an oven at about 100 °C.		
*DFO reacts with the amino acids in perspiration.		

Liqui-Drox

Ardrox P133D	200 mL
Liqui-Nox	400 mL
dH$_2$O	400 mL
Combine the ingredients and stir thoroughly. The solution should be thick and have a milky yellow color. (In time, solution will go clear; stir to return to milky color.) Store in dark bottle.	
**Shelf life: 6 months	
Procedure: Apply the solution with a small brush to the adhesive side of the tape. Brush until a lather is produced. Allow solution to sit on tape for about 10 s. Rinse the tape under a stream of water until liquid-drox is no longer visible. Allow tape to dry, then view under UV light. Ridge detail will fade within 12 h.	

Liqui-Nox

Tap water	20 drops
Liqui-Nox	20 drops
Black fingerprint powder	0.5 g
Procedure	
1. Mix the ingredients to create a foam with bubbles. 2. Use a Camel hair brush to paint the tape surface with the mixture. 3. Wait 30–60 s and rinse the tape under a gentle stream of tap water and allow to dry. 4. Photograph any developed detail.	

ENHANCEMENT REAGENTS ON WET SURFACES

Physical Developer

Stock detergent solution	n-dodecylamine acetate	3 g	
	Synperonic-N	4 g	
	dH$_2$O	1 L	
**Shelf life: 1 year			
Silver nitrate solution	Silver nitrate	20 g	
	dH$_2$O	100 mL	
**Shelf life: 1 year	Store in dark bottles		
Redox solution	Ferric nitrate	30 g	
	Ferrous ammonium sulfate	80 g	
	Citric acid	20 g	
	dH$_2$O	1 L	
**Shelf life: Indefinite			
Maleic acid solution	Maleic acid	25 g	
	dH$_2$O	1 L	
**Shelf life: Indefinite			
Working solution	Tray 1	Maleic acid solution	
	Tray 2	Redox solution	1 L
		Detergent solution	40 mL
		Silver nitrate solution	50 mL
	Tray 3	dH$_2$O	
Procedure: Place specimen in Tray 1 for 5 min. If bubbling occurs, keep specimen in tray until bubbling stops. Submerge the specimen in Tray 2 for 5–15 min on an orbital shaker. Place specimen in Tray 3 for rinsing. It can then be air-dried.			
*Sodium hypochlorite can be used in conjunction with PD. The solution darkens the latent prints and lightens the background. Mix sodium hypochlorite and distilled water in a 1:1 dilution. Dip the specimen into the solution for 15 s. Then place in a water rinse.			
**Shelf life: Indefinite			
*Physical developer is normally applied after the DFO or ninhydrin methods.			

Safranin O (Fluorescent Dye)

Safranine O	1 g
Methanol	1 L
Combine ingredients and place on stirring device for 15 min.	
**Shelf life: Indefinite	
Procedure: Same as above dyes. An optional rinse of methanol can be used to remove excess dye.	
*Used in conjunction with cyanoacrylate fuming and is very effective in the 500 nm range.	

Silver Nitrate

Water based	Silver nitrate	3 g	*For Harris' white powder lab
	dH$_2$O	100 mL	
Alcohol based	Silver nitrate	3 g	
	dH$_2$O	10 mL	
	Ethanol	100 mL	
Store in dark glass bottles.			
**Shelf life: 1 year			
Procedure: The solution may be dipped or painted on the test area. It must be dried and then subjected to high-intensity light or sunlight to develop prints.			
*Silver nitrate reacts with the sodium chloride (salt) content in perspiration.			

Small Particle Reagent

Molybdenum disulfide	30 g
dH$_2$O	1 L
Photo-Flo 2000	3 drops
Procedure: Mix thoroughly and dip specimen in a tray of the working solution. Gently agitate the tray; prints will develop within a couple of minutes. Remove the specimen and rinse with water. Let air dry at room temperature.	
**Shelf life: Indefinite	
*Small particle reagent detects fatty acids and lipids on nonporous surfaces, including damp surfaces. When rinsing with water, do not directly spray the prints.	

Sticky-Side Powder

Sticky-side powder	1 tsp
Photo-Flo solution	
Place the sticky-side powder in a beaker. Dilute with distilled water by 50%. Add Photo-Flo to the powder and stir until mixture reaches the consistency of thin paint.	
**Shelf life: Prepare as needed	
Procedure: Paint the solution on the adhesive surface of the tape with a small brush. Allow to set for 30–60 s, then rinse off with cold tap water.	

SCREENING TEST REAGENTS FOR OTHER BIOLOGICAL STAINS

Acid Phosphatase (Presumptive Test for Semen)

Buffer	4.1 g sodium acetate
	450 mL dH$_2$O
Adjust pH to 5.5 with glacial acetic acid. Make volume up to 500 mL with distilled water.	
Reagent I: Dissolve 0.25 g disodium alpha-naphthyl phosphate in 250 mL buffer.	
Reagent II: (Fast blue B) dissolve 0.25 g of fast blue B in 250 mL buffer.	
**Wrap in foil	
Stock solution: Freeze. Shelf life approx. 6 months.	
Working solution: Freeze 2 mL aliquots for use in upcoming lab. After lab, discard and refill with stock solution. This will help prevent contamination.	
Procedure: Take one drop of reagent I and add to cutting. Wait 10 s. Add one drop of reagent II to cutting. A purple color within 10 s indicates a positive for semen. Any color change after 10 s could be a false positive.	

Jaffe Reagent (Urine Presumptive Test)

Solution A (Jaffe reagent)	10% saturated picric acid (2—3 g picric acid in 100 mL dH$_2$O)
Solution B (5% NaOH)	5% NaOH solution in 80% ethanol
Store in amber bottles.	
Shelf life: 3 months	
Procedure: Extract cutting with four—five drops of distilled water. Add one drop of Jaffe reagent to cutting. Wait 10 s. Add one drop of 5% NaOH solution to cutting. An orange color indicates a positive for urine.	

Urobilinogen Test (Presumptive Test for Feces)

This test relies on the formation of green fluorescent zinc—urobilin complex. Urobilinogen is oxidized to urobilin, which is soluble in alcohol. In the presence of neutral alcoholic zinc salts, the green complex is formed.
1. Prepare test tube 1 with an aqueous extract of the stain. 2. Prepare test tube 2 with an aqueous extract of a positive control. 3. Prepare test tube 3 with an aqueous extract of a negative control. 4. Add three drops of 10% alcoholic mercuric chloride to each test tube. 5. Add three drops of 10% alcoholic zinc chloride to each test tube and shake 6. Examine under UV.
Apple green fluorescence indicates that urobilinogen is present
10% alcoholic mercuric chloride—10% (weight/volume) in EtOH
10% alcoholic zinc chloride—10% (weight/volume) in EtOH

Index

SECOND EDITION

THE CRIME SCENE A VISUAL GUIDE

Marilyn T. Miller and Peter Massey

The primary goal of The Crime Scene is to provide visual instruction of the correct way in which to process a forensic crime scene. By using photographs and video clips to show proper versus improper procedures the reader will be able to identify the correct principles required in process the scene.

The second edition of *The Crime Scene: A Visual Guide* presents knowledgeable chapters on the following: crime scene investigation, the various types of documentation, scene reconstruction and the value of evidence and proper evidence collection. Additionally, a companion site will host: video and additional instructional materials.

Key Features

- Coverage of techniques, documentation and reconstruction at a crime scene
- Shows side-by-side comparison of the correct process versus the incorrect process
- Online website will host: videos and additional instructional material

Authors

Marilyn T. Miller, EdD

Marilyn Miller teaches forensic science and crime scene investigation courses at the undergraduate and graduate levels. She is a Fellow in the Criminalistics section of the American Academy of Forensic Science, the Southern Association of Forensic Scientists and the American Chemical Society. Miller is a faculty member of the Henry Lee Institute of Forensic Science and the National Crime Scene Training Center. She has presented and taught as part of hundreds of forensic seminars across the United States. Before coming to VCU, she worked as a supervisor and forensic scientist for law enforcement agencies in North Carolina, Pennsylvania and Florida.

Peter Massey, MS

Peter Massey started his career at the Hamden, CT Department of Police Services rising to the rank of Detective. He retired in July 2003 after more than twenty years to become the Training Coordinator for the National Crime Scene Training and Technology Center at the Henry C. Lee Institute of Forensic Science. During his tenure as Training Coordinator, he was responsible for offering hundreds of advanced training courses to the law enforcement and forensic science community. Over his more than nine years at the University of New Haven he has taught courses in Criminal Justice and F[...] member in the Forensic Science Department, as well as an a[...]

ACADEMIC PRESS
An imprint of Elsevier
elsevier.com/books-and-journals

ELSEVIER